Cinema and Fiction

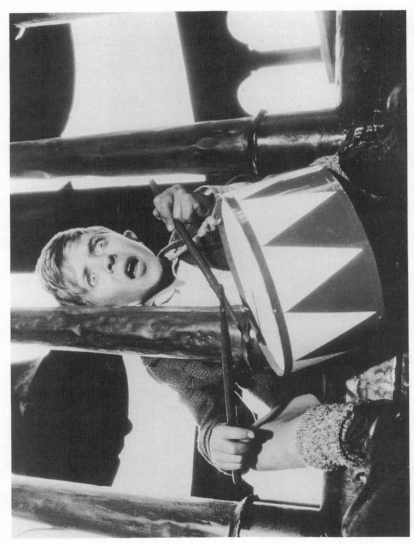

Gross and Schlöndorff, *The Tin Drum* (Photo courtesy BFI Stills, Posters and Designs)

Cinema and Fiction

New Modes of Adapting, 1950–1990

Edited by

JOHN ORR and COLIN NICHOLSON

EDINBURGH UNIVERSITY PRESS

© Edinburgh University Press, 1992

Edinburgh University Press
22 George Square, Edinburgh

Typeset in Century Text
by Pioneer Associates, Perthshire, and
printed in Great Britain by
The University Press, Cambridge

A CIP record for this book is
available from the British Library.

ISBN 0 7486 0356 5

Contents

Notes on contributors

JOHN ORR is Reader in Sociology at Edinburgh University where he teaches film studies. He has been a film and drama critic for the *Literary Review* and written extensively on modern culture, fiction and the theatre. He has recently published *Tragicomedy and Contemporary Culture* (1991) and edited *Terrorism and Modern Drama* for Edinburgh University Press. He is the author of the forthcoming *Cinema and Modernity* for Polity Press.

COLIN NICHOLSON is Senior Lecturer in English Literature at Edinburgh University. He has published widely on Scottish, American, Canadian and English writing and his forthcoming *Iain Crichton Smith: New Critical Essays* and *Landscapes of the Mind* are to be published by Edinburgh University Press and Polygon respectively.

RICHARD KILBORN is Senior Lecturer in Film and Media Studies at Stirling University. He has research interests in German Cinema and Radio and Television Drama. He is the author of *The Multi-Media Melting Pot* (Commedia, 1985) and the forthcoming *An Introduction to Television Soaps* (Batesford, 1992)

VASSILIKI KOLOCOTRONI was born in Athens, lives in Edinburgh, and is a doctoral student in English Literature at Glasgow University working on theories of modernism. She is a regular contributor to *Cine 7*, the Greek film Journal.

OLGA TAXIDOU works at the Ionic Centre for Hellenic Studies in Greece. She was recently awarded a PhD at Edinburgh University for her dissertation on Edward Gordon Craig and Modernist Theatre.

J. B. ELLIS is a Lecturer in English Literature at Edinburgh University where he teaches Film Studies.

CATHERINE FELLOWS is a freelance journalist and a recent graduate in English Literature from Edinburgh University. She is currently researching the Indian Film Industry.

JOHN IZOD is Senior Lecturer in Film and Media Studies at Stirling University. He is the author of *Reading the Screen* (1984), *Hollywood and the Box Office* (1988) and the forthcoming *Films of Nicholas Roeg* (1991).

JOHN BROWN is a screenwriter who has written a number of television series including *The Justice Game*. He was Assistant Director of the Scottish Film Council from 1970 to 1989.

ELISABETH LIDDEL has taught widely in Further and Higher Education in Scotland in the fields of Journalism, Mass Communications and Media Studies. She has also worked as Development Officer for Media Studies in the Scottish Education Department.

MICHAEL LIDDEL has published numerous articles on English and Media Studies, both of which he currently teaches at Bankhead Academy, Aberdeen.

FRANK GORMLIE is Senior Teacher in Media Studies and English at James Gillespie's High School Edinburgh. He has also served as an editor of the Media Education Journal.

RICK INSTRELL has been involved in media studies projects in Scotland since 1980. He teaches film study at Edinburgh University's Centre for Continuing Education, and is director of their Festival Summer School.

ROBBIE ROBERTSON is a researcher in both the literature and cinema of science fiction and currently works with the Scottish Consultative Council on the Curriculum in Edinburgh.

1

Introduction: Proust, the movie

JOHN ORR

In film history from 1930 onwards cinema and fiction have always closely intertwined, not only in the United States but throughout Europe and the rest of the world. Hollywood produced a set of classic adaptations in its classic period – *Anna Karenin, Madame Bovary, Jane Eyre, Wuthering Heights*, and in Europe Josef von Sternberg adapted Heinrich Mann, Jean Renoir adapted Zola and David Lean adapted Dickens. Hollywood now adapts Stephen King, Mario Puzo and Thomas Harris for global audiences, and trans-national co-productions of the eighties have brought Proust, García Marquez, Fowles, Kundera and other major novelists to the contemporary screen. On a more modest scale, film and fiction can now clearly work to their mutual advantage as in Bill Forsyth's recent adaptation of Marilynne Robinson's *Housekeeping*. The fidelity of Forsyth's version to the original novel not only allows his film great passages of visual imagination; it has also stimulated interest in a remarkable but previously underrated American novel. If the book was essential to the picture, the picture, in turn, has been vital to the creation of a wider audience for the book.

It is not just with the classics, the popular genre or the major author that adaptation has taken place. Literary adaptation has occurred at all levels, using short stories as well as full-length novels, resurrecting writers from obscurity as well as adapting best-selling authors of the moment. Literary and dramatic input has also worked in other ways. Screenwriters have been drawn from fiction and from the theatre to produce original screenplays, many of them working in close collaboration with the film's directors. Such is the current intensity of the tie-in, the intertextuality of the written word and the visual image in our electronic culture, that one is tempted to speak, as John Izod does convincingly in this volume, of 'literary and cinematic *fictions*' as the shared property of the book and the screen. On the other hand, a common mode of addressing the adaptation, the 'picture-book' as we

1

shall call it, is to assess how far the film can be seen as a credible or faithful rendering of the text. Does it do justice to the book or does it 'betray' its literary antecedent: that is, how is the question repeatedly framed by critics and viewers? Less often, but just as important, is whether we can speak of a picture-book *improving* on the literary text, even transforming it out of all recognition. Such an example is the celebrated anecdote of Howard Hawks and William Faulkner deciding to adapt the worst, in their opinion, of Hemingway's novels, *To Have and Have Not*, for the screen. They regarded it as not the best of his work, but as the greater challenge. An equally striking example is Luis Buñuel's decision to adapt *Tristana* from what he regarded as the worst story of his favourite novelist, Benito Pérez Galdós.

The picture-book is always a tempting project because film and fiction have two things in common. They are both narrative forms, and both are referential. Both produce stories which work through temporal succession. Both refer to, or connote, pre-existent materials. Fiction works through a pre-existent language, film through the raw data of the physical world which its cameras record.[1] In both cases, words and images give off associations which go beyond the immediacy of their language or their physical objects. For different groups of readers and viewers words and images may well connote many different things. But there are vital differences too between the picture and the book. In fiction, narrative language is used to describe consciousness, but the camera has no analogous convention for rendering thought. Conse-quently, although both use dialogue, the narrative language of feeling, attitude, and judgement in the novel often becomes more ambiguous and problematic when rendered through the image. It is also, some critics would argue, more limited. Film relies more on visual gesture and expression but cannot hope to replicate the complex fictive language of feeling purely through the look. Moreover the camera largely works from a series of fixed viewpoints. Though this can be changed with rapid cutting or tracking, none the less the fluid interchangeability of the point of view which is a feature of the classic novel up to Henry James is less easy. Although the techniques of voice-over can be used very effectively, as film noir shows by rendering sonically the hard-boiled prose of private-eye fiction, there is often no defining narrative voice.

For the picture-book, we thus find a major dilemma. The camera is not omniscient like the nineteenth-century narrator nor is its powerful intimacy as subjective as a stream-of-consciousness narrative. In short, the cinema cannot be Tolstoy and it cannot be Joyce. It does not deal well with a multitude of major characters or a panoramic view of the social world. Conversely, it cannot dissect the subterranean life of thought in all its verbal intricacies. It works best in a scaled-down milieu, in the close connecting links between the personal and the social. Moreover, it cannot usually absorb the sheer density of text which the full-length novel seems to demand as the price of fidelity to narrative. The novella and the short story are more often the right length for a two-hour feature film. The truly epic picture-book of the cinema is not the American or Soviet versions of *War and Peace* but Luchino Visconti's adaptation of Giuseppe di Lampedusa's *The Leopard* which takes a historical novel of the mid-twentieth century and transposes its modest length of two hundred pages to three very full hours of cinema.

The Leopard is illuminating in another way. Between its director and its author there is a shared historical frame of meaning. The picture-book is at its best when film and text are part of the same culture, part of the same age, yet also when some time has elapsed between book and film, when the picture-book is also a retrospective rendering of the text. Lampedusa and Visconti share, in the middle of the twentieth century, a retrospective of a part of the previous century's history in Italy. It is an achievement repeated, in a slightly narrower time band, by Bernardo Bertolucci's picture-book of Alberto Moravio's novel of Fascist Italy, *The Conformist*. The dates here are instructive. Lampedusa's novel was published in 1938, Visconti's film made in 1964. Moravia's novel was published in 1952, Bertolucci's film made in 1969. Orson Welles' picture-book of Kafka's *The Trial* is an example of extreme distance of this shared frame of meaning. The novel of 1912, a tragic fable highly prophetic of the police states, tyrannical bureaucracies and genocide in the Europe of this century, is transposed by Welles to a central Europe of 1960 which has 'come out the other side' of world war and entered the age of the nuclear bomb and the computer. In a similar vein, 1984 seemed an appropriate year for Mike Radford, the British film-maker, to adapt Orwell's futuristic novel of 1948, *Nineteen Eighty-Four*, to a vision of Britain mediated by contemporary experience.

At this point, perhaps, we ought to look further at the aesthetic objections to the picture-book, especially Alain Resnais' powerful reason for refusing to adapt literary texts. For Resnais, the written fiction brings a pre-existent weight to the cinema which burdens the process of film-making. His own solution, as one of the most literary of modern film-makers, was to opt for the original screenplay commissioned from major contemporary writers such as Marguerite Duras, Alain Robbe-Grillet, Jean Cayrol and David Mercer. As the writers concerned have testified, working with Resnais was a highly successful form of collaboration, one which linked their own developments in writing to innovations in film-making. Many critics have noted the close and fertile connection in France between the *nouveau roman* and the *nouvelle vague*. Thus Resnais' undisputed triumph as a film-maker of the literary screenplay not only shows the close relationship of cinema and fiction but also constitutes a challenge for the advocate of the picture-book. Is not the picture-book on this plane clearly redundant? We have major directors like Antonioni and Buñuel who have used gifted *literary* screenwriters such as Tonino Guerra or Jean-Claude Carrière. We have others like Welles, Bergman or Herzog who are gifted enough to write their own screenplays. All of them work from original screenplays which are later published as literary texts. Is not the picture-book by comparison simply a secondary offshoot of the cinema's tie-in with other forms of culture? Is it not a convenient shortcut, a flight from originality?

At one level, the answer must be yes, the picture-book often is secondary and derivative. At another level, the answer must be no. The culture of the picture-book cannot genuinely be separated from that of the literary screenplay, or of the current interpenetration of written and electronic media, the increasing symbiosis of different cultural forms. Moreover, it shows us what is all too often forgotten, the organic historical connections of word and image, of verbal and visual literacy which at their most basic, in television and newspapers, are both forms of collage.[2] All modern fiction, from Joyce, Kafka and Faulkner to Kundera and Pynchon, is a form of writing which has an awareness of the power of the moving image at this basic level. Conversely, the picture-book at its best transforms the important narrative text into an enduring cinematic image. At its most powerful, it illustrates the power of the text by persuading us to read it if we have not already done so. If we have, it graphically reminds us of textual power. On the other hand, the text chosen can be fairly marginal to its genre or to its author's work in general. For the film-maker it may not be a text at all, but merely an idea, a fragment, a treatment, an inspiration. It may remind us simply that all stories come from somewhere and have always been in circulation, in some form or other.

Despite the various crises – financial, artistic, political – in contemporary cinema, the picture-book remains a cogent force. *The Leopard, The Trial* and *The Conformist* were among the most powerful films of the sixties, itself one of the most important decades in film history. In the last decade two of the most outstanding films to be considered for any top-ten listing have been adaptations. The first is the Francesco Rosi/Tonino Guerra picture-book of the novel by Gabriel García Marquez *Chronicle of a Death Foretold* and the second the adaptation of Milan Kundera's *The Unbearable Lightness of Being* by Philip Kaufman and Jean-Claude Carrière, analysed here by Catherine Fellowes. Moreover fiction by John Fowles, William Styron, Margaret Atwood, Doris Lessing, Angela Carter, Ian MacEwan, Robert Stone and many other current writers has been adapted in the last decade. In addition, the new or revitalised genres of popular fiction, horror, crime thrillers, science fiction have fed directly into the American cinema either to provide obvious tie ins, as in the case of Stephen King or Thomas Harris. Such fictions can also be a source of new experiments in genre, as in the case of Jim Thompson's novels, *The Grifters* and *The Kill-Off*, or Stanley Kubrick's picture-book of King's *The Shining*, discussed here in an essay by John Brown.

The recent 'discovery' of Jim Thompson, who wrote his best novels in the fifties and significantly worked on the screenplays of two of Kubrick's best movies, *The Killing* and *Paths of Glory*, is an interesting match of popular genre and picture-book, showing the importance of shared meaning in the context of American modes of adapting. During the reign of the Hollywood studio code and its creed of compensating moral value for the graphic depiction of evil, Thompson's novels, with their terse lacerating ironies, were too challenging to become obvious screen properties. Indeed, as critics have noted, the total absence of a moral centre makes Raymond Chandler at times look sentimental. Thompson was a prophetic writer, a visionary of pure amoralism, an observer viewing criminality as the bedrock of modern American life and witnessing the moral paralysis it induces. The film-makers who have used him – Sam Peckinpah and Walter Hill, Stephen Frears, Maggie Greenwald – have responded both to the America of the present where crime is a mere fact of life and to its recent past, updating him and yet trying to retain that sense of continuity with an earlier, less frantic age. Yet reading Thompson and pondering his profound sense of the contradictions of criminality, it is those film-makers working at the limits of genre, not his movie-adaptors, who seem to match that Nietzschean irony and amoralism which strikes a raw American nerve.

Terence Malick's *Badlands* shot in 1974 but set in 1958, with its formal etiquette, its ironised literary voice-over, its casual juxtaposition of everyday pleasantries and psychopathic killing, is much closer to *The Getaway* than Thompson's adaptors. David Lynch's *Blue Velvet* more than matches the chilling eruptions of suburban menace in *The Kill-Off* as a horrifying present with past echoes. The fake nostalgia of fifties hit-records is uncanny in its casual power, while Maggie Greenwald's recent film version of *The Kill-Off* is in turn clearly influenced by Lynch's landmark picture. Lynch's more recent *Wild at Heart* has strong echoes of the *The Getaway* and *The Grifters* and Lynch's *mise-en-scéne* has uncanny parallels with Thompson's narrative prose. Lynch's return to the composed framing of classic studio melodrama, his self-conscious reverence for the spoken word as opposed to multi-layered sound track *à la* Robert Altmann, the demise of the zoom, his intense neo-Expressionist focus on the clinching gesture within the single shot; all these give us a stylistics of the recent past of the cinema haunting the American present. Just as Lynch recycles the classic stylistics of obvious meaning for a completely heretical purpose, namely to frame actions which are *inexplicable*, so for the nineties reader Thompson's narrative line with its formal proprieties and gentle dialogue constantly disrupted by existential terror correlates 'then' with 'now', a specific history repeating itself as the perpetual present.

Within the conventions of film noir, there are similar drawbacks and ambiguities over adapting. *Ossessione*, Visconti's 1942 unofficial picture-book of James Cain's *The Postman Always Rings Twice*, is far superior to Tay Garnett's official Hollywood version of 1946 with John Garfield and Lana Turner. Visconti's feel for exterior location, the unbridled and fluid sensuality of his camera-work, his unerring ability to render obsession at a visceral level contrast with a clumsily-framed Hollywood movie which is hidebound by the censorship code of the Hays Office and clearly ill at ease with exterior locations – the latter film in effect fails to get out of the studio. But the 1982 remake of the film by Bob Rafelson after the death of the code at the Hays Office, is little better. The challenge, of course, is to use exteriors more effectively, and to make sexually explicit the erotic encounter which the original film version could only fudge. But Rafelson's film has no sense of period and equally, no sense of love or obsession, which it merely replaces with kitchen table scenes of copulation. For a film which unerringly links eros, adultery, money and power into an unbreakable chain, as in Cain's novel, we have to look at Lawrence Kasdan's *Body Heat*, filmed from Kasdan's original screenplay. Set in contemporary Florida, Kasdan's highly erotic movie has self-conscious echoes of the whole noir history and uncannily evokes the forties at every juncture. Yet its sexual and financial mores are clearly those of its own period -- the eighties. Thus, like the films of Lynch and Malick, it comes closer to fiction by not adapting it, and closer to the past by engaging the present.

II

Another problem with the picture-book lies in its form. If it is to succeed, it has to be a work of transposition, yet if it is a work of transposition, does it not violate the nature of the original? The problem has been exposed recently by the lure of one of the great modern masterpieces of fiction, *In Remembrance of Things Past*. Is it at all conceivable to make Proust, the movie? Two assaults by the cinema on the Proustian edifice tell us much about the inherent risks of the picture-book. The first, *Swann in Love*, by Volker Schlöndorff, whose film version of *The Tin Drum* is discussed in this volume by Richard Kilborn, went for the modest task of adapting the first volume, *Swann's Way*. Scripted by Jean-Claude Carrière, Peter Brook and Marie-Hélène Estienne with a high degree of fidelity to narrative and dialogue, the film clearly shows why Schlöndorff prefers the first volume. It contains the one part of the novel where the presence of the Narrator is minimal, where he exists largely as a voice, a mere commentator. It thus becomes possible to eliminate him as a character from the film. The film turns to Swann instead, dissecting his erotic passion for Odette, a Parisian courtesan. Swann's passion is to be matched later in the novel by the Narrator's own for Gilberte and Albertine, but ends here in a happiness the Narrator can never attain. Swann's jealous obsession with Odette culminates in a marriage whose mutual advantages are social rather than personal. Odette gains status through her new position while Swann gains a social confidence from his marriage to offset the ethnic disadvantages of his Jewishness. Though Proust's narrative of Swann's life, as opposed to the life of his Narrator, works chronologically, the film version reverses the author's narrative sequence by starting with the climax to Swann's suspicions of Odette's liaisons with both men and women, and then tracing the early blossoming of their affair through flashback.

Yet there is a problem of reflexive narrative which Schlöndorff cannot resolve. In Proust's text, his Narrator, a persona of Proust himself, can exorcise the sufferings of sexual betrayal by transforming memory into an artwork, into a fictional narrative of his biography. For Swann, there is no such artistic fallback, and the reflexive Proustian quality of narrative is lost. The film cannot render memory as recollection, judgement, because Swann's persona is not outside the film, not part of the process of making it, while the narrator, as a literary device, has disappeared. The film cannot make up for it. Swann has no narrative voice, so that much depends on the iconography of the gaze. The face of the anguished Swann (Jeremy Irons) is pale and melancholy, at times desperate, at times diffuse, always passively haunted. That of Odette (Ornella Muti) is alert, composed, razor sharp, always focused on the tangible and the specific. We see things through Swann's eyes but see him through hers. It is a composed and balanced procedure, but also a romantic convention. The film as a commodified vehicle also forsakes fidelity of appearance to film stardom. Jeremy Irons is a photogenic Keatsian hero, not the carrot-haired eczematic Jew whom Proust describes in the novel. In a way Irons is made too passive a figure for film narrative, which is why for the audience the more gripping scenes are the appearances of de Charlus (a virtuoso performance by Alain Delon) as he mocks his own sexual predation.

The litmus test of Proust, the movie, comes however, with the movie which was never made but whose screenplay is preserved as a literary text in its own right. Harold Pinter's screenplay for Joseph Losey, a project of the early seventies, runs to 166 pages and contains 455 separate shots.[3] The ambitious project was never made because the massive financial backing needed never materialised. But the text remains a literary document rather than a technical shooting script, asking perhaps to be judged in the place of the images which it never engendered. It is a picture-book without a picture, stranded between novel and film. But it clearly shows the dilemma of Proust, the movie. Pinter rightly centres the narrative on the Narrator, whom he calls Marcel. His strategy is to start with the memories of Marcel in the last volume of the novel, *Time Regained*, written by Proust directly after *Swann's Way*, as Marcel visits the house of the Prince de Guermantes in 1921. It then reverts directly to the first volume, rendering Marcel's childhood at Combray and proceeding in largely chronological manner through the novel, now and again using flashback or repetition.

There is no voice-over, no obvious strategy of asserting narrative presence, of searching for a facsimile. As written, the screenplay narrative is imagistic and fragmented, a mosaic of remembrances which evolves gradually into an icy geometry of sexual betrayal. Pinter thus opts for no half-measures. Acknowledging that there is no way of replicating the narrative presence of Marcel, he chooses to objectify him instead, to make him a figure in a mosaic of sexual and social hypocrisies, a naive, gullible obsessive around whom hypocrites circle until some form of belated recognition dawns. Pinter's Marcel is at best a passive centre, overshadowed, like Swann in Schlöndorff's film, by de Charlus who is not only the central predator but also the central commentator on betrayal and rapacity in general. It is difficult to envisage Marcel on screen as anything other than a figure to whom things happen, and a figure who remains on the outside, an observer for whom screen presence would be very difficult to create. In the novel, acts of reflecting and recollecting, the narrator's retroactive imposition of a desperate reason upon the volatility of the emotions, is what gives the narrative its power. The power of first-person narrative, intimate yet discursive, and the Proustian epiphanies of memory are the magic gifts which atone for inaction, obsession, betrayal.

The narrative problematic also takes us back to the vexed question of a shared frame of meaning between author and screenwriter. Here of course, there is little shared frame of meaning. The problem which confronts Pinter here is the one posed by L. P. Hartley in *The Go-Between*, which Pinter also adapted for Joseph Losey, the past as 'another country'. What atones for this hiatus in Pinter's Proust screenplay, as it does in Christopher Hampton's adaptation of *Les Liaisons Dangereuses* are the complex cynicisms of seduction whose rites in this case, span classes, nations and epochs. The success of Hampton's adaptations, as both theatre and cinema, lies precisely in this appeal. In Stephen Frears' picture-book, Hampton dispenses with accurate social etiquette, while Frears uses his American stars, Glenn

Close, John Malkovich and Michele Pfeiffer to give his themes a more contemporary appeal, making a deliberate pitch for anachronism. The sexual and moral vices of the French aristocracy are now, Pinter and Hampton imply, those of the Western middle-classes in general who have shed their puritanical heritage. In the age of consumer capitalism bourgeois audiences can now share vicariously in ritualised, costume versions of their own sexual and politicial cynicism. Even the historical picture-book is a product of its own age but it works best when it does not self-consciously parade its anachronism. Thus a literary device, an omniscient narrator of the twentieth century commenting on the mores of the nineteenth, which works well for John Fowles in *The French Lieutenant's Woman*, is largely lost in Karel Reisz's picture-book equivalent. Pinter's ingenious doubling of the love affair between Charles and Sarah as an affair between the two film actors who are playing them is a parallel plot, a film within a film, which stands in for the omniscient narrator that cinema can scarcely render. But as a stand-in device, it is a secondary and rather contrived surrogate.

In Fowles' novel, the first-person Fowlesian narrator is too distant with his sharp anachronisms from his nineteenth century characters to be truly cinematic. On the other hand, Proust's first-person Narrator is too singular, obsessive, all-encompassing, locked into memory. Kafka is perhaps unique among the great modern writers in using a narrative structure, as opposed to single imagistic epiphanies, which suggests direct filmic potential. In *The Trial* his character-narrator has no omniscient knowledge and we see the world much as he does. Certainly we see things in the novel from no one else's point of view. Yet K is an objectified presence, a third person character-narrator whom we also observe, dispassionately, from the outside. As Citati puts it: 'Kafka adopted the paradoxical condition of totally accepting the character's viewpoint -- but at the same time he created a glass wall between himself and Joseph K.'[4] The camera in Welles' picture-book gives a genuinely Kafkaesque narrative because it taps the unique properties of the novel which correspond more vitally to the nature of cinema itself. So it is that we begin with *The Trial*.

Notes

1. For a fuller discussion of this problem see David Cohen *Film and Fiction: The Dynamics of Exchange*, New Haven: Yale University Press, 1979, p. 80: also Geoffrey Wagner *The Novel and the Cinema*, London: The Tantivy Press, 1975.
2. See Anthony Giddens *Modernity and Self-Identity*, Cambridge: Polity Press, 1991, p. 25.
3. Harold Pinter *The Proust Screenplay: 'A la recherche du temps perdu'*, London: Eyre Methuen, 1978.
4. Pietro Citati *Kafka*, London: Minerva, 1991, p. 108.

Part I

Political fiction and the cinema

2

The Trial of Orson Welles

JOHN ORR

The attitude of Orson Welles towards his filming of Franz Kafka's famous novel in 1962 has at best been ambivalent. He originally chose it from a list of fifteen novels given to him by producer Alexander Salkind, when he claimed he would have preferred financing for one of his own projects instead. During interviews after the film's premiere, Welles claimed he was not a 'Kafka' expert and that Kafka, anyway, was not necessarily one of his favourite writers.[1] The claim must be taken with some caution. Welles also stated that he had full editorial control over the final cut, freedom from Hollywood interference, and that *The Trial* was the best film that he had ever made. His use of transnational locations, a common feature of the Welles' *opus* – here in Yugoslavia, France and Italy – was a combination of necessity and design. Welles was forced to leave Zagreb before the end of filming there because of Salkind's unpaid debts. The disused Gare d'Orsay in Paris as a new location was an inspired choice born out of instant need, but its combination of vast Belle Epoque interiors and creeping decay made it a brilliant contrast to the bleak and brute modernisms of highrise Zagreb. While the novel never moves outside of Prague, the film never sets foot in it. After all, Prague was then ruled by a Stalinist regime which had banned Kafka and would, following the Soviet invasion of 1968, re-ban him even after he had been unbanned. Instead, Welles replaces the enclosed Kafkaesque city with the claustrophobias of a continent, the suffocations of the pre-war rule of Empire in Austro-Hungary with the chill apocalypse of a nuclear Europe in the age of the Cuban Missile crisis and the building of the Berlin wall. The future was already here and separating the start of the novel from the making of the film was the slaughter of two world wars.

The Trial of Franz Kafka is a tragic fable with the logic of nightmare. It is one of the great modern novels – and there are very few indeed – which seem to get inside the experience of dreaming. The novel is characterised by those sudden transpositions in space-time which

13

confront a fearful dreamer with the new, the unexpected, the unknown, yet seem a logical continuation of previous experience. In Welles, as in Kafka, one turns around the corner to face a new world. But the new is merely a continuation of the old through forms of connection, mental images linking places which have no obvious spatial continuity. For Freud these are provided by those forms of condensation and displacement present in the dream-work.[2] For Kafka, they are provided by the exterior logic of surveillance and terror in a police state. The dream-like journey of Joseph K. from arrest to execution was a vast premonition perhaps, of the totalitarian rule which convulsed much of central Europe for fifty years. At the same time it has the logic of a precise hallucination. Welles, ever-Promethean in his quest of the impossible, tries to combine Kafka and Freud in the cinema of nightmare. His Joseph K. is a dreamer whose web of dark associations is implicitly sexual. He is also a subject of the state who complies with rampant terror. Guilt in one domain triggers guilt in the other. In dying at the hands of the state, at the hands of a Law which is lawless, he is punished for his guilty desire by those who specialise in the liquidation of the innocent. They, for their part, have no intrinsic interest in sin at all.

There is another crucial and risky difference between book and film. Welles' Joseph K (Anthony Perkins) is an American anti-hero, one might almost say a Euro-American transplanted back into his continent of origin, Europe. Instead of the passivity of the dream victim who protests too little, his American accent protests too much. Welles thus raises the level of protestation already present in Kafka's text and turns it into a sign of aural guilt. K's outraged voice constantly explodes across a dubbed and dislocating sound-track. While Kafka leaves open the question of whether Joseph K is guilty or not, or indeed what guilt can possibly mean, Welles opts for a more unambiguous reading, but one whose filmic extension contains its own ambiguities. As film-maker, he deems his anti-hero guilty and this central fact defines the relationship of the film to the book. But the guilt is internal. In part the 'trial' of Welles's K is conducted by K himself. Let us make no mistake here. Welles is not trying to produce *the* definitive film version of a major artwork of the twentieth century. He is aiming instead for an original and contemporary translation of word into image, and of dialogue written and read, into dialogue spoken and heard; all this in synch with powerful and discordant images of nightmare.

When the film was premiered in Paris in December, 1962, some critics deplored what they saw to be Perkins' aggressive and inappropriate posture towards the authorities who eventually destroy him. Yet the tone of defiance is clearly there in Kafka's text and Welles evokes this aggression not only as defiance but also as unexplained guilt. In his view, Joseph K is guilty, sharing prior complicity in the system which persecutes him. The early morning visit by the sinister agents of the state is more 'familiar', more predictable to him than he is willing to admit. Perkins uses a set of nervous and hyperactive reactions, all of them highly mannered, to suggest that K anticipates it, that he is expecting it to happen. The return of the repressed here is both sexual and political. The police come to arrest him at the moment of waking, at that moment of vivid dreaming that we are most likely to retain thereafter in our daytime memory. The direction of the persecutors' entry in the film is not without interest. In a low-angle shot reminiscent of *Citizen Kane*, Welles has them burst through double doors from the adjacent apartment of Fraulein Burstner as if the act of entry were a sequel to the witnessing of the primal scene of K's implicit lust, and the gesture itself a metaphorical penetration. The act of intrusion is not only an arrest of his person but, as the film soon makes clear, an arrest of his desire. Later when Burstner returns, K's desire is made explicit, a sporadic lust encumbered by the proprieties of formal address and which absurd etiquette forbids to speak its name.

K's squat enclosed room with its low ceiling, his enclosed balcony outside high up in the apartment block, the propinquity of Fraulein Burstner's own room – one of the 'scenes' of K's unspecified crime; all suggest the claustrophobia of persecution without escape, guilt without exit. In Welles's narrative, film space now becomes a futuristic labyrinth down which his hero flees the guilt-accretions of the past, the encrustations of a time transforming itself into another dimension, or rather breaking any clear boundary between space and time, transforming itself instead into a single space-time continuum. Meanwhile the return of Fraulein Burstner (Jeanne Moreau) after the police depart confirms the mutuality of an attraction stronger in K who in turn is too inhibited to let it openly blossom. K's stumbling response to his arrest is in fact a series of Freudian slips which continue in the physically gauche manner he confronts the night-club singer in her room. Welles makes much here of the alternative route to her chamber, the 'path' down the outside corridor. His camera tracks back and forth with the decorum of front entry, and thus highlights the 'back entry' of intrusion. Later, when Burstner learns of the police visit and bodily pushes K out through the double doors, the sudden backward movement suggests sexual ejection. Previously, during interrogation K has referred to his phonograph as a 'pornograph' and a mark on the floor of his room made a dentist's chair as an 'ovular shape'. Later when the exhausted Burstner back from her 'supper show' casually remarks to him in the corridor outside 'It's been a long, hard night', K's low-key but bright-eyed reply is 'Yes – but . . .'

Welles constructs dream narrative by transposing theatrical devices to the screen. His film is full of dramatic exits and entrances but their spatial reference is filmic. K continually bursts through closed doors from enclosed spaces into open ones, from a space that is crabbed and finite to one which is vast and agoraphobic. And then vice versa. The door is a device to conceal what Burch has called 'offscreen space'.[3] It portends the anxious gaze upon the first sighting of the other side, the 'unknown' screen of dream logic blocking the scene that is about to ambush its dreaming subject. Welles's rejection of a natural plane of spatial continuity is crucial here. Wellesian entry is often movement in film recording to another place and another time, neither contiguous nor continuous. That is, it is movement to another place that seems to have no consistency with the place in which the hero is already positioned. If K is continually ambushed by the spectacle of the unknown, so are we. The unexpected is often not something which initially happens onscreen, but a threatening presence offscreen that is withheld and waiting to be unveiled. It is shielded from our view not just by the cut, but by the doors whose opening precedes the cut. The cut then becomes the jump in the space-time passage of the dream.

In his re-arranging of chapter sequence, Welles proceeds from Chapter 1, the arrest, to Chapter 4, the encounter with Fraulein Burstner's friend, then back to Chapter 2 where K enters the packed gallery of the court, then onto Chapter 5 where he witnesses the flogging of his police interrogators. The alterations enable Welles to image the logic of discontinuous space, where mental association works through its physical negation. By dint of a sudden cut, K literally bursts out through the closed doors of Burstner's room into the unfolding spaces of the vast office arena, and the camera's long forward-tracking shot lends to K's stride the rhythms of power and control which contrast with his ignominious ejection. The low horizontal structure of Burstner's room is replicated among the clatter of countless typewriters but width and depth are now limitless and the echoing noise of the machines adds to the optical openness of receding space. Yet within a moment, K pitches himself back into the dark enclosed space of 'the broom closet', a storeroom where he unveils his birthday cake for Fraulein Burstner and is caught in the act by his boss. The connotations of 'cake', 'bake', 'surprise', 'present', 'oven' metonymically framed within a secret womb-like space are obvious enough. K, again stammering with guilt, is again caught *in flagrante delicto*. Guilty intent is then re-iterated through its iconic opposite when he goes back out onto the office floor and sees his young cousin, Irmi, through a glass partition which acts as a sound barrier, blocking off her voice but not the frantic gestures to capture his attention. Wide-shot deep-focus is used here to suggest transparency of dark sexual motive through glass. Again his boss rebukingly 'catches him in the act' of communicating with his fifteen year-old cousin who is framed in long shot behind glass between their hostile profiles. But having quickly dispatched her, K reasserts his power by returning to his elevated desk above the work-floor. A tilting crane shot from behind unveils his spatial relationship of dominance over desk-bound clerical slaves, their backs alone visible to us as their Olivettis rattle away with deafening noise.

In switching instantly from the office arena back to K's apartment, Welles undermines the fragile iconography of K's bureaucratic power. He cuts to an exterior shot of K trailing after Fraulein Pittl, a crippled friend of Burstner who is leaving the apartment block with a trunk full of Burstner's possessions. Again K, asking after the strange disappearance of Burstner, guiltily denies to the strange woman his own 'guilt by association'. But Welles's masterly tracking shot subtly undermines his protestations. The shot is a long crescent-shaped dolly across the wasteland in front of high-rise Zagreb, unveiling for the first time the ubiquity of massive concrete towering up in rectangular blocks out of the middle of nowhere. It is the first time we really see the outside of K's apartment block, but then again there is no establishing shot, no general view, so we do not really see it at all. At any one instant, we do not 'get' the whole picture. As we see the brute buildings loom in close proximity to the apartment block, the latter has already disappeared from the frame. The long shot of the cripple has been referred to as the film's 'Mother Courage' shot. But aside from any homage to Brecht, it makes K even more abject than its peripatetic cripple. The constant creak of her crippled leg drowns his questions and protests. She never looks at him as she lectures him and he finally takes up the trunk and wheels it himself.

Again with his sudden cut to the theatre auditorium, from brute modern to old world baroque, Welles rings the changes. But when K goes outside to meet his interrogator about the court, the brief composure of auditorium vanishes. K wanders through labyrinthine spaces which are derelict and decaying, exterior and interior at the same time. Surveillance is not necessary, the state go-between tells him. 'They aren't going to follow you. That isn't their job.' For K's nightmare passage already matches the trajectory of flight, a flight in which he has no need to look over his own shoulder. He is watched without being watched, as if all his movements were invisibly monitored. Welles makes secular here the total gaze of Kafka's pitiless and trascendent God, who sees everything that K does not. In both instances, the overt gaze has become redundant. The same two men he passes are the ones who will later kill him. As he makes his way to the courtroom he strides past gaunt, wraith-like creatures without a backward glance, passive victims in vast open spaces who look like displaced inmates of Auschwitz, and who remind us, if not him, of his

potential fate. The long sweeping shot centred around a vast cloaked
statue which captures this Wellesian anachronism, this post-Holocaust
epiphany, is awe-inspiring in its execution. The absence of looking (at
the victims), mirrors the absence of watching (no obvious surveillance).
But as surely as the audience sees the former, it senses the latter and
shares complicity in K's fate.

The packed courtroom scene is a reprise perhaps of the election
address of Charles Foster Kane, but with a difference. Here the audience
is live, not part of a matte projection and Welles uses side- and reverse-
angles to establish the tense relationship of K and his audience.
Moreover K, though defiant, is on the defensive, not the offensive like
the triumphant Kane. Welles visually reproduces Kafka's description of
the packed gallery, but introduces his own melodramatic touch. The
crowd are immediately aware of K while in Kafka's novel they at first
take no notice of him. Here K defends himself vehemently but no one
takes any notice of him. Instead they get their fun by watching the
student grab his wife, Hilda (Elsa Martinelli) who has previously
guided K to the courtroom, and carry her off out through the door. As
Cowie suggests, the violent manner of her abduction is another clue to
the violent fate which will befall him, the audience's reaction to it a sign
of indifference towards his own fate.[4]

The next sequence reaffirms the narrative thread of nightmare.
Politics becomes sexual, sex becomes political. The policemen who have
interrogated K in his apartment are now being interrogated in turn by
their superior. For this is a police state where the chain of 'guilt' spreads
like a bacillus up the chain of command. Welles' *mise-en-scène* is sado-
masochistic. Those minions who used arbitrary power are now its abject
victims. The policemen are tied and whiplashed by their boss in the
office storeroom already established as a primal scene of guilt. In
overblown empathy K 'acts out' each blow as if he were himself the
victim, while the blow itself is not that of the boot or the fist but that of
the whip on the bare torso of the victim; while filmed in such a tight
space with an off-angle hand-held camera, the weapon seems to be that
of the light-bulb, hit by the interrogator each time he strikes and arcing
tightly through the cupboard darkness. Here the transparency of light
itself is literally 'striking' – the motion of the bulb, the tight arc of the
destroyer. The ray of light thus becomes an encased weapon. K escapes
through the door in a cut to an exterior profile shot which shows the
victims desperately tugging at his sleeve and his flight is a dream
passage back into the power of authority, as he strides purposefully to
meet Uncle Max. The tracking long shots and crane tilts of the office
arena are repeated. He is thus re-established. But the sequence tells us
his elevation will not last. As work finishes and the clerks all leave,
another tracking shot takes K and his uncle at right angles through the

milling, departing throng. The separation of K from his workers is dissolved in the chaos of contrary bustle and movement.

K's first visit to the advocate echoes the motif of open and closed spaces, cutting almost immediately from the tight shot of Leni's eyes peering out at K through the letter flap on the front door to the dusty palatial apartment of the bed-ridden Hastler played by Welles himself. Typically Hastler's face is withheld until after direct contact with K. His voice is heard before he is seen. A low-angle shot from the bottom of the bed conceals his portly frame. A hot flannel applied to his face hides his features. Yet Hastler 'knows' about K's case already, just as everybody else 'knows'. The confidential visit is a charade since nothing can any longer be said in confidence. The sexual motif continues with K's attraction for the advocate's secretary and its nature has been keyed in during the sequence with his uncle at the office. They both walk along a vast railed balcony housing a mammoth computer which Max suggests could hold the secret to the nature of K's trial. The computer is referred to as a 'she', seen as identical by K with 'love' and 'terror'. Love and terror are synonyms for the promise/threat of female desire which Leni (Romy Schneider) embodies. At one level Leni is the dream attraction of the instant object of desire and here Welles shifts away from Kafka's play with the grotesque ugliness of the webbed fingers through the high-lit glamour of Schneider's face and the siren lure of her guttural voice.

Yet he does not abandon it entirely. For K the lure of the defect in a beautiful woman is a compelling perversity and also connotes, perhaps, the challenge of the breaking of the membrane in the first act of penetration. The link is strengthened by its timing. Leni remarks 'Look, skin between my middle fingers like a web', just after she asked K about his girlfriend and has obviously seen a photo of Burstner: 'She's not so young.' Thus the defective membrane is linked indirectly to the 'double doors' of Burstner's room and then precedes Leni's act of seduction in the dusty book-strewn library which looks for all the world like a garbage tip. The shot sequence here is fascinating. Welles films Schneider's overtures from a low angle as she turns suddenly to force K to the ground. In the sudden motion we see Perkins' legs tip up into the bottom of the frame as he flies backwards out of shot. Welles then cuts to a high-angle long shot in which their flying tangled bodies are spread among the open pages of the scattered books. To complete sexual role-reversal, we clearly see K's limbs wrapped around his seductress as he falls to the ground under her. There is a jump cut to a low angle profile in medium shot of their upper bodies; K's eyes are almost closed as if on the edge of pleasurable exhaustion. Thereafter he wraps his coat around them both. As they talk, Welles cuts back to an even higher angle in which their bodies seem to be part of a strewn textual wasteland, where they are literally indistinguishable from the detritus which surrounds them. The sequence suggests through the constant talk which is both distraction and anxiety, that K's nightmare seduction has turned into a wet dream, that the moment of impact on the ground is that of ejaculation, and that the indecipherable movements of the bodies under the coat may well be the vain attempt of Schneider to re-arouse his spent desire. The involuntary pleasure of dream thus becomes the failure to sustain reality which is what, increasingly, K cannot do.

More temptation occurs immediately after in K's encounter with the wife of the student who had been carried off to great laughter during the initial session of the trial. Welles shoots her in the deserted courtroom from the back of the podium in reverse angle towards the open door at the back. Most of the chairs have cleared. The place is barely recognisable. The familiar has been rendered unfamiliar by the 180° change of angle. The sexual lure is sustained when Hilda returns to beguile him, claiming as her husband catches them talking together: 'I'll come back soon and you can do with me whatever you like.' But the politics of sexual encounter feed straight into the hero's paranoia. 'This could be a trap', K asserts. He toys with the idea of seduction of the woman as an act of revenge on the student and on the magistrate of the court. But he is by now the victim of seduction, not its perpetrator. The act of seduction, female on male, has now become associated in his mind with the act of surveillance. To be seduced and to be watched are adjacent acts of devouring, and both are forms of temptation.

Welles' juxtaposition of surveillance and sexual desire is partly wilful, the filmic innovator playing with the constants of the written text. Images of desire distract from the narrative and highly verbal quest for justice. But the relentless quest for justice also distracts from the images of desire. As spectators we cannot live through the erotic threat to K embodied in sequential images of different woman whose presences are disconcerting, while following with equal attention the labyrinthine paths of K's legal pursuit of 'his case' through different and discontinuous spaces, through mismatching corridors and rooms. Dream-logic combines the two but reason drives them asunder. Welles thus attenuates the dissonance of the text, playing image and voice-off against one another. Yet the subtle underplaying of the sexual fix makes it clearly the subtext, a series of restrained allusions which accrete throughout the film, while the justice quest devolves into the logic of nightmare. In the screenplay the words are largely Kafka's. In the film the images largely belong to Welles.

The quest here is clearly an imagistic nightmare. The journey between places, between rooms that K makes in searching for knowledge about his case, always disorients. The spectator shares his vertiginous sense of a path towards the unknown where the route itself is rendered unfamiliar. In the second visit to the courtroom Welles uses a long reverse-angle take from the platform for the first time to render the familiar unfamiliar. Shadows fall from the open door at the back onto the vast floor and the power of the place as a tribunal of the state is thus dissipated, and made to seem absurd. This is followed by long, dizzying shots outside in the corridor, tracking and hand-held, of court supplicants and endless library shelves, as K threads his way outside. K emerges outside through pillars of a baroque Italian church to meet his cousin, Irmi, then takes a few steps forward to become centred in the bleak glass towers of new Zagreb before bidding her farewell amidst the cool horizontal lines of a suburban Italian factory.

The return to Hastler's apartment echoes the return of the sexual fix after the disarray of space-time mismatches. K arrives at a time when Leni is clearly seducing Bloch (Akim Tamiroff), an older dishevelled client of Hastler's whom, it appears, she locks up in a maid's room and treats as a slave. The small seedy room echoes the enclosed space of the storeroom. As the two clients of Hastler scathingly discuss their lawyer together in almost identical waistcoats, it becomes clear that Bloch is K's double, an older version of what will happen to K if he allows himself to remain Hastler's client, a version in other words of Joseph as an old man. An intimate medium shot establishes Leni in the foreground slightly in front of the two men until she finally leans her head back between them. Not only does the shot suggest her domination over them, the seductress of both, but the undignified hold on the shot which captures the tension in the face of both men while nothing seems to be happening hints at a possible act of masturbation taking place out of frame. At one level the discourse is legal. Bloch has laughingly told K he has five advocates and Bloch is the least important of them, but sexual innuendo remains. 'So you sleep in the maid's room?' K inquires. 'She lets me have it,' Bloch replies, 'It's very convenient.'

As K struggles with Leni to get through to Hastler's musty bedchamber, and confront the indolent advocate, the metaphoric connection of guilt and sexuality is intensified. In the bedchamber Hastler informs K that Leni finds all accused men attractive and treats them as sexual prey. 'She makes love to all of them', he continues, 'and when I allow her to, she tells me about them to arouse me.' Moreover, Hastler claims to K that if an advocate 'has the right eye' he can 'see' all the guilty men and be attracted by them. The statement once more links surveillance with desire. Leni's seductions of the accused are forms of surveillance by proxy in which the bedridden Hastler 'keeps an eye' on his charges by envisaging the details of their sexual slavery which Leni verbally imparts to him. The final humiliation of Bloch occurs when Leni beckons him forward to kiss the advocate's hand. But the framing is wilfully ambiguous. From the end of the bed Bloch seems almost to be crawling under the coverlet to burrow between Hastler's thighs. A quick cut to a reverse angle from the top of the bed shows the angle of his body slightly altered, so that he pulls Hastler's hand out from under the cover and demeaningly kisses it. For a brief moment it appears as if he was about to kiss a different part of the lawyer's anatomy. Here the camera shot avoids crudity of gesture and also suggests another metaphor of abjectness, echoed in K's derisive comment that Bloch 'is the advocate's dog'. His action is that of a blind, obedient pet snuggling up to his master's side. This is the cul-de-sac too of the bureaucratic victim, of a man whose case is hopeless. 'To be in chains,' Hastler proclaims ominously, 'is sometimes safer than to be free'. Seeing Bloch's humiliation, K does break free. He leaves the lawyer's apartment never to return.

The wasteland of K's abortive seduction by Leni is Hastler's disused library, a legal wasteland, a veritable desert of piled-up archives and ancient books strewn with dust. It is the written legacy of the law in all its manifold, bureaucratic complexity, of all the abandoned statutes which are irrelevant and fallen into disuse. The act of seduction amidst the book pile is, on the one hand, an act of sacrilege, a defiance of the official sacredness of the law. On the other it is a visceral defiance of the deathliness of the dead text which has no application to living things. Yet Welles' montage suggests something further, a third possibility. A long shot after the first thrust of seduction shows the furtive couple to be indistinguishable from the carpet of open and disordered texts on which they lie. It is as if in the failure of their desire, they have become at one with the shattered canvas of the law which fails to give their bodies definition. The intended act of sacrilege has been literally swallowed up by the objects of its contempt. The archaic text dominates the living body.

The visit to Titorelli, the portrait painted of judges is a *mise-en-scène* which maintains fidelity to Kafka's story and dialogue but establishes an image-sequence uniquely Wellesian in its execution. K is pursued by a gang of teenage girls up a spiral staircase and ladder into a tower which leads onto the painter's attic studio. The sequence is a reprise of the Expressionist image of phallic ascent which also recalls the ascent of the church tower in Hitchcock's *Vertigo*. The images of sexual role-reversal, K as the pursued, females as predators, are intensified by filming the painter's studio as a latticed cage in which K is the human specimen watched through wooden slats by female 'vultures' whose laughter is like the shrieking chatter of birds. 'A dreadful little claw reaches up and seizes me,' Titorelli tells K with great distaste as he plucks off a girl's hand reaching in through one of the wooden apertures. Thus K is the domesticated prey in a human zoo and the girls bird-like spectators, whispering gleefully: 'He's taken off his jacket'. Titorelli reaffirms the image by showing K the portrait of justice he has painted for the Court but which we never see. It is a portrait of Justice with wings and scales and a bandage over its eyes, but also of Justice as a 'Goddess of Victory'. For K however, with one eye on the peering girls outside, it is like 'the Goddess of the Hunt in full cry.' Welles constantly cuts back and forth here from K and the painter to close-up shots of single eyes peering at them between the slats. The secret police may be nowhere in sight but the act of surveillance has reached the limit of its power and intimacy.

Titorelli tells him that 'these girls belong to the court.' Their watching thus becomes a form of surrogate surveillance, desire mediating the political. Both the girls and the court wish to destroy him in different ways, the girls to tear apart his body, the court to rip him open body and soul. But the watching is also a function of K's guilt, as his nervous demeanour and his flickering eyes reveal. Moreover, Welles plays off the reverse-angles of watching against the formal plot-line. All the while K and Titorelli are discussing the difference between ostensible acquittal and indefinite deferral of the case, both of them final forms of bureaucratic nightmare. The first ensures that K's dossier circulates indefinitely as he is constantly acquitted and then re-arrested, 'ostensibly free' but always a prisoner. The second entails an endless stalemate in which his case will never be taken to a Higher Court which alone has the power to judge him innocent but remains inaccessible. The eternity of injustice is not then the brutal act of execution but the eternity of waiting and the eternity of guilt, the constant failure ever to be proved innocent. But outside the protective veneer of Hastler and Titorelli, who can provide the torture of deferral, there still lingers the brute possibility of summary execution.

K's pursuit by the teenage gang of girls after he leaves the studio is spectacular proof of this possibility. By this time his paranoia is already rampant. In the studio sequence Welles self-consciously and wilfully plays on Freud's view of paranoia as a repressed fear of being watched or caught out in the act of homosexual desire. The presentation of Titorelli as camp, effeminate and inquisitive, aided by Welles' own dubbing of the painter's voice in a fruity Southern English accent, clearly suggests his approaches to K over portrait paintings is a form of sexual overture. There is more than a hint that the watching girls may be there in the hope of witnessing a gay seduction. 'We're going to see a lot of each other, eh, Joey boy!' Titorelli smugly suggests. This in turn echoes and strengthens the previous scenes of sado-masochistic torture and Bloch's grovelling to Hastler. But by this time K is already in flight. The spatial dislocation of the cutting is oneiric and powerful. K leaves the attic studio with its tight tower-like structure to find himself straight away in the library of the law courts with its low horizontal structure. His rapid flight along its tight, ground-level latticed corridors – a spectacular quickfire backtrack – cuts abruptly to continued chase through even narrower underground tunnels with airshafts where the girls, still pursuing, are running over the ground above and peering down at him. The camera trajectory is swiftly horizontal in all three sequences but the cutting is between different vertical planes -- tower, ground-level, subterranean. The tunnelled flight thus suggests detumescence without gradual descent. Space-time co-ordinates dissolve in the blind flight through the labyrinth of nightmare. It is not merely that K's paranoia brings him back down to earth. It actually takes him underground and threatens to bury him alive.

At this point Welles again excels himself. Yet another optical *volte-face* conjures agoraphobic desolation out of claustrophobic terror. K escapes out onto the vast open piazza of an Italian city, empty, nocturnal, forbidding. He is suddenly small, defenceless, vulnerable in this urban desert. A reverse-angle reveals the priest on his pulpit outside a huge cathedral whose pillars are covered in rivets. The priest is looking down at him, both the church and the figure towering over him. As Hastler arrives in pursuit of K Welles brings back the visual slides on the fable of entry to the Law with which, as narrator, he introduced the film, and which in the novel occurs in the sermon of the priest. Welles thus dramatised the sermon as an image-sequence on a screen which is then framed reflexively as a screen-within-a-screen. The designs were composed and patented on a pin screen by Alexandré Alexeieff[5] and Welles uses them now in a set on which K and Hastler are framed in turn as figures in the flesh and as silhouettes. They watch the images and contend between them over their meaning. K is first framed in silhouetted profile against the screen as if he is the 'man from the country' who in the fable begs admittance, and Hastler the guard who gives him no entry. Then the positions are reversed. Hastler is shown in silhouette and finally K is shown fully lit in full face against the now empty screen. The latticed slides echo the previous image of flight through the corridor. The 'visual aids' are 'particular delusions' which turn 'lying into a universal principle'. At the moment in which moral fable becomes formally paramount Welles deconstructs the discourse by producing images stressing what Deleuze has called in Welles 'the powers of the False', the path of deceiving nightmare beyond the moral journey, indeed beyond all good and evil.[6]

Yet, as Naremore has pointed out, Welles still brings his Western and specifically American conception of justice to bear on the film.[7] K remains a defiant hero who pursues justice to the end and refuses to die, as Kafka makes him die, 'like a dog'. To the Priest who calls him 'my son', he defiantly retorts 'I am not your son'. There is then a logic of justice to his defiance, in which he realises that even if his own case is lost, it does not condemn 'the entire world to lunacy'. Though Wellesian morality is more discursive and less oblique than Kafka's in its use of the word, though it centrally engages the issue of the law and justice as moral facts, the ambiguous power of the image contradicts this semiological transparency. The space-time image of K's flight is one of tragic doom, the defiant individual cry drowned in images of bleak, tragic necessity. We know K will die and Welles is not furnishing us with exemplary heroism but with a visual pathos. As the secret police take K away in a montage of marching shots through the city and suburb to the deserted quarry which matches Kafka's dream topography of old Prague, the fidelity of Welles's narrative to Kafka's text is extraordinary, even though the ending itself is transformed, post-Auschwitz, with the body of the hysterical but defiant victim blown up by dynamite into the dust of a mushroom-shaped cloud. It retains that quality of the novel which stresses brute and summary execution after the long never-ending passage towards trial in which no advance seems to have been made.

The final defiance of K undermines Welles's stated view of him as a guilty 'little bureaucrat'. In the quarry K rejects the chance to use on himself the knife which the secret policemen pass back and forth across his prone body, and tells them 'you'll have to kill me.' But the defiance itself is flawed by the clear link, in his case, between guilt and protest. The hyperactive figure of Anthony Perkins is obviously disappointing for those who wish to see K as a passive and noble victim, and Welles is all too aware that someone like Antonioni would film the novel very differently, as is evident in the coolly apocalyptic tone of *L'Eclisse*, made at the same time as *The Trial*. Instead Welles forgoes the temptation of statuesque passivity which runs counter to the dream-momentum of Kafka's narrative, and opts for the constant image of defiance-in-flight. Here it was surely a stroke of luck for cinema history that the Salkinds ran out of money at the very moment Welles wished the Yugoslav authorities to finance very elaborate sets for the court scenes and other interiors. Instead the vast open spaces of the derelict Gare d'Orsay are both exterior and interior in their feel and look. Certainly they provided acres of empty floor-space for tracking and the imaginative design upon half-formed fixtures that makes the work of Jean Mandaroux so visually compelling. The imaginative use of a disused space which is half-formed and half-deformed, and which bears the trace of human intention in its architectural shapes but simultaneously dissolves them, is vital to the look of the film, and one which preformed studio sets could never have captured. It is small wonder that with total control of a contemporary project for the first time since *Citizen Kane*, Welles would call it his best and most satisfying film. It had the camera mobility and vast open spaces of location shooting which the earlier masterpiece lacked. But Welles also had the final cut and the editorial control he missed so much in *The Lady from Shanghai* and *Touch of Evil*.

The impact of the film upon the modern cinema has been powerful and profound. Like *Touch of Evil*, it inspired a new generation of European film-makers to address the fluidity and plasticity of the film image, and to see the image as a form of durational movement in which nothing 'ever stops'. The tight-suited Perkins, constantly on the move as he is framed in low-angle medium shot or profiled in long shot, is seen as a lone desolate figure enclosed in tight, nightmarish spaces or else dwarfed by huge forbidding surfaces; all these were to inspire Bernardo Bertolucci in his famous adaptation of Alberto Moravia's novel *The Conformist*, where he too uses the Parisian landscape of the Gare d'Orsay. His fascist anti-hero Marcello Clerici has the same taut and tight appearance, the same motor-anxiety of the reluctant conformist, the same restless movement towards unknown destinations, and the same guilt. The general nightmare of the bureaucratic police state is translated back into a specific dream-reverie of the age of Mussolini. The bisexual sub-text of Welles surfaces more explicitly in Bertolucci as oneiric Freudian melodrama, a dream-reverie of forbidden desire. In American cinema too, as Kolker has pointed out,[8] Kubrick and Scorcese have followed Welles' Kafkaesque example in the filming of *A Clockwork Orange* and *After Hours* for very different purposes; the former using tracking to *recuperate* cinematic space rather than decentre it, while the latter turns the labyrinth of *The Trial* into a Manhattan yuppie's nightmare. Unlike Bertolucci's highly original film, both are more obviously derivative and both make compromises, turning inspiration into idiom and dislocation into mannerism. But then neither had the power of the original or, beyond that, the power of the written masterpiece which inspired it.

For here we have the rare case of one masterpiece inspiring the creation of another. The paradox is that of a film adaptation of an artwork transforming itself into an artwork that exists in its own right, and yet somehow still has to be understood as 'a film version' of the book. In retrospect both artworks are now cultural facts and there can be no invidious comparison between the book-as-original and the film-as-artefact. Their connection is unprecedented and perhaps will never again be matched, but the paradox remains – they cannot be discussed without being compared. Yet on an aesthetic level, there is no longer any comparison between them at all. If anything, one can only hope Welles's film comes to be more accessible than it has been over recent years and that, in some ideal world, it can be seen by all those who have read the book. On the other hand, it should not and indeed cannot be seen merely as a visual incentive to those who have not read the book in the way, for example, that it is possible to watch Shakespeare on stage without having read the play that is being performed. The book comes first, the film second despite the current temptations of our audio-visual culture. Yet aesthetically the film stands on its own and the puzzle continues. The paradox of influence and intertextuality this particular film represents can, unlike most other adaptations, never be resolved.

Notes

1. See Welles's remarks in a 1963 interview: 'Orson Welles talking to Juan Cobos, Miguel Rubio and José Pruneda' in Andrew Sarris (ed.) *Hollywood Voices*, London: Secker and Warburg, 1971, p. 149. For more detailed descriptions of the production background to *The Trial*, consult Frank Brady *Citizen Welles*, London: Coronet Books, 1991, p. 528: and Barbara Leaming *Orson Welles*, Harmondsworth: Penguin, 1987, p. 459.
2. See Sigmund Freud *The Interpretation of Dreams*, Harmondsworth: Penguin, 1976, pp. 383–414, 417f., 650f.; also Christian Metz *Psychoanalysis and Cinema*, London: Macmillan, 1982, p. 178.
3. Noel Burch *Theory of Film Practice*, Princeton, NJ: Princeton University Press, 1981, p. 38.
4. Peter Cowie *The Cinema of Orson Welles*, New York: Da Capo Press, 1983, p. 159.
5. *ibid.*, p. 166.
6. Gilles Deleuze *Cinema 2: The Time-Image*, London: The Athlone Press, 1989, p. 137.
7. James Naremore *The Magic World of Orson Welles*, New York: Oxford University Press, 1978, p. 189.
8. Robert Kolker *The Cinema of Loneliness: Penn, Kubrick, Coppola, Scorcesse, Altmann*, New York: Oxford University Press, 1980, pp. 84, 223.

Filmography

The Trial (Paris Europa Productions/FI-C-IT/Hisa-Films, 118 minutes, 1963.) Starring Anthony Perkins, Jeanne Moreau, Romy Schneider, Akim Tamiroff, Else Martinelli, Orson Welles. Director of Photography, Edmond Richard; Camera operator, Adolphe Charlet; Edited by Yvonne Martin, Denise Baby and Fritz Mueller; Art director, Jean Mandaroux; Music, Jean Ledrut and Tomaso Albinoni; Produced by Alexander and Michael Salkind; Written and Directed by Orson Welles.

3

Filming the unfilmable:
Volker Schlöndorff and *The Tin Drum*

RICHARD KILBORN

Of all the works to be produced by the post-war generation of West German novelists none has had quite the same impact as Günter Grass' *The Tin Drum*. When it first appeared in 1959, it was as if a whirlwind had blown through the literary scene. Not only was it seen as an important contribution to the ongoing task of 'coming to terms with the (German) past' (*Vergangenheitsbewältigung*), but the story was told with a sureness of touch and exuded such creative energy that it was difficult to believe that this was Grass' first novel. The work also created a great stir in that it explored and depicted in graphic detail areas of sexual and religious experience which had traditionally been surrounded by many taboos. Grass' own view of the work was that he had been attempting to capture 'the reality of a whole epoch, with all its absurdities and contradictions', focusing on the 'confined world of the petit bourgeoisie', but also on the wider public sphere where 'the most fearful and monstrous crimes' had been committed.[1]

Given this combination of factors – the epic breadth of the novel, coupled with the bold manner of its telling – *The Tin Drum* was generally thought to be unfilmable. Indeed almost sixteen years were to elapse before the Munich-based producer Franz Seitz finally persuaded Grass -- on the strength of a fifty-page treatment he had prepared -- that a film version of the novel was feasible. Not surprisingly Seitz turned to someone with a proven track-record in adaptation to direct the film, his choice falling on the German director Volker Schlöndorff. It also soon became clear that this was going to be one of the biggest projects yet to have been undertaken by a West German production team.

Work on the film – which had a large budget of over 6 million marks – began in 1977 and location shooting took place in Yugoslavia, Normandy and Gdansk/Danzig in the course of 1978, with studio scenes being shot in Berlin. The film was premiered in the Spring of 1979 and later that year it received the Golden Palm award at the Cannes film festival (jointly with *Apocalypse Now*). In the following year it received the

28

ultimate accolade, being the first German film ever to receive a Hollywood Oscar.

The present essay reflects on some of the processes by which Grass' work was translated from page to screen, and reflects on some of the special difficulties of filming a novel which since its publication had acquired almost legendary status. At the same time an attempt is made to set *The Tin Drum* in the context of Schlöndorff's other adaptation work, most notably *The Lost Honour of Katharina Blum*, the film which before *The Tin Drum* had done most to establish Schlöndorff's reputation as a director who could be relied on to combine box-office appeal with an ability to tackle serious contemporary issues.

As already suggested, Schlöndorff had already gained a considerable reputation as a film-maker specialising in the adaptation of literary works. His first full-length feature *The Young Törleß* (1966) had been adapted from the 'novella' of the same name by Robert Musil. This film, which was generally well received, encouraged Schlöndorff to produce more adaptations including film versions of Brecht's *Baal*, of Marguerite Yourcenar's *Le Coup de Grace* and of Heinrich Böll's *The Lost Honour of Katharina Blum*, that probing satirical account of a particularly critical phase in the development of the Federal Republic. This latter film was both a commercial success and also got mostly good critical reviews. It was this combination which doubtless persuaded Seitz that Schlöndorff was the film-maker best qualified to rise to the challenge which *The Tin Drum* presented.

There has been considerable speculation about why Schlöndorff should always have felt so drawn towards adaptation. Before giving an account of how *The Tin Drum* itself was adapted for the screen, we shall therefore consider one or two of the observations which Schlöndorff has had to make on the subject. When asked to explain the special fascination that literary subjects have had for him, Schlöndorff has often made the point that from an early age the reading of books acquired for him the intensity of 'real life' experience. For Schlöndorff then there have been good grounds for turning to literature as the point of departure for much of his film work. An additional, and possibly more telling reason for his commitment to adaptations is the director's conviction that the adapting of literary works fulfils an important democratising function. In Schlöndorff's view 'moving literature out into the market-place' is a most worthwhile project, since it reduces the possibility of literature acquiring the aura of a remote, high-culture object.[2] Such popularising beliefs have important implications for the whole manner in which Schlöndorff approaches any adaptation project. It has meant that for him the priority in adaptation will lie not so much in preserving the literary qualities of the work in question as in producing a version in which – whilst some of the original contours may still be visible – the primary aim has been to create a new artwork which seeks to make its impact solely by cinematic means.

In further reflections on the subject, Schlöndorff has always been ready to concede the more 'opportunistic' reasons for producing adaptations.[3] He happily acknowledges that in some measure all adaptations seek to capitalise on the currency established by the original work. Thus part of the economic calculation is the opportunity to rekindle the interest which the work first created. This being the case, it might be thought that there would always be a direct correlation between the reception of the book and the impact or success of the associated film. As Schlöndorff has pointed out, however, bestselling books have not always – indeed very rarely – been converted into blockbuster films. Accordingly his own motivation for wanting to produce film versions of such well-known contemporary works as *Katharina Blum* and *The Tin Drum* was not the fact that they had acquired the status of contemporary classics but that they tackled subjects which in his opinion were worthy of extended feature-film treatment.[4]

An additional explanation of Schlöndorff's fondness for adaptation has to do with his basic attitude to the business of film-making. In stark contrast to his West German contemporaries such as Herzog and Syberberg, Schlöndorff has always adopted a decidedly non-auteurist, almost artisanal approach to the film-making process. As John Sandford has remarked: 'Schlöndorff is not given to technical experiments, avant-garde mannerisms or innovations; his work is polished and entertaining, and his films contain in abundance . . . elements of audience appeal'.[5] It was these qualities which persuaded those who contributed to the large, multi-million mark budget of *The Tin Drum* that Schlöndorff – perhaps more than any other German director of his generation – could be relied upon to produce a film which reconciled commercial and artistic imperatives.[6]

Adapting *The Tin Drum*

In Grass' novel the narrative is presented as a retrospective account, as Oskar, the novel's diminutive narrator and chief protagonist, reflects back on the course of events which have led him to his present (mid-fifties) situation: that of an inmate of a Düsseldorf mental asylum. It is in this confined environment that the reader first confronts Oskar and it is from this vantage point that Oskar – employing the first person form – begins to conjure up the elaborate and kaleidoscopic pageant of past events. This initial perspective quickly gives way, however, to a different mode of address in which Oskar becomes a player in his own drama and is referred to in the apparently more detached third person form. From now on the novel constantly oscillates between first and third person narration, leading to that delightful and teasing uncertainty on the part of the reader as to how much is the product of Oskar's fertile imagination and how much can be treated as a more accurate chronicling of allegedly historical events. From the outset it was clear that this constantly shifting narrative focus would be one of the first things to be sacrificed in the course of transferring the work from page to screen.

Quite apart from the stylistic complexity of the work, the sheer magnitude of the novel in itself created a major challenge to Schlöndorff and his team. Any adaptation is necessarily going to involve a considerable degree of reduction, but in the case of *The Tin Drum* it was obvious from the start that the production of a version for the commercial cinema would necessitate a more radical paring-down. Another major misgiving was that the imaginative force of the novel had been of such striking intensity that any adaptation would by comparison appear as the palest of shadows. A particular fear in this respect was that once rendered concrete in the form of a more or less straightforward, linear narrative, so much of the original work's tantalising allure would be lost that the whole adaptation exercise would not be worth the time and trouble invested.[7]

The task of adapting *The Tin Drum* for the screen was thus daunting by any standard, even for a director as well versed in the business as Schlöndorff. The latter had, however, learned a good deal from the experience of working on other large-scale adaptation ventures, in one of which at least he had made serious errors of judgement. The film in question *Michael Kohlhaas* (1969), adapted from Heinrich von Kleist's well-known 'novella', was a clear attempt on the director's part to achieve an international breakthrough. To these ends Schlöndorff deliberately stripped away many of the identifiably German aspects of Kleist's original story and produced a fast-moving, and often gory adventure yarn, with little or no indication of the historical context. The casting of well-known international stars such as Anna Karina in the role of Kohlhaas' wife also confirmed Schlöndorff's intentions, as did the film's working title *Man on Horseback* with its promise of action-packed, Western-style entertainment. The film itself not only drew derision from the critics, it also failed at the box-office, and Schlöndorff was left to reflect ruefully on what had gone wrong. His conclusion was that: 'A German film, precisely in order to be competitive at the international level, must be especially German. I don't believe you can produce films synthetically by gathering together the best components from all over the place, and then thinking you'll end up with something worthwhile'.[8]

The bitter lesson of *Michael Kohlhaas* was something Schlöndorff did not forget in all his future film-making. There were, however, other equally important learning experiences before he came to make *The Tin*

Drum. Perhaps the most significant of these was producing a film version of Heinrich Böll's short prose work *The Lost Honour of Katharina Blum*, not only because it gave Schlöndorff the opportunity of working in close collaboration with one of West Germany's best-known contemporary authors, but also because the work in question addressed one of the most pressing socio-political issues of the day: the wave of State authoritarianism which had begun to sweep through the Federal Republic in the late sixties and early seventies. This had brought uncomfortable reminders of still darker periods in Germany's past, in the same way that Grass' novel had done fifteen years previously. Böll's salutary tale of 'How violence can arise, and what it can lead to' also encapsulated the feelings of many thinking West Germans at the time and Schlöndorff clearly identified with many of the sentiments contained in the *Katharina Blum* text. In particular he shared Böll's feeling that the mood of near-hysteria being stirred up by the sensationalist, right-wing *Bild-Zeitung* not only posed a serious threat to civil liberties but threatened the very foundations of the fledgling West German democracy. The task of producing a successful adaptation of *Katharina Blum* clearly profited from the fact that both Schlöndorff and Böll shared the same sense of outrage at what was happening in the FRG. Thus Böll – far from adopting any very proprietorial attitude to his work – proved a very co-operative collaborator and fully accepted the need to produce a script where the complex, mosaic-like narrative of the original was rendered down into a simple, linear account which follows a strict chronological sequence.

With Schlöndorff's *Katharina Blum* project – unlike his earlier *Törleß* and later *Tin Drum* adaptations – only a relatively short time elapsed between the appearance of the original work and the making of the film. This, coupled with the fact that Böll's story so clearly relates to a set of near-contemporary events, had important implications for how Schlöndorff tackled the adaptation. In particular it meant that he felt he was not so constrained by the need to produce a 'faithful' adaptation of the original work and was more concerned about conveying the work's socio-critical message. As Schlöndorff himself remarked at the time: '*Katharina Blum* is not a film version of a novel in the same way that *Torleß* was. What is of importance is the subject-matter . . . What interested us was not the literary quality, but the issues raised . . . I see the whole project more as an engagement with matters of topical concern rather than the film version of a novel'.[9] With the *Tin Drum* adaptation on the other hand Schlöndorff was aware that he confronted a very different sort of challenge, not least because of the special aura which the novel had acquired in the eighteen years since its publication. As Schlöndorff observed in the diary which he kept at the time: 'All those who are working on the film feel that this is more than just another film adaptation'.[10] He noted further that he was initially more apprehensive than he had been with Böll's work that he would be able to do justice to the dynamism and energy of Grass' novel, where at one moment the reader is being carried away on an extravagant flight of fancy, and the next is confronted by a passage of sobre realism in which the narrator has assumed more the role of objective chronicler. Both Grass and Schlöndorff, however, recognised from the outset that a film version of *The Tin Drum* could only work properly if one dispensed with the device of having everything recounted retrospectively by an omniscient narrator.

More than a year's work went into the production of a script which met with the approval of all concerned. Grass himself played an active role in producing this blueprint and wrote much of the dialogue.[11] By the beginning of 1978 Schlöndorff and his team had succeeded in creating what the director called 'an autonomous narrative structure for the film'.[12] Franz Seitz in his initial treatment for the film had attempted to reproduce something of the original complexity of the novel by having frequent recourse to the flashback technique. By contrast Schlöndorff opts for an altogether simpler structure in which the highly convoluted narrative of the novel has given way to a chronological presentation of events which homes in on certain key episodes in Oskar's life. These are aligned in a manner which at times resembles the individual acts in a cabaret performance. (Schlöndorff himself once used the term 'Nummernrevue' to describe the film, suggesting that he too thought of the film as a series of 'numbers' all bound together and orchestrated by the small but indomitable ring-master Oskar.[13])

Oskar remains the central protagonist in all these episodes or acts, but compared with the novel, which ranges freely hither and thither in space and time, the cinema audience has a much stronger sense of involvement in a developing drama. The manner in which the audience relate to the narrator/protagonist has likewise undergone a decisive shift. In the novel the narrator Oskar is a highly ambivalent figure, embodying on the one hand qualities of malice and on the other those of child-like naivety and innocence, as a result of which readers are by turns attracted and repulsed by his character. In the film the relationship which the audience is allowed to develop with the diminutive Oskar is one in which there is a much stronger sense of identification. This identification is signalled at the start of the film when we are addressed by the disembodied voice of the child Oskar informing us that what follows is going to be a story in which he is centrally involved. The voice-over device continues to be used throughout the rest of the film both as an economic way of providing background information and also as a means of bridging the gap between episodes which are temporally and geographically often far removed. It also gives Oskar the opportunity to provide us with his quirkily subjective interpretation of events. The pattern is set in the opening sequence of the film as squeaky-voiced Oskar begins to probe into his parental origins, to the visual accompaniment of an illustrative series of images. As his grandmother Anna sits alone in the middle of a potato patch in the Kaschubei, she gives temporary refuge under her voluminous skirts to the alleged arsonist Joseph who is on the run from the police. This act of mercy results in the birth nine months later of his mother Agnes. In a later scene where we are witness to Oskar's own birth (a key scene in view of his many later attempts to seek solace in any womb-like enclosure!), the voice-over again ensures that we are closely aligned with Oskar's point of view even at the critical moment when he is expelled into the world.

The audience's sense of identification with Oskar is further reinforced by the decision – reached at an early stage in the adaptation process – to have a child, rather than a dwarf, play the part of Oskar. As Schlöndorff has observed: 'It was always our idea not to make a film with a dwarf (as protagonist). This would have led to people saying: this is all about dwarfs' problems and these don't interest me. Each one of us, however, can look back on his own childhood. With hindsight it is a period we would have liked to have been able to extend. You can, moreover, (easily) identify with a child'.[14] In another diary entry Schlöndorff casts further light on why he chose to focus on the child-like, as opposed to dwarf-like, aspects of Oskar. 'I'm looking for the Oskar in myself . . . The film will be more the description of a child's relationship to adults than a description of the typical milieu of the petit bourgeois in the 1930s, with which I have no direct connection'.[15] (Unlike Grass, Schlöndorff – who was born in 1939 – had no direct experience of the Third Reich.) The only problem which arises out of having Oskar as the audience's main point of identification, however, is that his own actions inevitably appear more understandable and legitimised than those of Oskar in the novel. By the same token the behaviour and demeanour of many other characters frequently appear to teeter on the brink of caricature.

Though Oskar remains emphatically a child throughout the film, he is far from being the epitome of child-like innocence. This had not a little to do with the choice of child actor to play the eponymous drummer-boy. Twelve-year old David Bennent, who was given the awesome responsibility of taking on the role, brought a rare combination of qualities to the part. As one critic observed at the time: 'he (Bennent) combines a physique several years below (his actual age), suggesting by turns the tantrum-prone child and the wiliest of seedy old men.'[16]

The selection of Bennent also brought other advantages in that the former's large, protruding eyes corresponded exactly to how Grass himself visualised the character. All this lent credence to the idea that Oskar – far from being an ugly dwarf or gnome – was a child who of his own volition and as an act of protest – simply decided to stop growing. At the same time the young actor's maturity of visage made it easier for audiences to accept that Oskar – having continued to grow 'inwardly' – can act in ways that are commensurate with ongoing mental and emotional development.

Though Schlöndorff ensures that the audience, generally speaking, is aligned with Oskar's point of view, it would be wrong to suggest that we see the world exclusively through his eyes. Schlöndorff himself – when asked about the ways in which he was seeking to position the audience in the film – observed that one doesn't reproduce the child's perspective by simply lowering the camera to slightly less than a metre above ground level.[17] His aim in *The Tin Drum* was to attempt to capture something of the *emotional* impact which the behaviour of adults has in a child's eyes, and this was to be achieved as much through the shaping of the narrative as the placing of the camera. In short, for Schlöndorff the perspective from which events are viewed in the film is not child-like in an optical sense but in a spiritual or intellectual one.[18]

Of central importance in any adaptation is the extent to which the production team has succeeded in finding an appropriate visual language for what in the original was expressed through purely verbal means. As we have already had occasion to comment, a special feature of Grass' work was the plethora of different literary and stylistic devices he employed. A particular characteristic of the novel is the virtuoso manner with which the author switches between these various styles, to the point at which the work appears at times to be simply a rapturous celebration of the powers of language and at others to be more like some grotesque parody of conventional literary forms. In an attempt to capture something of this stylistic multiplicity of the original, Schlöndorff has carefully selected a number of specifically filmic devices which carry something of the same resonance as the various literary tropes Grass employs in the novel. In this way Schlöndorff not only avoids the danger of falling into an inappropriate, 'plodding' type of naturalism, but also ensures that the full resources of cinema are employed to exploit the spectacular (in its literal sense) potential of the *Tin Drum* narrative.

What then are some of the specific ploys that Schlöndorff uses to create this effect of stylistic diversity or kaleidoscopic spectacle? When he first read the novel, he had, for instance, been reminded of 'the coarse outlines of early woodcuts', whilst other parts brought to mind scenes

from a 'Kasperletheater' (Punch and Judy theatre).[19] For Schlöndorff
the cinematic point of reference for both of these was the early days of
the silent, especially the Chaplin films. It therefore comes as no surprise
that certain scenes in *The Tin Drum* – particularly some of the opening
sequences – should exhibit many of the features we associate with early
cinema. Little Oskar bears more than a passing resemblance to 'the
Kid', whilst the officers who chase Oskar's maternal grandfather seem
to be straight out of the Keystone Cops. As if to accentuate these
allusions, Schlöndorff also uses a series of editing techniques (e.g. the
iris-out and dissolve devices) in these early scenes which deliberately
evoke an 'early cinema' style.

Other episodes in the film carry with them a different set of
associations. In the birth sequence, for instance, audiences will recognise
certain features with which they will have become familiar through the
horror movie. Likewise one or two of the more dramatic exchanges in
the film, such as the spirited defence of the Polish post-office, draw
upon many of the conventions of the American Western. By contrast
other scenes in *The Tin Drum* bring echoes of 'classic moments' of film
comedy, such as when Oskar intervenes to persuade the band playing
at the Nazi rally to switch from a march rhythm to a Viennese waltz
with delightfully farcical consequences. In addition to these more
obvious stylistic or generic allusions, German commentators have also
drawn attention to the close parallels between some of the landscape
scenes in Schlöndorff's film and the 'Heimatfilme' of yesteryear (those
nostalgic and sentimental effusions which had acquired such a dubious
reputation ever since they were used to support Nazi ideas on race
during the 1930s).[20]

The examples cited in the above paragraph provide ample evidence of
Schlöndorff's endeavour to find cinematic equivalents for the stylistic
diversity of the novel. The director's understandable insistence, however,
that everything be shaped according to the dictates of film has
inevitably exposed him to the charge that the losses incurred in the
process of adaptation far outweigh any potential gains. The standard
line of argument is that so much of the original has had to be abandoned
that the film is at worst simply a piece of commercial exploitation and is
therefore wholly redundant, or it is at best a mildly entertaining
diversion which can in no way lay claim to anything like the same
cultural importance as the original. What critics who argue thus forget,
however, is that audiences who go to watch *The Tin Drum* in the
cinema are themselves not primarily concerned with how faithfully it
reproduces the spirit of the original novel. Any assessment of its impact
is more likely to be formed by relating the form and subject of this film
to a set of expectations derived from their own cinematic experiences.
Thus, when at the end of the film the narrative doubles back on itself

and the train passes the same potato-field that we encountered in the film's opening sequence, most members of the audience will judge this to be an entirely appropriate ending within the given parameters of mainstream cinema (this is in spite of the fact that in opting for this ending the film-making team has brought down the curtain on events some ten years earlier than is the case with the novel!)

In the final analysis film operates within an entirely different signifying system to literature. In George Bluestone's phrase: 'the filmed novel, in spite of certain resemblances, will inevitably become a different artistic entity from the novel on which it is based'.[21] In establishing the criteria for judging the success of a film, one should therefore be primarily guided by its impact as a film. Judging by the box-office figures *The Tin Drum* clearly found an audience who responded very positively to its filmic qualities. Remarks made by Grass himself, who after all one might have expected to be one of the film's sternest critics, are in this regard most illuminating. Expressing his feelings on first seeing the film, he maintained that it was a 'highly charged piece of work' and that as he sat watching 'he completely forgot the book and saw only the film'.[22]

Notes

1. Grass in an article published in the *Münchner Merkur* of 24.10.1968 and cited in *Die Blechtrommel als Film* by V. Schlöndorff and G. Grass, Zweitausendundeins, München, 1979, unpaginated.
2. Lewandowski, Rainer *Die Filme von Volker Schlöndorff*, Olms Presse, Hildesheim/New York, 1981, p. 24.
3. It is also worth remarking that the climate of film-making in West Germany in the sixties and seventies, with reasonably generous subsidies available for worthy, non-controversial subjects, was especially conducive to the making of film adaptations, especially those of the established classics.
4. Lewandowski *op. cit.*, p. 23.
5. Sandford, John *The New German Cinema*, London: Eyre-Methuen, 1981, p. 37.
6. Further evidence of Schlöndorff's desire to reach out and capture the attention of the largest possible audience is provided by the number of film/television co-productions in which he has become involved.
7. Grass himself recollects several instances of people suggesting ways of adapting his work which would have resulted in grotesque distortions of the original. He even recalls one American producer who wonders whether it was strictly speaking necessary to have Oskar stop growing at the age of three!
8. See Sandford, *op. cit.*, p. 39.
9. Interview with V. Schlöndorff in: *Film-Echo/Filmwoche* no. 23, 23 April 1975 (my translation).

10. Schlöndorff, Volker *Die Blechtrommel. Tagebuch einer Verfilmung*, Frankfurt/Main, 1979.
11. The collaboration, where possible, of the 'original' author on an adaptation project was something Brecht claimed was one way of guaranteeing that the transposition process did not become an act of commercial exploitation. To Brecht's mind the presence of the author would ensure that what he termed the 'social tendency' of the work was not neglected.
12. Schlöndorff, *op. cit.*, p. 50.
13. Schlöndorff, *op. cit.*, p. 38.
14. Schlöndorff, *op. cit.*, p. 24.
15. Schlöndorff, *op. cit.*, p. 94.
16. Jan Dawson, review in *Monthly Film Bulletin*, June 1980, vol. 47, no. 557, p. 107.
17. Schlöndorff, *op. cit.*, p. 25.
18. *ibid.*
19. *ibid.*, p. 44.
20. Hans C. Blumenberg *Kinozeit*: Aufsätze und Kritiken zum modernen Film 1976–1980, Frankfurt am Main, 1980, p. 206.
21. *Novels into Film* Berkeley: University of California Press, 1961, pp. 63–4.
22. Schlöndorff, *op. cit.*, p. 122.

Filmography

The Tin Drum (A UA/Franz Seitz/Bioskop/Film Polski Production West Germany/France 1979.) Starring David Bennent, Mario Adorf, Angela Winkler, Daniel Olbrychski; Production Design by Nico Perakis; Cinematography by Igor Luther; Music by Maurice Jarre; Screenplay by Jean-Claude Carrière, Franz Seitz, Volker Schlöndorff from the novel by Gunter Grass: Directed by Volker Schlöndorff.

4

A Dry White Season:
The personal and the political

VASSILIKI KOLOCOTRONI and OLGA TAXIDOU

> Opening Lines: 'I used to think of him as an ordinary, good-natured, harmless, unremarkable man. The sort of person university friends, bumping into each other after many years, might try to recall, saying: "Ben Du Toit?" Followed by a quizzical pause and a half-hearted: "Oh, of course. Nice chap. What happened to him?" Never dreaming that *this* could happen to him.'

> Opening Shot: Two young boys, one black one white, playing ball in a field, as credits fall -- Cut -- next shot: scene in black beer-hall, sudden entrance of young black agitators, speech, police raid, violence -- Cut -- rugby game at white boys' school, Ben and family watching.

In looking at the points of contact and difference between two connected artworks which deal with the issue of apartheid this essay assesses the effectiveness of each, and the ways each chooses to *mediate* such an issue. *A Dry White Season*[1] makes an interesting case-study of artistic transposition from one medium to another. Any shift from book to film presupposes and effects a change of emphasis, a narrowing or extending of viewpoint, the inclusion or exclusion of key voices, the positioning of respective audiences, and finally, a set of choices both narrative and political.

Both film and book establish from their opening 'scenes' the parameters which will determine their stance. The novel introduces Ben from an immediately internal perspective, that is, from the position he occupies in the enclosed white world. No direct sign of conflict here. Rather, the 'analysis' presented by the narrator who is called upon to reconstruct Ben's story is one which focuses on the personal and psychological. Relying on the well-established literary convention of point of view which presents us from the first paragraph onwards with the 'psyche' of the leading character whose subsequent development we are invited to follow, the book stresses the individual rather than the collective. The presence of the narrator (a journalist friend of Ben) seems to serve more than one purpose. His narrative frames Ben's story, providing the introduction, commentary and conclusion to it, as it appears in Ben's diaries. He thus becomes the first reader of the story; a presence that supposedly distances and objectifies. He is interposed between the story as told by Ben and the reader. While trying to avoid psychological identification with the 'hero', this technique of the intermediary here also serves to glorify the process of telling/writing thus, in a sense, deferring the moment of action. This additional voice, rather than opening up the central point of view, is subsumed by it as the journalist appears as yet another aspect of Ben. Finally, his voice, enlightened though it may be, simply adds to the pervasiveness of the white mediation of the story. The issue here is not the exclusion of the black perspective but its ultimate subjugation and reduction to the white personal experience.

Following an opposite narrative direction, the film begins by setting its own terms and by placing the racial issue at the forefront of its concerns. The shot of two boys, one black, one white, playing in an idyllic and seemingly innocent, carefree world is undercut by the sudden juxtaposition of the sequence of racial violence in the township beer-hall. This shift posits one of the main themes which the film explores: the passage from 'innocence' to 'awareness', to the experience of institutionalised violence and to political consciousness. This is cinematically reinforced by the use of the shock-effect technique – the effect created by the abrupt, repeated juxtaposition of homely and violent scenes, setting the tone for the presentation of, and confrontation with political oppositions which the film works through. Only after the initial shock and hint at conflict are the main characters sketched out; their position and assumed 'innocence' foregrounded through their relationship to broader, collective issues. The racial scene in the beer-hall is thus cut to the rugby game at the white boys' school -- where violence is just a boys' game – and the first appearance of Ben and family. Hardly a 'protagonist', Ben is for the audience but a representative of the white world of South Africa.

Ben (Donald Sutherland) is a middle-aged history teacher whose seemingly happy middle-class life takes a dramatic turn when he gradually decides to get involved in an investigation of the circum-stances surrounding the death of a black school cleaner, Gordon Ngubene (Winston Ntshona), following the disappearance of the latter's son, Jonathan (Bekhitemba Mpofu). With the help of Stanley Makhaya (Zakes Mokae), a street-wise black taxi driver, and Melanie Bruwer (Susan Sarandon), a liberal journalist, Ben is led deeper and deeper into the world of apartheid. His growing awareness and commitment bring him into conflict with the brutal powers of oppression of the Pretoria regime. His safe world falls apart as he finds himself increasingly estranged from his personal and social background. Having lost all security and innocence, Ben is killed.

Remaining to a large degree 'faithful' to the central plot of the book, the film none the less redefines the use and purpose of characterisation by recasting as *types* the psychologically rounded characters of the book. It also digresses cinematically by adding weight to minor characters in the book in order to exploit more fully their narrative potential. The inclusion, for instance, of the Marlon Brando cameo as the maverick lawyer Ian MacKenzie gives rise to a 'courtroom melodrama' scene which concretises institutionalised injustice both in the context of Gordon's case and in its cinematic references to the standardised codes of this Hollywood sub-genre. Another way in which the film 're-writes' the book is through the inclusion of various points of view, not necessarily those dominant in the book. Whereas Brink's text 'tells' the story through the perspective of a middle-class white male as it is mediated through the narrator's third person narrative, the filmic text allows for a space of dialectical interaction between seemingly opposed and conflicting perspectives. Furthermore, the novel's narrative stance, distanced as it may claim to be, is nevertheless internalised and subjective. Conversely, the film's use of point of view, shaped by the specificity of the medium, interchanges objective with subjective narrative positions in both its camera work and editing techniques. The point of view technique, as it appears in the film, does not merely rely on character narration and narrow subjectivity. The film claims to construct a point of view that in Eisensteinian terms portrays 'an attitude towards the thing portrayed'. Thus in the place of a psychological narrative the film posits a political one.[2]

Ben is the central consciousness of the book, a middle-aged history teacher, whose mild and liberal ways seem to conceal an underlying dissatisfaction with the world around him. This malaise is hinted at in the relationship with his wife which, as the reader is led to surmise through the information provided by the narrator/journalist friend, is going through the difficult phase of a 'mid-life crisis'. In its political and personal ramifications, this crisis seems to lead him towards an 'adventure', with all the connotations that the term implies. Ben's commitment and awareness go hand in hand with his personal tensions and, in many respects, derive from them. It is chiefly through personal interactions that he reaches an understanding of issues that both transcend his immediate environment and challenge his initial liberal complacency. His relationship with Gordon, the school's black cleaner, whose son's Afrikaner education Ben is subsidising, is originally one of philanthropic patronage. It gradually becomes a form of political companionship into which Ben is drawn after his hesitation, and disbelief

is shattered by an increasing disillusionment with the Afrikaner state.
Ben's political involvement, however, is treated in the text more as a
man's quest for truth than as a radical questioning of the powers that
be. The questions Ben asks are of a metaphysical and religious nature.
His is the voice of a disenchanted humanist, fallen from grace, as it
were, desperately clinging to those 'universal' values that this present
corrupt state of things seems to deny him:

> Everything one used to take for granted, with so much certainty
> that one never even bothered to enquire about it, now turns out to
> be illusion. Your certainties are proven lies. And what happens if
> you start probing? Must you learn a wholly new language first?
> 'Humanity'. Normally one uses it as a synonym for compassion;
> charity; decency; integrity. 'He is such a human person.' Must one
> now go in search of entirely different sets of synonyms: cruelty;
> exploitation; unscrupulousness; or whatever? Darkness descending.
> (p. 161)

The text deals with Ben's disillusioned liberalism as a form of
metaphysical angst by alluding to biblical and historical references,
namely the motif of the 'dry white season'. This is allegorically made to
signify both a persistent memory from Ben's childhood in a 'virgin'
African land and the plight, likened to a curse from God, that has
befallen the South African present. He writes in his journal:

> What had happened before that drought has never been particularly
> vivid or significant to me: that was where I first discovered myself
> and the world. And it seems to me I'm finding myself on the edge
> of yet another dry white season, perhaps worse than the one I knew
> as a child. (p. 163)

> Everything permitted you is pure grace. For any moment of the
> day or night they may decide to pounce . . . And the mere fact that,
> from day to day, from one hour to the next, you can say: *This day,
> this hour is still granted me* – becomes an experience so intensely
> marvellous that you learn to praise the Lord in a new way. Is this
> the way a leper feels as he takes leave of his limbs one by one? Or a
> man suffering from a terminal cancer? Oh it is a dry season. But
> infinitely precious in its own way. (p. 223)

Finally, the text constantly reminds us that Ben's confrontation with
the South African state is triggered by his essentially humanist reaction
to the injustice and cruelty inflicted upon Gordon and his family and is
further manifested and glorified in what becomes a human *rapproche-
ment*; the understanding and taking upon oneself of another man's
suffering. When asked by Stanley, 'Why bother about Gordon?', Ben
replies:

'Because I knew him. And because –' He didn't know how to put it; but he didn't want to avoid it either. Lowering his glass, he looked into Stanley's eyes. 'I don't think I ever really *knew* him before. Or if I did, it didn't seem to directly concern me. It was – well, *like the dark side of the moon*. Even if one acknowledged its existence it wasn't really necessary to live with it.' A brief moment, the suggestion of a smile. *'Now people have landed there.'* (p. 96 [emphasis added])

Interestingly enough, the analogy drawn here between Ben's coming to 'know' Gordon and his world and the metaphorical sense of 'exploring' a distant and unknown territory, is revealing in terms of authorial concerns. Ben is portrayed as the agent of more than a process of knowing; his 'journey' into the 'dark' world of racial injustice is one of 'exploration' and 'charting' of a seemingly remote and thus mysterious land. More significantly, this land awaits colonisation. Brink's analogy is, therefore, less than innocent as it draws quite comfortably and unproblematically on a set of assumptions that reinforce a colonising discourse. The process of 'othering' which is at work here posits Gordon and black South Africa as that empty space which can only be concretely realised through representation and appropriation by a colonising 'discovery'. Indeed, apartheid itself only comes to exist after Ben discovers it through Gordon.

Accordingly, Brink's authorial project seems to be based on the same theme of journey and exploration. It is fair to assume here that the main personae of Ben and his journalist friend act as guises for Brink's own role and also help to foreground the role of the writer and the act of writing. Ben's exploration and discovery are handed over in written form to the journalist-facilitator, who in turn transmits this knowledge to the reader and the world in an act of dissemination of the written word. Correspondingly, Brink, in a gesture of glorification of the role of the writer as 'explorer' and 'map-maker', identifies his project in the following terms: 'There are two metaphors I can think of to express the function of the writer in a repressive society. Both have to do with map-making' (p. 166). In a theoretical essay, Brink parallels the writer's 'mission' to the plight of a certain corporal Martens who, after being sent to the Cape of Good Hope by the Dutch East India Company, was threatened by that same company with imprisonment for volunteering to draw a map of the then *terra incognita*. Brink goes on to establish the following connection:

The parallel is startlingly obvious. The strange territory explored and mapped for the first time; the assiduous cartographer offering his map to the world and threatened, to his dismay, with thirty years in chains should he disclose; and the long lonely years afterwards, during which he continues to draw and redraw his map, refining it all the time in order to correspond more and more closely to the land he has explored. Here is the writer slaving away in his ceaseless attempt to draw the map of his vision of truth, risking his liberty in order to offer the world a view of itself.[3]

Brink's story fails to acknowledge that the explorer's lonely and misunderstood venture is a direct result of an historical process of colonisation; a fact which might help put in perspective his company's refusal to have the map drawn and thus offer its exploits to competition. More important, however, is the absence of any real or historical consideration for the actual land (including its people) which was there to be mapped; the assumption being that it exists as a result of its reconstruction by the cartographer. 'Refined' and 'enlightening' as it may be, this representation conceals and displaces an act of exploitation. The fact that in Brink's formulation, the map reflects the vision of truth of its maker, ultimately exposes the whole enterprise in both its actual and metaphorical sense as a self-glorifying appropriation. In the second metaphor for the act of writing, Brink further elaborates his view of the writer as a privileged mediator:

> The writer is not concerned only with 'reproducing' the real. What he does is to perceive, below the lines of the map he draws, the contours of another world, somehow a more *essential* world. And from the interaction between the land as he *perceives* it to be and the land as he knows it *can* be, someone from outside, the 'reader' of the map, watches – and aids – the emergence of the *meaning* of the map. It remains a map: it is not the world itself. It offers no protection against the rigours of the world. (*ibid.*, p. 169)

As a metaphor for the act of writing, 'map-making' establishes the unreality of the mapped object; it is there insofar as it can help reveal inner truths and reflect them at a safe distance from any engagement with the real world. In a certain sense, Ben is the inadvertent explorer embarked on a journey of map-making of the unmarked territory of his own land, whereby the mappable objects are not only the history and geography of the land but also its inhabitants.

Stanley Makhaya acts as Ben's 'guide' on this journey. Invaluable for his knowledge of both worlds, Stanley's experience is that of a go-between; he is a survivor, negotiating the two worlds without fully trusting either. His is more the voice of the cynic than that of the revolutionary. In narrative terms, he is a 'facilitator', there to promote the adventure, to guide and protect the hero in his encounters. He is both the shield that wards off potential dangers and the spark that ignites crises: in both cases, the action is promoted and the hero draws closer to the truth. The scene, for example, where Stanley appears uninvited at Ben's family Christmas dinner, drunk and indignant, leads to the final breakdown of Ben's already delicate domestic life. Forced to take sides and to realise that there can be no happy and harmonious co-existence of the two worlds, Ben finally sees that there is a direct link between his professional and family life and the institutionalised injustice perpetrated by the state. It becomes startlingly clear that his position in his immediate environment is in complicity with a broader political practice of violence. As a liberal, Ben wakens with a sense of profound guilt. This loss of a sense of belonging is made up for by the gain of a more fundamental human companionship with Stanley, presented in the text as one that transcends race and history. In a scene where this bonding is almost ritualistically sealed, Ben and Stanley discover their common 'ground':

'Why?' asked Stanley. 'This is your place, isn't it? It's your city. You made it.' Ben shook his head. For a long time he sat staring at his pipe-smoke in silence. 'No, it's not my place. Where I grew up' – he smiled briefly – 'you know, I was fourteen years old before I put shoes on my feet. Except for church. You should have seen my soles, thick and hard from walking in the veld watching the sheep.'

'I looked after the cattle when I was small.' Stanley grinned, revealing his strong white teeth. 'We used to have great fights with *kieries* down at the water.'

'We fought with clay sticks.'

'And made clay oxen. And roasted tortoises.'

'And robbed birds' nests and caught snakes.'

They both burst out laughing, without really knowing why. Something had changed, in a manner inconceivable only a few minutes earlier. (p. 85)

Merging the two voices into an essentially human and almost 'aracial' discourse, the text unproblematically elides historical and political difference. Stanley here enacts another aspect of his role as facilitator, that of the great equaliser whose humanity is foregrounded in order to highlight Ben's unquestionable links with the land. In the passage quoted, both men inhabit a utopian and prehistoric *topos*. Again Brink's theoretical concerns confirm this literary treatment:

the image of two opposing nationalisms may be a simplification, especially if it omits to explore the surprising amount of common ground between Afrikaners and Blacks. After all, both carry collective memories of a tribal, nomadic past: both have been shaped through struggles for independence, and both, in their acknowledgement that 'land and community (are) inseparable', share a profound allegiance to the physical and metaphysical presence of Africa.[4]

As if this weren't true for the rest of the world, Brink, nevertheless, fails to identify his point of view as that of the liberal who finds solutions in the essentials.[5] This is a view that lays claims to universal truths, while remaining a singular vision. It is this vision that positions Stanley in the text as human but also, in interspersed descriptive details, as the 'noble savage'. Seen through the eyes of Ben, he is occasionally exposed to the mildly repelled 'civilised gaze': 'Stanley crossed his massive legs. One trouser leg was pulled up, revealing a red sock above the white shoe' (p. 84). 'The big man stared at him intently for a moment, then leaned over to take one of the cups, adding four teaspoons of sugar . . . He made a slurping sound as he tested the heat of his cup on his lips.' (pp. 86–7)

This gaze is also a 'male gaze', one which is cast on – and posits – a female 'other' as an object of appropriation and reconstruction. As is the case with the 'racial other', the female exists in Brink's text only to the extent that it can facilitate, trigger, unleash the protagonist's desire for growth and fulfilment. Ben's political awakening is thus simultaneously a sexual one. Melanie Bruwer is here the female and therefore sexual equivalent of Stanley: her role is to bring out yet another aspect of Ben's suppressed humanity, in this case his masculinity. Their encounter becomes yet another avenue for Ben's discovery of his true and better self. With Melanie, Ben is all he can be, sharing the same political commitment while gaining the deeper insight that only sexual fulfilment can allow. Melanie is therefore reduced to an object of Ben's male desire, there to comfort and reassure, and simultaneously to be, as it were, explored and conquered. In Ben's discourse, the ability to position Melanie at the other end of his gaze becomes the ultimate 'reward':

> She was naked. I stared at her in utter silence. She was clearly timid; fearful, I think, that I might find her provocative. But she made no attempt to turn away. She must have known that it was as necessary for me to gaze as it was for her to be gazed at . . . What mattered was that in her nakedness she was making herself available to me. The incomprehensible gift of herself. What else do we have to offer? (p. 272)

This adoring gaze is anything but innocent. Melanie's character is a construct which allows for the displacing and transposition of issues peripheral to the story at hand yet central enough for the symbolic working out of Ben's internal conflicts. In a scheme where analogies are drawn between the personal and the political, Melanie is set up as one who is entangled and victimised. In telling her story to Ben, he is predictably shocked when she reveals that her own politically and personally formative experience was rape:

> After a long silence he asked, aghast: 'Didn't it muck you up completely? That time in Mozambique – didn't it make you feel you'd never be the same again?'

'Perhaps I didn't want to be the same.'

'But for someone like you – the way you grew up – a girl, a woman?'

'Does that really make a difference? Perhaps it even made things easier for me.'

'In what possible way?'

'To get out of myself. To free myself from my hangups. To learn to ask less from myself.' (p. 133)

He apparently learns from this experience. The blatant use of rape and of the victimisation of woman as the figurative illustration of yet another painful awakening further highlights this character's naiveté. The case made here is not so much for sympathy as for fear and fascination: perhaps another instance of the female posited as the locus of dark and mysterious sexual powers. Moreover, the profound sexism that this discourse perpetrates is not only manifested in the trivialisation and distortion of female sexual experience, but more significantly in the refusal to see that this is another more pervasive version of the exercise of power; a power that the discourse claims to stand against. The effect on Ben of Melanie's rape story is one of enablement and release: it is almost as if he recaptures a sense of lost innocence, as if the violence inflicted on Melanie's body carries Ben back to a unity with a primordial past:

And now it was inside *him* it was happening, the sudden loosening, like a great flock of pigeons freed from a cage. Without trying to stop or check it, encouraged by her own confessions and by the lived-in ease of the room in that comforting dusk which made confidence possible, he allowed it to flow from him spontaneously, all the years he'd cooped up inside him. His childhood on the Free State farm, and the terrible drought in which they'd lost everything; the constant wandering when his father had a job on the railways, and the annual train journey to the sea . . . (p. 133)

Ben and Melanie discuss the question of rape more than once in the book. In these exchanges, Ben again assumes the role of the one who is 'educated', in a familiar narrative pattern of role shifting. He thus learns from Melanie that: 'It's only when you fully appreciate your body that you can also accept its insignificance.' (p. 193) This insistence on rape as a violent act and its psychological implications is significant in terms of the text's authorial concerns. The appropriation of a woman's voice and the supposedly authentic experience it conveys, provides the raw material for further 'exploration' and 'colonisation', the metaphorical context on which Brink himself draws when outlining the role of the writer. We have already discussed these terms, their problematic connotations and their unproblematised use by the author; we need to point out, however, that this indulgent discursive exercise, using rape in the guise of a contemplation on the human condition, is as objectionable as it is revealing: Ben's interest in Melanie's story amounts to a fascination not far removed from pleasure and desire. In drawing yet another 'map', this time of the female body and sexual experience, the text, however 'honourable' its intentions may be, enacts those very power structures it initially sets out to criticise. Moreover, this attitude is manifested not solely in the fictional and evocative rape stories, but also in more familiar and straightforward patronising and essentialist remarks of the type Brink voices in his theorising elsewhere:

> it is an important reminder of the vital role played by women in the struggle for liberation – from sexism as much as from racism. Some of these speakers, like Winnie Mandela or Albertina Sisulu, are famous throughout the world; others are near-anonymous. But in bringing to the South African struggle the acuteness of their female observation, their compassion, and the directness of their experience, they provide a testimony and an inspiration indispensable to the situation.[6]

The discussion of the text so far has focused on aspects of characterisation and narrative choices which highlight the overall orientation of the book. Concentrating on the personal and the universal rather than the historical and political, *A Dry White Season* makes an intervention of a liberal and in that sense limited kind. Despite its pretensions, and to a certain extent because of them, the book is caught up in the paradox of its position: the revolutionary potential of a white middle-class liberal stance. As one critic puts it, Brink's novel signals 'The revolt of the reasonable . . . far more deadly than any amount of shouting from the housetops'.[7] This hyperbole can only be read as a rhetorical gesture that reduces a whole history of very real struggle. Indeed, this telling coinage sums up the political proposition put forward in and by the book. This seemingly paradoxical formulation posits any direct political intervention as 'un-reasonable' and therefore potentially ineffective, while reassuringly affirming the validity of the occasional explosive act by the otherwise thoughtful citizen and thus untypical 'revolutionary'. The use of the term 'revolt' here echoes the Camusian notion of an individual space and choice for continual resistance: 'Revolution is not revolt . . . [Revolt] is the total, obstinate, almost blind at the beginning, refusal of an order which brings men to their knees. Revolt is primarily the heart'.[8] In fact, Brink himself refers to that concept both in his theoretical works and in his fiction. A debate on the validity of this political position is beyond the scope of this paper, but the term 'revolt' does lend itself to interpretations that privilege the universal and humanist over the collective and the political. In his analysis of Camus's political writings, Jonathan King elaborates on the term 'revolt':

Revolt is the individual's instinctive refusal to submit to a power
which he deems excessive or unjust . . . Revolt thereby creates and
reveals values, not only for the individual, but for all mankind. It
assumes 'total' human complicity. If the slave says 'no', he says
'no' not only *against* his master, but *for* his master. Revolt creates
values which are purely human, based on an instinctive sense of
inviolable justice and freedom.[9]

Preferring the form of the political parable to that of the internalised
individual journey, Euzhan Palcy's *A Dry White Season* radically re-
reads all the assertions put forward by the book and proposes an almost
new version of the same story. This determines both the structural/
narrative strategies and the stance of the film-maker. As a result the
film appears more stylised in form, less psychologically analytical in
characterisation, more didactic in the positioning of its audience. This
is not necessarily a limitation since it is used as an effect rather than as
a rhetorical gesture. The film has a story to tell and a specific message
to convey. Unlike the book, the latter is more important than the
former.

Treating the story in the form of a parable creates a set of narrative
possibilities absent in the book. Instead of projecting the singular point
of view of a central protagonist, the film positions its hero within a
typology of characters and promotes the action through a series of
symbolic interactions. Rather than allowing the story to unravel through
the internalised vision of Ben, the film sustains a multiple focalisation
by positing all characters as types in set situations. In doing so, it
attempts to promote a collective point of view against which isolated
incidents and relationships are interpreted. The filmic version re-creates
the world of *A Dry White Season* in terms of representative roles and
relations, with everything and everyone standing for a given and
recognisable side and where there is no space for pseudo-philosophical
rambling. Instead, from the opening scene we know that Ben's world
will inevitably crumble as he becomes politically involved. Similarly,
the world of those around him is affected as they themselves are forced
to take sides. Ben's family in the film is not merely a narrative foil,
there to facilitate his progression from frustration to heroism, but
rather consists of concrete and identifiable types who also have political
decisions to make. The device which more significantly allows for these
parallel stories to be told is that of narrative coupling. These couples
are formed in terms of structural relations that help promote the action
and constantly shift the point of view.

Thus the film develops its characterisation in terms of set structural
units, such as father/son, teacher/student, oppressor/oppressed, black/
white. As the story evolves, characters occupy more than one position
within a narrative couple, in the same way that they shift from one

couple to the other. Ben's relationship with his son Johan, for instance, is originally mirrored in Gordon's relationship with Jonathan, so that the father/son couple functions as an aspect of the black/white parallel unit. However, when the film reaches its final resolution with the killing of Ben, Stanley takes over the role of the father for Johan, whereby the father/son coupling merges with the black/white and thus subverts the original distinctions. These couples also exist in the book, but perform a restrictive function, merely thematic and not narrative. They are there mainly to promote character development – chiefly that of Ben – rather than of action or perspective. For this reason, they are fixed and static and do not allow for transpositions from one couple to another. Conversely, this device in the film is not reductive, but serves to de-personalise and de-psychologise the characters by inserting them into a scheme where ideology can be inscribed and read.

The film also chooses to omit certain scenes and themes crucial to the book. The sexual encounter between Ben and Melanie, with all its sexist ramifications, is totally excluded in the screenplay. Melanie here is not a catalyst for Ben's emotions but a concrete type in her own right. Her role is that of the white woman who has actively taken a position in the context of South African politics. In that role, she is narratively coupled with Ben's wife Susan, rather than sexually coupled with Ben. She acts to highlight both her involvement in the struggle and, conversely, Susan's stance and conscious decision to protect her white South African world. The fact that the positions of the two women are opposed, does not imply that they have to be sexual rivals, as in the book, but rather that they, as all other characters, represent personal and political choices. As a result of this reworking, Ben's character is more sympathetic in the film, in the sense of a more credible transition from the safe world to the political adventure. Accordingly, his relationship with Stanley is effectively reinterpreted in the film. In terms of positioning within narrative couples, Stanley proceeds to occupy the successive roles of teacher (to Ben), father (to Johan, after Ben's death), and finally, of the 'avenging angel', who administers justice and channels emotional and political release on behalf of the audience. Consistent to the form of the parable, the film offers a final resolution which the book does not reach: Ben's murder is taken a step further in the film, with Stanley's corrective gesture in killing Stolz.

It is characteristic that the film chooses to end thus, with an act of political violence which, by countering the institutionalised violence of the State, is presented as the 'moral of the story' and is endorsed as a realistic political choice. From another perspective, this may be seen as another Hollywood 'happy ending', as a gesture, that is, of comfort and reassurance for the audience. The 'killing off' of the villain is, of course, a generic convention but it is one with which the film chooses to comply not only in order to alleviate the cinematic tension, but more significantly to lead the 'story' to its logical conclusion. Ironically, the cinematic convention which the film employs opens up possibilities for more 'readings' than the one offered in Brink's novel: whereas in the book Ben's death is treated as the inevitable conclusion of this protagonist's adventure, in the film his killing seems to provoke an immediately active reaction which contextualises both killings within a political framework – where the death of the hero is not necessarily the end of the story. The slow-motion sequence of Stolz's death provides this ending with significant emphasis, suggesting that this is the real climax of the story. Accordingly, the final image of the still close-up of Stanley's face is an ambiguous comment: his action ends this, 'our' story, but is by no means the 'final word'. Stanley thus becomes the potential protagonist of the sequel, one that is not to be acted out on a screen.

A Dry White Season is, formally, a true 'Hollywood movie'. As such it relies on recognisable and tested formulae. It is by no means cinematically adventurous, in the sense of an exploration of the medium. This alignment with the structural conventions of the political thriller in its Hollywood version seems to be a choice rather than an imposed limitation. This means working with a popular cinematic form and endorsing it to the extent that it conveys a particular political message. More specifically, the inclusion of the 'courtroom melodrama scene' featuring Marlon Brando's star-quality performance is, on the one hand, a box-office attraction, while, on the other, also relies on Brando's well-known commitment to the anti-apartheid movement.[10] As is also the case with the 'happy ending' (seen by some critics as an easy way out), the acceptance of such conventions may result in the weakening of the critical position of the film. However, this is a risk that the film seems to consciously take while at the same time promoting a specific reading of the conventions used. The danger of assuming total control over such conventions and of manipulating the audience accordingly is, in this case, successfully balanced by the clarity and consistency of the film's political stance.

We are thus faced with two ways of 'telling' one story. The literary text proceeds through introspection and a sense of personal closure; the filmic text rewrites and comments on it through a structure of elimination and shifts of emphasis. Both attempt to deal with the political and are thus specific interventions. Their power as texts and as mediating agents, however, is constantly undercut by a set of parameters both within and outside their medium. On the one hand, Brink's novel foregrounds the limitations of its chosen mode, in its very dealing with the political through a humanist idealisation, while, on the other, the film, despite its critical stance, is still determined by the industry of which it is a product. The paradox of a Hollywood 'cause movie', in other words, is one that this film cannot escape. In this context, MGM's donation of £1,000 to 'a non-political organization' (Amnesty International), is solemnly announced in the video release of the film, as a token of the industry's acknowledgement of the reality that inspired the film. This is, however, a political reality and one which the film manages to voice, despite MGM's noble gesture and claim of power over its target audience. The validity of what it says is being constantly and actively judged, on screens worldwide and, more importantly, in the streets of South Africa.

Notes

1. André Brink, *A Dry White Season*, London: Flamingo, 1979. The film of the same title was directed by Euzhan Palcy (MGM, 1989).
2. Sergei Eisenstein, 'The Structure of the Film' in *Film Form*, trans. Jay Leyda, New York: Harcourt, Brace and World, 1949, pp. 150-51. For further discussion of point of view in film see Edward R. Branigan, *Point of View in the Cinema: A Theory of Narration and Subjectivity in Classical Film*, New York: Mouton Publishers, 1984.
3. André Brink, *Mapmakers: Writing in a State of Siege*, London: Faber and Faber, 1983, p. 167.
4. André Brink, 'Two Tribes Divided by a Common Heritage', *The Independent on Sunday*, 17 June 1990, p. 17.
5. We are dealing here with a particular strand of liberalism which defines itself in the context of the Afrikaner struggle against British imperialism. Afrikaners' claims to the South African land are thus historically seen as part of a 'national war of independence' and, in André Brink's view, theoretically justified. For further discussion of the issue of Afrikaner nationalism and of the role of the Afrikaner liberal, see Patrick van Rensburg, *Guilty Land*, Harmondsworth: Penguin Books, 1962.
6. From Brink's review of Diana Russell's *Lives of Courage: Women for a New South Africa* ('Two Tribes Divided by a Common Heritage', *op. cit.* note 4).
7. From *The Guardian* review of *A Dry White Season*, quoted on the back cover of the above mentioned edition.
8. Albert Camus, quoted in Jonathan King (ed.), *Albert Camus: Selected Political Writings*, London: Methuen, 1981, p. 12. Our translation.
9. *Ibid.*, pp. 16-17. For further discussion of some of the problems in Camus's formulations, see Edward W. Said, 'Narrative, Geography and Interpretation', *New Left Review*, no. 180, March/April 1990, pp. 81-97.
10. This complicity with Hollywood does not necessarily imply an 'equal partnership'. It is not coincidental that, according to Marlon Brando, MGM reneged on its initial agreement with the star to make a significant contribution (equivalent to his

fee, amounting to $11,000,000, which he was to donate) to an anti-apartheid organisation. This controversy apparently forced Brando to give his first public interview in fifteen years, a fact which, of course, drew more attention to the film.

Filmography

A Dry White Season (A Paula Weinstein/MGM Production, US 1989.) Starring Donald Sutherland, Janet Suzman, Zakes Mokae, Jurgen Prochnow, Susan Sarandon, Marlon Brando, Winston Ntshona, Thoko Ntshinga, Bekhitemba Mpofu, Rowen Elmes; Screenplay by Colin Welland and Euzhan Palcy from the novel by André Brink; Directed by Euzhan Palcy.

5

Peter Weir's version:
The Year of Living Dangerously

JOHN ORR

The average viewing of a full-length feature film, between ninety minutes and two hours, is shorter than the average reading time of a full-length novel. Moreover the kinetic impact of the big screen movie through simultaneous camera mobility, source sound, sound-track, special effects, montage, music, voice-over and dialogue can all work to make the image linger within the diegesis, or time-frame, of film narrative. Hence Hitchcock, for one, preferred the short story to the novel as the literary fiction which best converted to the big screen, and the recent successful collaboration between Angela Carter and Neil Jordan in the writing and filming of two of her stories as *The Company of Wolves*, seems to confirm this. The finished literary product carries an immense baggage of preformed knowledge and emotion, often constricting the spatial and temporal extension of the image. Its fiction is *there* before the screenplay, let alone the shooting of the first sequence. At novel length, fidelity to the text often involves omitting through compression the half-truths of partial representation which then become condemned as artistic sins. A better strategy at times, is the move away from the full-length text because of its own limitations, but this often works only because the written text is inferior to the visual text it then becomes.

Such is the case with Peter Weir's adaption of Christopher Koch's novel *The Year of Living Dangerously*.[1] Only four years elapsed between the Australian publication of the book in 1978 and the screening of the film version, distributed by MGM, in 1982. Like Carter with Jordan, Koch worked closely with Weir on the adaptation of his text but the results were considerably different. Though Koch's name appears on the screenwriting credits along with Weir and David Williamson, he withdrew from the project well before its completion, a disillusioned man.[2] Yet in spite of this breakdown between author and film-maker, I want to argue here that Weir's movie is one of his best, and certainly one of the most accomplished English language movies of the early eighties.

The success of Weir's film is due to his skill in transforming rather than translating. He turns a text which veers between journalistic sensationalism and documentary fiction into an organic melodrama, to which all the many naturalistic details are strictly subordinated. Koch's novel, which won the National Book Award for Australian literature, is a vivid and dynamic but largely unstructured piece of fiction, good on detail, but often slapdash and unfocused. Weir brings to the film a structure of feeling that depends on *the absence* of a preformed literary structure, a task obviously impossible with a major novel. Here he simplifies action but also adds in the best traditions of melodrama, a genuine air of mystery which goes beyond the political plot. His film visually integrates all the connected elements of conscience, surveillance, violence and desire and yet still leaves us at the end, as all his best pictures do, with the sense that all has not been revealed. Certainly, the screenplay shows great fidelity to the text at times, retaining much of the original in voice-over and dialogue, yet in retrospect, it seems inevitable that Koch should not have tolerated the direction the movie was taking. For Weir was changing it out of all recognition.

The novel is set in Indonesia in 1965 and takes its title from one of the speeches of the country's dictatorial ruler, President Sukarno, who has established his reputation as one of the leaders of the post-colonial Third World. In trying to forge a new radical, anti-imperialist Indonesia, Sukarno has exhorted his followers to embrace 'The Year of Living Dangerously'. But Sukarno himself was living more dangerously than he knew. He had to strike a delicate balance between the PKI, the world's third largest Communist Party and the conservative Muslim generals who ran his army. He was eventually deposed, just after the film ends, by a bloody civil war in which half a million communists and their sympathisers were killed.

The strength of Koch's novel lies in its feel for history and political intrigue. It trades brilliantly on first-hand observation of a country on the brink of disaster, with all the urgency and excitement of good investigative journalism. But it tries to do too much without the right literary resources. Its narrative at times is like reporter's copy and its characters talk in obvious clichés. The relationships of the central characters are strangely lacking in intensity.

The novel's main theme is the morality of investigative journalism, but it never distances itself sufficiently from its subject matter. It is written too much in the idiom of the journalists it portrays, so that the Anglo-Saxon newshounds hanging around the Wayanga Bar of Jakarta's one hygienic hotel are described very much in the language they use themselves. Koch compounds the error by using a narrative form which gambles on the author and his readers sharing an obvious consensus about complex experiences. This, for example, is Koch's first presentation of Billy Kwan: 'There is no way, unless you have unusual self-control, in disguising the expression on your face when you first meet a dwarf. It brings out the curious child in us to see these little people.'[3] The limited language, the uncertain tone, let Koch down badly. Because his generalisations seem contrived, he lacks the conviction to speak for us as readers.

Introducing Jill Bryant, the British Embassy attaché, he shows his limitations even more. The Australian journalist Guy Hamilton first meets Bryant through Kwan. Here is Koch describing her from Hamilton's point of view, trying to suggest the sexual frisson Guy experiences as she takes off her glasses:

> But the young woman continued to smile at him, her chin resting on her hand, her gaze almost tender. Her dark blue eyes had none of the diminished appearance common to many people who have removed their glasses; they obviously had an astigmatism, being slightly unfocussed, and this gave them the dazed look which usually signals great affection or sexual excitement.[4]

The description is neither physically evocative nor does its clumsy prose capture the rhythm of Guy's growing attraction. In Weir's film, Bryant is played by Sigourney Weaver who does not wear glasses and whose eyes are always in focus. In Weir's close-ups or medium close-ups, her gaze is a constant presence in the film, casual but always alert, languid yet sharp and lyrical. The difference is at one level that of emphasis, but at a deeper level one of form. Koch's powers of description do not measure up to Weir's camera which transforms Bryant into a photogenic image, not passive, but active, intelligent, sensual. In Koch's instant, uncertain psychologising, Bryant has no real nature. But in the film she has the visual presence on which all cinematic character is based, in which the look and the glance and the gesture give expression to personality. For Koch, she is merely a cipher, only an accompaniment to male camaraderie. In Weir's film she is in many ways Hamilton's iconic equal, a formidable screen protagonist.

In the novel the centrepiece is the male bonding between Hamilton and Billy Kwan, man and dwarf, reporter and cameraman, the Australian Englishman and the Chinese Australian. Koch has suggested that Guy and Billy are doubles of one another.[5] While enlarging that dimension of doubling, the film turns the central relationship into a triangle of outsiders -- Bryant, the attaché who is almost certainly a spy, Kwan the Chinese-Australian who can 'pass' for being Indonesian, Hamilton, the raw, abrasive Australian with little trace of English gentility or discretion. Through Kwan, Guy establishes himself as a top newsman by getting an interview with Audit, the secretive leader of the PKI, has an affair with Bryant in the brief period before her return to Europe, and during the army coup escapes to rejoin her at the airport after being blinded in one eye by an army officer outside the Presidential Palace. Kwan meanwhile turns against Sukarno his former hero, and is thrown to his death from a hotel window by security agents while staging a public protest. All three are powerless to alter Indonesia's historical fate.

The book's main stylistic weakness is its inconsistent narrative. For the most part, Koch uses a first-person narrator who plays little part in the action and often gets conveniently forgotten. The character of Cookie, a fairly anonymous journalist, is a transparent and clumsy device: a convenient witness who happens, unconvincingly, to be in the right place at the right time. At other times when Koch wants us to see things from Guy or Billy's point of view, he forgets Cookie altogether. As a result the novel has little focus and no genuine centre. In the film, Weir dispenses with Cookie. He makes Kwan the centring point of view through narrative voice-over and through the prominence of his dossiers on the other characters and the political crisis. The film reveals, where the novel bombards with information. Weir cleverly transforms information into surveillance, which through its great visual power, becomes the object of the narrative, not part of an excessive clutter of narrating devices. While the camera shows Kwan's hands flicking through his dossiers, his voice-over reads the information they contain. The effect on the viewer is to create greater intimacy but also greater distance from Billy, just as Weir distances us from Billy's political hero, Sukarno, a figure whom Guy meets in the novel but who, in the movie, is merely seen leaning over the balcony of the presidential palace.

There are, as one might expect, crucial omissions in the film. Weir opts to avoid the complexities of a political intrigue which provide obvious pitfalls for film narrative. We are told nothing of Sukarno's withdrawal from the United Nations, the importance of the Jakarta-Peking axis or Sukarno's threatened invasion of Malaysia, to whose territories he had laid claim. But if the film skips much political detail, it also avoids the damage done by Koch's lame capitulation to the spy genre. Koch's Hamilton is a James Bond fan who gets involved in an Ian Fleming sub-plot which damages the novel's credibility as serious fiction. Kumar, Guy's secretary, turns out to be the secret lover of a Soviet woman spy who tries to entice and then kill off the Australian because he has discovered from Jill Bryant the existence of a secret arms shipment to the communists from China. Weir replaces this sub-plot by a dream sequence in which Guy imagines he is being strangled in a swimming pool by Kumar's attractive sister. The nightmare clinches his growing suspicion that Kumar is secretly PKI. But Weir humanises the communist secretary, making him determined and ruthless but also self-effacing and compassionate.

As we have seen already, Koch regarded doubling as a central feature of the novel. Another is the symbolism of the Wayang, the Javanese shadow puppets whom he tries to infuse with elaborate meanings. Traditionally such puppets act out morality tales from the *Bhagavad Gita* and other Hindu epics. But neither the doubling motif nor the Wayang symbolism gives the novel the structure it evidently seeks. Koch offloads too much irrelevant detail about the Chinese-Australian and the 'English' Aussie, Hamilton, without capturing any genuine sense of rapport in their relationship. This is precisely what Weir does. Mel Gibson plays Guy as a de-Anglicised rough-edged diamond, yet it is Linda Hunt's Oscar-winning performance as Kwan which establishes the uncanny rapport between them. In visual terms the doubling of the two is established through the motif of seeing, of the journalist as active voyeur. Kwan tells Hamilton, 'I'm your eyes', and proves it by filming a PKI demo over the crowd outside the American Embassy, sitting on Guy's shoulders. But Billy is more than just cameraman and sidekick. He witnesses more than Hamilton wishes to see, and his eyes become the source of conscience which opposes the amorality of Guy's ambition and desire.

Koch's use of Wayang is more ambitious. He tries to construct a complete political allegory out of it, using one of the plays in the Wayang theatre's Pandara cycle for exact literary parallels. Here, Arjuna, one of the puppet figures, becomes Hamilton, while Somar the dwarf-clown, a God in disguise, becomes Kwan. Around the Wayang opposition between Left and Right, captured in the shadow-play of the puppets on the wall, Koch builds his political symbols. Audit, head of the PKI, represented by the Wayang of the Left, holds court at Party HQ while Kwan eventually supports Islam, the Wayang of the Right, urging Sukarno to do likewise.[6] As Kwan's political double, Sukarno is a version of the Direck-God who manipulates the shadow-puppets, balancing Left and Right. Given that the Wayang of the Left stands for evil and the Wayang of the Right stands for good, Koch's own political preferences become clearer. Kwan's disenchantment with Sukarno and his move to the Right is a clear path that Hamilton is meant to follow.

Yet Koch's use of allegory is too schematic and as the novel progresses, his instinct is to turn allegory into melodrama. The chaos of Sukarno's Indonesia defied any neat packaging of divisions into Left and Right and the crucial scene of Hamilton's political conversion simplifies the political issues concerned. On his way back from witnessing the PKI's 'Long March' in the countryside, Guy sees the start of a Wayang puppet-show which 'converts' him to the 'right and the just'. Billy's tragic death accelerates his moral growth. Discarding the expediency of the ruthless newshound, he partly atones for Billy's death by turning into a modern version of Arguan, a noble crusader of good. His escape at the end of the novel and re-uniting with Jill is seen as a kind of redemption for which Billy is the human sacrifice. Through Billy's death, his more active double is made whole.

Weir significantly alters the allegory in the film. No 'conversion' takes place. Guy remains amoral, refusing to make judgements or take sides even after the trauma of witnessing Billy's death. Weir instead creates in his central character something absent from the novel, an erotic interweaving of ambition and desire. The newsman's craving for the big scoop, his hunger to uncover all hidden knowledge is matched to his ruthless and compulsive desire for Jill. Unlike the novel where the affair tails off as a confused sub-plot, Weir seeks to give us a visual rendering of the dangerous relationship between politics and desire. In that sense the film recalls Orwell's *Nineteen Eighty-Four* where the opposition of politics and passion is worked out through the secret, doomed opposition of Winston and Julia to the dictatorship of Big Brother. Thus in his frightening dystopia, Orwell still uses a fairly traditional romantic convention. But while there is a strong element of romanticism in Weir's film, there is also something more. He is not interested in oppressed ideals but in the flaunting of lack of ideals, the Anglo-Saxon 'high' of living dangerously amidst the labyrinthine and partisan intensities of the Third World.

The means of achieving this structure of feeling is through the omnipresent cinematic gaze, which is close to Alfred Hitchcock's remarkable *Vertigo* in technique. The cinematic gaze has no real equivalent in literary narrative. Through Weir's direction it becomes the visual sign of watching, surveillance and desire. Through the eyes of Billy Kwan, the gaze itself is situated uneasily between conscience and desire, between the urge towards morality and the intensity of feeling which thrives upon its absence. This is the core of the film's succinct, intriguing ambiguity. It plays on the prevalence of forbidden seeing. As Guy's cameraman, Billy tries to make his gaze political by filming the violent demo against the American Embassy. The demonstrators try to seize his camera and Guy, in trying to protect the film, is slashed in the leg with a knife. But if Billy watches others on Guy's behalf, he also watches Guy himself. When Guy discovers his dossier amidst the files in Billy's bungalow, he momentarily assumes his friend to be a spy with unknown allegiances. It is a deepening ambiguity the audience takes with it into its 'witnessing' of the love affair which it watches partly through Billy's eyes and must imagine, like him, the act of love-making between Guy and Jill the film never permits it to see.

The ambiguity deepens even further with the 'watching' of conscience.

On his first night in Jakarta Billy takes Guy into the slums of the city near the hotel and his voice repeats Tolstoy's famous question 'What then must be done?' His answer is a visual metaphor that paves the way for the ever-present gaze, telling Guy 'to add his light to the sum of light'. But Hamilton's eyes, though they come to 'see' poverty and famine and write them up in his despatches, are still the eyes of a reporter. 'We can't afford', he tells his friend, 'to get involved.' But Kwan does. His voice-over is an appendage to his gaze, passing judgement on those he has witnessed in action. Guy cannot see in the same way. When he goes to the Presidential Palace, Kwan warns him to take his sunglasses off at the gate, as Sukarno's guards claim to know an assassin by his eyes. Mel Gibson's eyes burn for knowledge as later they will burn with desire for the woman who has turned down Billy's proposal of marriage. But they make no moral judgement. They cannot finally distinguish right from wrong.

As outsiders, the triangle of Billy, Guy and Jill have to keep their eyes open to know what is happening in a situation which changes from moment to moment. But they also watch each other. And the Indonesians watch them, balefully returning their gaze. The two Anglo-Saxons, paid in different ways to watch the populace are here watched in turn as their conversation skirts round the ethics of their own watching. As their affair starts, the image of the surrounding gaze intensifies. Like the crowd, Weir's camera focuses on the outward and public manifestations of a private and secret desire. It catches too the double-take of those who watch the affair begin to flower, their embarrassed pretence at not watching which merely intensifies the sense of scrutiny. The house-warming at reporter Wally O'Sullivan's bungalow begins the process, but it not only plays upon discreet watching. It also trades on the studied aversion of the gaze.

Weir's flair for exact context can be seen in his choice of music. The scene in Koch's novels has the party-goers dancing to the Beatles, historically right for 1965 when their raw energy had won them global acclaim but wrong for the mood of the picture. Weir uses Jerry Lee Lewis singing *A Whole Lotta' Shakin' Goin' On*, a more sensual and subtle intimation of erotic encounter. The point is that neither Guy nor Jill take up the impulse to dance with each other, but elaborately avoid each other's company, talking and dancing with others. As Jill dances with Billy and then with Pete Curtis, a Canadian journalist who is Guy's whoring alter ego, the lecherous cynic he could easily become, Guy's watching and her looking back are confined to brief discreet glances, unacknowledged.

When the couple belatedly meet at the end of the party, it is clear their encounter is orchestrated by Billy, who is framed sitting between them, looking up from one to the other as they speak in close-up, but also, like a puppet-master, manipulating the tension between them over Hamilton's forthright exposures of starvation for his paper. As Palombo has pointed out, Billy can be seen as writing the scenario of their coming affair in which both are idealised and narcissistic projections of his thwarted self.[7] When he withdraws from politics, disillusioned, and recklessly destroys his own life, the couple are then thrown back on their own resources. The encounter is subtly melodramatic, Hitchcockian in its visual simplification and purification of complex passion in the interest of narrative tension. The pattern of manipulation and doubling is suggestive of *Vertigo*: the political espionage that both cools and fires passion echoes *Notorious*. As the encounter ends in a sudden but chilling silence, Kwan looks studiously away, as if disavowing his puppetry but also his empathy with their nascent desire.

Prior to this the party's *mise-en-scène* has already set up the pattern of doubling. Kwan has come dressed as Sukarno, his idealised political double, in a deliberate echo of the photograph Guy has seen on the wall of Billy's room. Guy in turn is the handsome successful double of the diminutive cameraman Jill has gently spurned. Kwan thus incites his erotic double to succeed where he has failed. 'And so it begins . . .', his voice-over narrates at the start of the next sequence. Thereafter the absence of his gaze is just as uncanny as its former presence. Having prompted Guy to go to an Embassy party where Jill is bound to attend, he becomes, like Gavin Elster in *Vertigo*, the manipulator who disappears out of sight. Arriving late at the reception, Guy corners Jill on a balcony and launches into his postponed embrace as curfew approaches. It is the culmination of her evasion of him over several weeks, the triumph over the obstacle to eros which Weir turns into pure and powerful melodrama. Again she rejects the scandal of his embrace, but then as he is about to leave, joins him in his car. In the next extraordinary sequence, Weir follows Hitchcock in *North-By-North West* in celebrating the triumph of desire over corrupt power as pure cinematic illusion.

Compelled into extraordinary movement by the hypnotic motif of Maurice Jarré's music, there follows the first of the two central erotic scenes in the film. As his car engine fails to start, Guy hears the passenger door open and shut. The car swerves off under the rebuking gaze of the colonel. In the snatched and sensual embraces the couple share in the moving car, mutual daring and exhilaration match the defiance of politics to the defiance of passion. As the car approaches an army roadblock the intensity of the embrace increases, as finally the machine bursts through the flames and the spaced petrol drums in a triumphant surge of phallic penetration. The running of the blockade is not just erotic bravado, but a flaunting of supreme indifference to all authority, all politics and finally all morality. Weir cuts suddenly from the car speeding round the bend to the car stationary the next morning. Its chassis peppered with bullet-holes, it is being examined by Billy outside his bungalow. The camera follows his gaze from the damaged car to his house where he presumes the couple are. The gaze that cannot 'see' them making love has already seen enough, seen that they are not only using his house, but by implication his room and his bed.

Guy is now victor over his two doubles, the moral and diminutive Kwan, the large, loud-mouthed but morally diminished Curtis. The affair feeds off the proximity of danger but also revels in *not* having to make a political choice, not needing to take sides. The attraction to its Western audience has a sting in its tail. To identify fully with Guy and Jill which is the easy temptation, also involves a conscious association with their lack of principle. Weir refrains from liberalising the consciences of his Western heroes to make them morally acceptable as recent British directors have done in *The Killing Fields, A Passage to India, The Mission* and *Under Fire*. The film confirms the Anglo-Saxon failure to penetrate the world of Asia, the redundancy of empty liberal gestures, the marginality of Anglo-Saxons in fact in the vast, fragmented world of the Pacific Rim. This is brought home when Guy is powerless to prevent Billy's death.

Throughout the film, motifs of watching and doubling have the taut symmetry of images trading on their evocative repetition, images confirmed by the stylistic excess of the face in close-up. At the same time Weir's simultaneous economy of montage and fluidity of movement recall the classic masters of Hollywood; not only Hitchcock, but also Howard Hawks and Nicholas Ray. Yet his political theme also moves away from classic stylisation towards a more candid and chastening view of the relationship between the West and the developing world to be found in Antonioni's *The Passenger*. It thus avoids the loud and cheap panaceas of films like Oliver Stone's *Salvador*. At the same time it is clearly a film that echoes the Australian director's own obsessions, in particular the unnerving sense of the Pacific world as permanently 'other' and mysterious, and unamenable to the platitudes of Anglo-Saxon civilisation.

Here the events of the second half of the film double and echo the first half just as *Picnic at Hanging Rock* returns compulsively to the haunting scene of the schoolgirls' mysterious disappearance. The knife wound Guy suffers in the PKI demonstration is doubled by the soldier's gun butt which blinds him in one eye as he tries to get to the Palace during the coup. Without Jill, he becomes the lewd and boozy double of the lecherous Curtis, dancing with his crony in an Indonesian bar to Little Richard's *Tutti frutti* in what is a clear travesty of the ritual at Wally's house-warming. Jarré's musical roadblock motif repeats itself not in movement at speed, but in Jill's slow-motion walk through pouring rain to warn Guy about a Chinese arms shipment to the Communists. The mesmeric slowness of her movement up the stairs to his office, the slow forward zoom of the camera onto the couple's prolonged hypnotic embrace reverses the speed of eros after the quickfire seduction of the car scene. The embrace is still secret, like the secrecy of the information she confides to him and the corrupt power of politics as warning and temptation makes it sensual, a trigger to the lovers' pact of danger and desire.

When Guy uses the secret to try and obtain another scoop and not, as Jill wants, to escape from impending civil war, it becomes clear that he has betrayed Kwan's faith in him. Billy's role remains crucial. Weir at this point remains faithful to the novel and resists the temptation of turning his 'Wise Fool' into 'Cunning Voyeur'. Billy not only sees, but judges on principle. For his principles, he dies. Although the incident of his death follows the book, Weir resists the temptation to place Kwan as a supporter of the Muslim generals. His role is ambiguous. He is an idealist but also in Jakarta a fish in water so that the inattentive viewer could falsely think him to be Indonesian. Weir makes his disenchantment with Guy coincide with his disillusion over Sukarno. The voice-over where he condemns Guy is haunting because it is choked with his own emotions of sadness and despair: 'You have changed. You are capable of betrayal. You have grown addicted to risk . . . Why can't you give yourself? Why can't you learn to love?'. Later, confronting Guy with his risk fixation in front of the PKI graffiti of the city's slums, his censure is more chilling and explicit. 'I gave her to you and now I'm taking her back . . . I believed in you. I made you see things. So did Jill. I created you.' At the end it is the dwarf alone who has tragic stature. The death of the 'Wise Fool' is alone tragic. For when others fail his dreams, Kwan, the failed puppet master, must destroy himself.

Kwan is the central figure in both novel and film but Weir deepens his tragic ambiguity. The choice of Linda Hunt as Kwan – for which she won an Oscar – was an inspired piece of casting which produced one of the best performances of the decade in the cinema. Her portrayal of Kwan presents us with a tragic enigma we can never resolve. Looking back to the novel after the film, Koch's character is too transparent, too earnestly presented, too much a person of surfaces despite the author's excessive allegorising. But Hunt's androgynous acting shows us the dilemma of a man who has the talent to see but lacks what he most desires, the capacity to control things. His attempt to stage-manage Guy and Jill is as doomed as his wish to influence Sukarno. He becomes a redundant puppet-master powerless to alter a passion destined to run its course without him.

The film's other major triumph over the book lies in the transformation of Jill Bryant from a short dumpy and promiscuous heroine drowned by

Koch in frenzied description to a tall, casually tough, career woman. Here Weaver gives her a languid self-assurance which is at times intimidating while remaining – a rare feat for an American actress – quintessentially English and middle-class. Like Guy, Jill has her own addiction to risk which Weir stresses by compressing the action into the few weeks left to her before her departure for Europe. Her addiction is an erotic mirror of Hamilton's own recklessness in which, narcissistically, she dictates the tough terms by which he has to win her, and watches with cool excitement as he battles to overcome them.

The motif of watching becomes here more glamorous and less disturbing than in Hitchcock. Weir's film is very different from the deathly romanticism of *Vertigo* where James Stewart's gaze is an obsessive pathology and Kim Novak's persona a dream-like apparition. Weir is not aiming here for the oneiric quality of Hitchcock as he does earlier in *Picnic at Hanging Rock* and *The Last Wave*. Moreover, he uses the closures of melodrama to recuperate the normal, to force eros to give way to moral realisation. Billy's death is a sacrifice which exorcises the gaze and blunts the raptures of narcissism, just as the murder of Harrison Ford's black partner in *Witness* is the necessary spur to the detective's necessary act of retribution against his own kind.[8] Both sacrifices, as in all good melodrama, force the necessity of action upon the reluctant hero and finally redeem him. Thus Weir departs from the loose fabric of historical veracity which the film at times invokes. In getting Guy and Jill out of Indonesia, it gets us out too and leaves the 'good Asians', in this case Kwan and Kumar, to suffer the consequences. In that sense it compromises itself. But in another sense, the process of 'getting out' was an experience only too real. Too wise to try to film in Indonesia, Weir filmed on location in a Muslim area of the Phillipines and the crew left in a hurry after threats from inhabitants convinced that the film was anti-Muslim.[9] The rest of the exteriors had to be filmed in Australia. For Weir it was indeed 'the year of living dangerously'.

Notes

1. C. J. Koch *The Year of Living Dangerously*, London: Sphere Books, 1981 (first published by Michael Joseph, 1979).
2. Les Murray 'The year of living dangerously'. Seminar given at the Commonwealth Writers' Conference, Edinburgh July 1986.
3. Koch *op. cit.*, p. 3.
4. *ibid.*, p. 49.
5. See the interview with Koch in *Kunapipi* vol. 8, no. 1, p. 19.
6. Hena Maes-Jeliniek 'History and the mythology of confrontation in *The Year of Living Dangerously*' *Kunapipi*, vol. 8, no. 1, p.29.
7. See the comparison of Weir's film with *Vertigo* by Stanley R. Palombo 'Hitchcock's *Vertigo*: The dream function in film' in Joseph Smith and William Kerrigan (eds) *Images in Our Souls:*

Cavell, Psychoanalysis and Cinema, Baltimore: Johns Hopkins University Press, 1987, p. 55.

8. For a general discussion of redemptive sacrifice in film melodrama, see Christine Gledhill 'The melodramatic field: An investigation' in C. Gledhill (ed.) *Home is Where the Heart is: Studies in Melodrama and the Woman's Film,* London: BFI, 1987, p. 5.

9. For more details, see Robert Winer 'Witnessing and bearing witness: The ontogeny of encounter in the films of Peter Weir' in Smith and Kerrigan *op. cit.,* p. 101.

Filmography

The Year of Living Dangerously (An MGM/McElroy and McElroy/ Peter Weir Production. Australia 1982.) Starring Mel Gibson, Sigourney Weaver, Linda Hunt, Michael Murphy, Bill Kerr, Noel Ferrier: Art Direction by Herbert Pinter; Cinematography by Russell Boyd; Music by Maurice Jarre; Edited by Bill Anderson; Screenplay by David Williamson, Peter Weir and C. J. Koch from the novel by C. J. Koch; Directed by Peter Weir.

6

Nineteen Eighty-Four and *1984*

J. B. ELLIS

Adaptations of novels for the screen have been a fundamental source of material for the cinema and for television throughout the history of both media. Indeed, before either television or cinema were invented, novels were often adapted for the stage. We are so used to this process now that it has become normal for the book of the film or television series to receive special promotion by its publisher at the time of the release of the screen version. However beneficial this may be to the publishers (and to living authors), the tacit assumption that the novel is merely the script of the film needs some examination. George Orwell's *Nineteen Eighty-Four* and Mike Radford's *1984* – the makers of the film helpfully did not choose the same title as the novel – provide a convenient pairing, a study of which should lead to a clearer idea of what the two forms share and where they differ.

Some classic novels have been filmed frequently. Dickens, for instance, has been particularly popular, especially so in the silent days. In Britain since the fifties, this field has been largely taken over by television, with the BBC in particular frequently showing series based on classic novels by Dickens or Jane Austen, some of which have been filmed several times. The fashion for such adaptations is underlined by the success of *The Jewel in the Crown*, or *Brideshead Revisited* and of many others. In most cases, the screen version assumes a special status as *the* version of the book, and its images and characterisation and construction influence our subsequent reading of the novel. On the other hand, if we are already familiar with the book before we see the filmed version, we tend to pay particular attention to whether or not the film diverges from the book. Criticism of the film often concentrates on its shortcomings as a faithful representation of the novel. This is only natural, but is based on the assumption that the book *can* be faithfully represented in another medium.

Narrative is the normal mode of film, and, in discussing adaptation, Fulton remarks that the 'way a novel tells a story – primarily by description and narration – is comparable to the way a film does – primarily by pictures'.[1] However, this very verbal/visual opposition must be kept in the forefront of any discussion of an adaptation of a novel to the screen. In the film, the pictures will dominate over all else. As Panofsky pointed out as long ago as 1934, 'the basic fact [is] that a moving picture, even when it has learned to talk, remains a picture that moves and does not convert itself into a piece of writing that is enacted.'[2]

1984, in fact, follows the narrative of the novel very closely, although, naturally, it has had to be condensed. To take one chapter (Part Three, Chapter I) as an example, Winston's early experiences in the Ministry of Love are reduced to a single barked command from the telescreen and Parsons's brief presence in Winston's cell. The novel at this point covers a much longer period of time – several days at least – and includes incidents that involve several other prisoners, among them the drunken woman who could have been Winston's mother, Ampleforth the poet (who has been excised from *1984* altogether), the woman who 'seemed to shrivel and turn a different colour when she heard the words . . . Room 101',[3] the chinless Bumstead whose face is smashed in for daring to reach for a piece of bread, and the 'skull-faced' man who begs not to be taken to Room 101. In the film, this last role is given to Parsons, but the brutality to Bumstead is omitted altogether, as is the general sense that Winston is one victim among many. These excisions may have been primarily made because of the necessity of reducing the novel to a film with a two-hour span, but they also bring the advantage of emphasising Winston's plight even more. He is at the centre of events at this point, rather than being an observer of them (and thus providing our means of being told about them). Similarly, the removal of much of Orwell's detail in Part One about Winston's daily work does not affect the general presentation of it. In any case, this sort of detail can be very successfully presented by purely visual means, as we shall see.

Orwell divided *Nineteen Eighty-Four* into three parts, the first of which introduces us to Winston Smith and to the life of Oceania in 1984. The second starts from the girl's (Julia's) passing of her note to Winston and centres on their relationship up to the raid on the room over Charrington's junkshop, but it also gives considerable space (Part Two, Chapters V, VI, and VIII) to Winston's growing association with and subconscious dependence on O'Brien. The third deals with Winston's interrogation, torture, and 're-integration' at the hands of O'Brien. Each Part is divided into numbered chapters, and each of these has an identifiable narrative function. Part One, Chapter IV, for instance, gives us the details of Winston's work, Part One, Chapter V the canteen scene, and so on. One of the main differences between *1984* and *Nineteen Eighty-Four* (as between most, if not all, films and their books) is that the film's narrative is much more fluid and continuous than it needs to be in the novel. The audience will experience the film in a single sitting, so that the subdivisions, which we accept in novels because they allow us some control over the pace at which we absorb the story, have to be suppressed in favour of a fluent narrative style that creates the whole arch of the narrative as a single continuity.

In fact, Orwell has given the film-maker considerable encouragement in this by making use of Winston's memory and his dreams to break up the surface of the sequential narrative. In the first chapter, that morning's Two Minutes Hate is recalled as he starts his diary; in the third, there is his dream of his mother's death and of the Golden Country; and the writing of his diary recurs throughout Part One, recording for us his independence of thought and the existence of his memory as a mark of this individuality. As he asks himself during the canteen scene, while the Ministry of Plenty's announcement is made about the raised chocolate ration which he knows to be a reduced one, 'Was he, then, *alone* in the possession of a memory?'.[4]

The position from which the novel is perceived by the reader is very close to Winston's own. It is not told in the first person, but all the events centre on Winston and we only understand them and the other characters in so far as Winston himself does. We are enlisted on his side by his very individuality, which we believe ourselves to share. His puzzlement at the world in which he lives is ours, too, because we are being introduced to it for the first time. In the film, also, this relationship between us is established, indirectly at first, as we identify with the only face at the Hate Meeting (which opens the film, before the credits) that does not fully submit to the emotion of the occasion; and then, more fully, as the diary entries are spoken as a 'voice-over', thus moving in the direction of – but never reaching – the intimacy of first-person narrative. This mode of presenting the story 'without the perceptible intervention of the author' is common in both modern fiction and the film.[5] It differs greatly from the two principal methods of narration in earlier novels. The first of these is the omniscient narrator, who not only presents but openly comments on the materials of the novel (Jane Austen is a good example); such omniscience, although arguably inherent in the camera's eye, is rarely attempted in the cinema, where an insistent authorial voice is a distraction from the pictures on the screen. The 'indirect first-person' (as we may term it) which we are discussing is less different – but still significantly so – from the second type of novel narration which is that of the first-person narrator, such as Esther in her part of *Bleak House*, Pip in *Great Expectations*, or Holden Caulfield in *The Catcher in the Rye*. These extreme first-person narrators are difficult to capture on film because the camera inevitably shows them to us from outside, as moving pictures, and will tend to treat them on – perhaps to reduce them to – the same level of reality as all the other characters. For instance, the BBC version of *Bleak House* (1984) made no attempt to present Esther as a first-person narrator. She appeared as 'externally' as all the other characters, with the result that the tension between the two styles of narration in the novel, between subjective and objective, personal and impersonal, ignorance and knowingness, which makes the book so unusually powerful, was completely lost. Even if Esther had been given a voice-over, the contrast between events as seen by her and events as seen by the third-person narrator could probably not have been sustained by the camera. Because Winston is a narrator of neither of these types, he transfers fairly easily to the screen, where we both see with his eyes and observe him from outside.

In the novel, there seem to be three main ways in which we are led to identify ourselves with Winston. The most obvious has already been mentioned – his writing of a diary, together with what it contains. Our rejection of the society which Winston serves is thus annexed to Winston's own hesitant revolt. The film captures this element unobtrusively, picturing Winston's solitary dedication. His expression over his diary is relaxed, as it is not when he is at work or in the canteen. Secondly, Orwell makes him express his independence and his revolt against Big Brother's world through his sexual relationship with Julia ('that was the force that would tear the Party to pieces').[6] Their shared hours together in the room over Charrington's shop are the nearest that Winston can get to the Golden World of which he dreams. This the film presents faithfully enough, but it is worth asking whether the effect is the same in book and film. This is partly to do with the passage of time, for such scenes were more shocking in print forty years ago and did not appear on the screen at all; whereas for the film audience of today they are common currency, so that they affect us less powerfully. Although the film repeats the significance of their relationship from the book, it carries less weight with us than does the now-familiar screen nakedness. The absence of Winston's former wife from the film also slightly simplifies his sexual psychology. Admittedly, the incident with the prostitute occurs in the film, but that passage in the book is fused with his memories of Katharine. In the film, his love for Julia has no predecessor, and Katharine's Party-derived frigidity is displaced to the meeting of the Anti-Sex League that follows his first visit to Charrington's shop.

There is a third aspect of the novel, closely related to Winston's own individuality, which does not, however, seem to appear in the film. This is the gently subversive satire of much of the narrator's (or is it Winston's?) treatment of the detail of the world of London in 1984. In Winston's Department at Minitrue, for instance, there is Ampleforth:

> with very hairy ears and a surprising talent for juggling with rhymes and metres . . . engaged in producing garbled versions – definitive texts, they were called – of poems which had become ideologically offensive, but which for one reason or another were to be retained in the anthologies.[7]

And Syme's relentless logic about the future progress of Newspeak, as the literature of the past is rewritten:

> Even the literature of the Party will change. Even the slogans will change. How could you have a slogan like 'freedom is slavery' when the concept of freedom has been abolished? The whole climate of thought will be different. In fact there will *be* no thought, as we understand it now. Orthodoxy means not thinking -- not needing to think. Orthodoxy is unconsciousness.[8]

The version of this conversation in the canteen in the film does allow Winston an expression of mild puzzlement, but the novel can make the point more boldly: 'One of these days, thought Winston with sudden deep conviction, Syme will be vaporized. He is too intelligent. He sees too clearly and speaks too plainly. The Party does not like such people. One day he will disappear. It is written in his face'.[9] Similarly, there is sardonic satire in the famous opening sentence of the book ('It was a bright cold day in April and the clocks were striking thirteen'); and such passing details as the re-use of Nelson's Column for Big Brother's statue and St Martin-in-the-Fields for 'a museum used for propaganda displays of various kinds – scale models of rocket bombs and Floating Fortresses, wax-work tableaux illustrating enemy atrocities, and the like'[10] intermittently create a certain ironic detachment in the novel. The more idiosyncratic views of Winston noted above are at times almost surreal. Of Mrs Parsons, 'a woman of about thirty, but looking much older', 'one had the impression that there was dust in the creases of her face',[11] an observation he returns to more than once. This satirical touch which provides important evidence of human feelings is most prominent in the first three chapters of the book, but is not present in the film (even early on), the whole of which looks at the future far more solemnly, a viewpoint clearly governed by the final scenes of the story. In fact, it is the very presence of the book itself as a symbol in our consciousness ever since it was written that has prevented the film-makers from allowing this at times slightly quizzical Winston of Part One from co-existing with the bewildered and isolated Winston who has become so well-known through his experiences later in the novel.

Another facet of this subtler picture is the very full quotation from Goldstein's book that Orwell provides (close to a tenth of the novel).

The two extracts from the book are a brittle but penetrating satire on the human race (and on the mid-century balance of world politics) and are arguably the best part of the novel; they certainly lie very close to the heart of it. Orwell refused to allow the Book-of-the-Month Club to cut them, together with the Appendix and other passages, from their edition;[12] and Crick has pointed out that Goldstein's critique owes much to the ideas and political stance of the P.O.U.M. leader, Andrés Nin, which Orwell sympathised with.[13] Crick is uncomfortable about its presence in the novel but Williams thinks it is fully justified.[14] It is concrete evidence for Winston of an organised opposition to the regime and, as such, a prop for his hitherto insubstantial revolt. It gives the force of intellect to his sexual resistance, and is to be set (once more ironically) beside his daily occupation of rewriting history. As a written text in the novel, it is as tangible as is Winston's diary, but it implies, as does the whole concept of the Brotherhood, a more real alternative to the Party than the gesture of 'From the age of uniformity, from the age of solitude, from the age of Big Brother, from the age of doublethink – greetings!'.[15] Winston's confidence is strengthened by reading it; 'after reading it he knew better than before that he was not mad',[16] and so do we. The reading of the book which we share with Winston in the novel lulls us (and him) into a security which the voice from the concealed telescreen shatters.

Clearly, such a large portion of the film could not have been devoted to extracts from Goldstein's book. It has been reduced essentially to a single short passage about the purpose of war, ironically spoken by Winston as we watch a telescreenful of heroic war images and then continued (as in the novel) as Julia and Winston lie in bed. In the film, the significance of Goldstein's book is thus somewhat muted. This is largely because books do not seem to be able to figure powerfully as icons in films. Philip French has remarked that there is in this a difference between music or painting and books: 'The obvious difference between playing a piece of music or exhibiting a painting and showing a book is that the former is a thing itself and the latter can only have a meaning if the spectator knows it.'[17] As spectators of the film we cannot, of course, already 'know' Goldstein's book, and nor can we be introduced to it in the detailed way that Orwell permits himself in the novel. Consequently, in the film Goldstein's book has lost a good deal of its significance. It is merely a proscribed work, and reading it an act of insubordination, with none of the satiric reference to the real world outside which hangs around its use in the novel.

In the article just quoted, French is, of course, discussing the appearance in films of already-existing works of art, but the point is true, too, of the visual and aural aspects in *1984*. It goes without saying that it is in the nature of film to make its primary impact visually, and

1984 is very successful here. The drabness of dress and the squalor of the living conditions so essential to presenting the repression and conformity of the future totalitarian state (but so influenced by conditions in Britain when Orwell was writing) are deftly translated to the screen. Grey, blue and brown predominate throughout: even the faces of men and women seem drained of colour. The telescreens present their images in faded sepia (which underlines their functionalism) and small details from the book such as the pursuit of razor-blades, the non-functioning lift, the blocked sink, and the Victory cigarettes whose tobacco falls out when they are taken from the packet, help to convey a wholly persuasive setting in which the blank-faced workers live out their lives. The only clean and well-dressed members of society seem to be the children in the Spies. O'Brien's flat, admittedly, is well cared for, but it is still drab and monochromatic. The only bright colours in the film occur in the red of IngSoc's insignia and the sash of the Anti-Sex League, and, on the other hand, in the bright greens of Spring in the countryside to which Winston and Julia escape.

Film has the great advantage of being able to present such significant detail without needing to draw attention to it. The slogan 'BIG BROTHER IS WATCHING YOU' has, of course, become well-known since 1949, but in the film it can be and has been omitted, because the penetratingly severe/friendly face staring from the poster and screen makes the same point effortlessly. Similarly, Ogilvy, the war-hero whom Winston creates, exists in purely visual form in the film; the 'thing itself' has meaning.

It might, then, be appropriate to discuss here one visual element that seems to be a failure. In the novel, when Winston finally reaches Room 101, we are as shocked as Winston is that his final torture is to be by means of rats. Only once before has a rat appeared, in Charrington's room, and we may well have forgotten (as, in a sense, Winston has) his fear of them. This incident is not used in the film, which has, however, rather over-insistently brought rats into Winston's recollections of his childhood, including one particularly unpleasant shot of them on a woman's corpse, while O'Brien stands with the boy Winston looking at her. By the end of the film, we have been too thoroughly prepared (especially since the rats are another feature of the book that has become common knowledge) for the full horror of them to remain. In any case, it is also true that the imagining of the rats of Room 101 by the reader of the novel is bound to have a more powerful effect on him than their visual presentation has on the audience of the film. It is not seeing them that is so terrible, but thinking of them. There are ways, therefore, in which images can (paradoxically) be a drawback in a film.

There is one final aspect of the film that deserves brief mention – its use of known actors in the leading roles. Each novel has a unique set of characters, but films often use familiar faces. At the time the film was made, the face of Suzanna Hamilton was not known, so she represents solely Julia, as do the nameless faces of the minor characters, whereas the faces of Richard Burton, John Hurt and Cyril Cusack have a penumbra of earlier performances around them. Consequently, we do not need the camera to pause on Hurt and Burton in the opening sequence for us to note who will be the central characters of the film. Furthermore, although Hurt's performance is very fine indeed, perhaps his face is too tortured, too sensitive? It is hard to believe that Winston's rebellion took so long to be noticed, when he is clearly so different from his fellows. He appears throughout as a victim, with a facial expression usually far more subtle than the norm of dull passivity in those around him. Burton had less of a problem here, for O'Brien must seem enigmatic, neither clearly sympathetic nor clearly hostile. Burton's face exactly captures Orwell's O'Brien: 'strong and fleshy and brutal, it was full of intelligence and a sort of controlled passion before which [Winston] felt himself helpless; but it was tired'.[18] Films are often seen as vehicles for film stars, who appear in similar roles (maybe even as themselves?) time after time. Burton's performance in *1984* seems to be one that exactly fits the role of O'Brien, so that we forget the actor's other appearances on the screen, and see only O'Brien.

In 1940 and 1941 Orwell contributed film criticism to *Time and Tide*, but not with much conviction.[19] Indeed he seems to have feared the power of the mass media. One of the stultifying aspects of society he lists in his outline for 'The Last Man in Europe', which was to turn into *Nineteen Eighty-Four*, was 'Films'.[20] In the novel, the power of film is pointed to in Winston's first diary entry, which consists of his account of the carefully constructed newsreel of the bombing of a ship full of refugees 'somewhere in the Mediterranean' (pp. 10–11); and the dominance of the telescreen is a central feature of the totalitarianism against which he writes. For all this, *1984* is, on the whole, a not unsuitable companion to *Nineteen Eighty-Four*. Some of Orwell's points it makes more succinctly and with immediacy, some it cannot present, but it shares and expresses the same humane belief in the individual, and records his destruction by the machine of the state with an equivalent compassion and horror.

Notes

1. 'From novel to film' in John Harrington (ed.) *Film And/As Literature* Englewood Cliffs, NJ: Prentice Hall, 1977, p. 151.
2. Erwin Panofsky 'Style and medium in the motion pictures' in *ibid.*, pp. 286–7.
3. George Orwell *Nineteen Eighty-Four*, Harmondsworth: Penguin, 1984, p. 186.
4. *ibid.*, p. 50.

5. Robert Richardson *Literature and Film*, Bloomington: Indiana
     University Press, 1972, p. 19.
 6. Orwell *op. cit.*, p. 103.
 7. *ibid.*, pp. 36–7.
 8. *ibid.*, p. 45.
 9. *ibid.*, p. 45.
10. *ibid.*, p. 81.
11. *ibid.*, p. 20.
12. See Bernard Crick *George Orwell: A Life*, London: Secker and
     Warburg, 1980, p. 386.
13. Crick, *op. cit.*. pp. 225, 246.
14. *ibid.*, p. 263; Raymond Williams *Orwell*, London: Fontana,
     1984, p. 97.
15. Orwell *op. cit.*, p. 25.
16. *ibid.*, p. 171.
17. 'All the better books' *Sight and Sound*, 36, (1966–7), pp. 38–41.
18. Orwell *op. cit.*, p. 209.
19. Crick *op. cit.*, p. 259.
20. *ibid.*, Appendix A, p. 408.

Filmography

1984 (An Umbrella/Rosenblum/Virgin Production GB 1984.)
Starring John Hurt, Richard Burton, Suzanna Hamilton, Cyril
Cusack, Gregor Fisher, James Walker: Production Design by Allan
Cameron: Cinematography by Roger Deakins: Music by Dominic
Muldowney: Edited by Tom Priestley: Screenplay by Michael
Radford from the novel by George Orwell; Directed by Michael
Radford.

7

The Unbearable Lightness of Being on film

CATHERINE FELLOWS

Milan Kundera's novel *The Unbearable Lightness of Being* (1984) is possibly the most important novel to have been set in Prague since Kafka's *The Trial*. Written in exile after the invasion of the city by Soviet forces in 1968, Kundera's retrospective look at the psychological and philosophical impact of the experience has an ironic detachment not present in Kafka's earlier, prophetic vision of totalitarianism: and yet there is discernable continuity. Both novels have an originality and depth of vision dependent upon their immersion in political events of historical magnitude. The formal innovation that Kundera is celebrated for internationally is a reaction against dogmatism, specifically that of the communist state. With its ability to evade and undermine so real an opponent. *The Unbearable Lightness of Being* re-establishes language as a significant locus for struggle, and because of its essential pluralism, a powerful means of resistance.

Novels of the stature of *The Unbearable Lightness of Being* have seldom been successfully adapted for cinema. With modernist authors it is common to assume that since their perceptions are inextricable from their explorations of language itself, any attempt to transpose them to another medium would be futile. It is unusual then that Philip Kaufman's screen version of the novel is so satisfying, particularly as it abandons the novel's achronology; even more unusual that Kundera should have been a major contributor to the film. In an interview with Graham Fuller, Kaufman reveals that Kundera's judgement was so sure that he, the director, allowed the author a free hand:

> Kundera became an unofficial consultant once production began in Lyon, and it was he who suggested the use of Czech composer Janecek's plangent piano quartets which function as a major subtext in the film . . . he (Kundera) was so unerring in his tastes that I just tended to follow his suggestions.[1]

Kundera's novel endorses a highly modern and problematic conception of reality which is also consonant with the actual processes of the film medium. For as Keith Cohen states: 'Cinema can be seen as the epitome of twentieth century relativism . . . Rather than becoming more complete and more all-encompassing, or more efficient through automation' the representation of reality that the camera offers 'is full of deletions, ellipses, and partial views'.[2] On one hand it approximates raw, unaccommodated vision, and on the other, in the way that it 'endows these "rescued fragments" with special significance, and combines them in an order at odds with their lived sequence', it exposes the extreme artifice of our habitual manipulations of what we see. In his novel, Kundera evokes visual experience as the decisive context for his observations about perception. The recalcitrance of what we see, constantly undermines any claim for inevitability we might make for our interpretation. If one considers Kundera's emphasis on the physical origins of such concepts as lightness and weight, on the ubiquitous influence of the soul/body dichotomy and the symbolic potential of photography, it should come as no surprise that at the time of the 1968 invasion, he was Professor of Film at the University of Prague. His very use of language would appear to be influenced by the multi-dimensional, analogic nature of the film medium. Describing his writing, Kundera talks of:

> a new art of 'novelistic counterpoint' capable of blending music, philosophy, narrative and dreams; a new art, a radical honing that allows the inclusion of the vertiginous complexity of the world without the loss of architectonic clarity; and an essayistic art that does not attempt to bear an apodictic message but rather limits itself to a hypothetical, ludic, or ironic point of view.[3]

The film medium is relevant to modern fiction because it can challenge the easy fluidity of traditional verbal narrative and its assumptions about the real. If an adaptation of such fiction is a sensitive rendering, it is usually because of the *limitations* which critics cite as evidence of film's inability to equal verbal language: for example, that the past or future can only be evoked from the standpoint of the present or that actions cannot be explained in the process of representing them. In this case one might wonder how a screen adaptation that omitted Kundera's 'most interesting character' could be really effective.[4] It is the first-person narrator, after all, who provides the context of comment, speculation and counter-example in which the principal action – the story of Tomas and Tereza – is embedded. Cut loose from this rich textual patterning, there seems to be scant material for a self-sufficient narrative. It could also be argued that the narrator is indispensable to the novel's most interesting preoccupation, the connection between fiction and the way people narrate their own realities. Yet despite the fact that the film's hauntingly melancholic atmosphere bears little resemblance to the ironic, sometimes complacent tone of the novel,

Kaufman's film seems sensitive to its source; as sensitive in its adoption of a more conventional narrative structure as it is in its scrupulously faithful depiction of details.

In a perceptive essay in *Sight and Sound*, Terence Rafferty describes Kaufman's film as being characterised by 'a kind of fidelity that's different from what we're used to: it's faithful to the novel as it exists in the mind of a reader, rather than to the novel as some kind of autonomous entity, or to a notion of the author's intent'.[5] This somewhat enigmatic statement hints at a crucial experiential element in the novel which the film echoes. A vital effect of the novel's structure is to generate a struggle in the reader which replicates both the essence of its philosophical disquisitions, and the fictional experiences of the characters which illustrate them. The novel's lack of chronology, its constant 'digressions', intrusions and disclaimers, conspire against the reader's impulse to 'believe' in the fragments of the story. Yet, assaulted by their author and minimal as they are, these fragments have great poignancy and beauty. We, as readers, cling tenaciously to our sense of the aesthetic, just as Tereza, the photographer, allows hers to determine her life, and doggedly adheres to her sense of artistic value even after she has experienced its shortcomings. In this way Kundera is simultaneously demonstrating the anomalies of our *narrating* approach to life, its illogicality and its inescapable power. The paradoxes we are actively struggling with as readers approximate those which define us as perceivers in life itself; the paradoxes which generate the richness of our everyday existence and constantly confound us.

The film has no need to play such elaborate games. As Robbe-Grillet says of film in general: 'The essential characteristic of the image is its presentness . . . by its nature, what we see on the screen is in the act of happening, we are given the gesture itself, not an account of it . . . The camera becomes an "existence" that appropriates and becomes in the film a point of view . . . [which] passes in a way to the spectator himself'.[6] The film can offer the spectator the (simulated) visual experiences of its characters, allowing him to feel the fragility of the illusion in which he remains enclosed. On screen, the absence of the mediator becomes a perceptual advantage. As we bathe in the modulating flow before our eyes, we are experiencing the lightness of being, the ultimate contingency which must always characterise screen fiction, and our reaction to it; our imposition of the weight of significance upon it.

From the outset Kaufman's picture declares both its loyalty to its source and its difference from it. Our first experience is of the sound-track, the most obvious indication of the multi-dimensionality of the medium. At once an array of conflicting associations is introduced: the cooing of doves – ideal, tender, romantic, calm; municipal bells –

historical European city; cackling laughter -- scepticism, mockery, frivolity; and jaunty music – optimism, teasing irreverence, glee. Kundera's equivocal style is evoked, and yet key cinematic characteristics are in focus, namely, simultaneity and embodiment. Filmic sounds effectively no different from their real-life equivalents assault our eardrums. Kaufman follows this with a dramatic close-up of a female face, the owner of which is nonchalantly smoking. In doing so he provides an impressive contrast to Kundera's opening, namely the discursive disclaimers of the narrator. It is as if Kaufman is acknowledging from the start the irrepressible nature of figures active on a screen. The assuredness of this image, its sheer presence, suggests there is no point in using Kundera's tactics to convince his audience of the fictionality of his creatures. For they are already alive on screen as part of the filmic illusion.

The effect of the opening sequences is exaggerated. Even if we fail to register its homage to Czech film-makers of the period, the comedy routines are conspicuous as a patient strains up from the operating table to gawp at Tomas' current girlfriend 'taking off her clothes' at the doctor's irresistible command. This scene, of course, is a direct reference to Milos Forman's *The Fireman's Ball*. Later at the provincial hospital another nurse swooning at Tomas' irreverent sawing of someone's skull to the rhythm of the civic band outside has the same effect. The pleasure derived from these comic scenes comes from believing that the irreverent hero is not cowed by life, but is a free-thinking, free-acting individual. Yet Tomas would just look silly if he were merely blowing up balloons in time to a patriotic song. Our reaction as spectators reveals that if we admire the gall of the performer it is because we remain cowed by that which is being made light of, the power of the State, illness, and death. In these original scenes, the film is exploiting conventions of its *own* medium to convey the problematic coexistence of lightness and weight, and showing the inextricability of that coexistence from modes of narrative.

An array of details, a pair of flirtatious girls, the dark glasses, contribute to the atmosphere of levity. As the camera draws into the courtyard of the spa hospital with Tomas' car, the surreal sight of a group in dressing gowns prancing silently in slow motion (we hear only the sound of Tomas' car, as though we were inside) is as disturbing as it is amusing. Likewise, the profusion of dispossessed bodies, disembodied groans and whispers, and disorientating steam present a picture at once naturalistic and surreal. Kaufman is not just introducing the concept of soul/body duality that is to play a major part as the film unfolds, but is provoking the feeling of it for the spectator on a visceral level. It is important for the movement of the film that we should witness the detached, choreographed eroticism of Tomas and Sabina's affair in Prague before Tomas' meeting with Teresa changes the scene irrevocably. The world of surfaces in which meaning is construed, dissolved and reformulated in endless variations is the world in which Sabina and Tomas play, fascinated by new constellations, the object, the bowler hat for example, mutating within their extended performance. Sven Nykvist's cinematography is exquisite here, his camera's inventive search for new angles and poses outstripping that of the lovers themselves.

The transformation of Tereza from novel to film could not be more marked. The film is admirable in its ability to use her persona to introduce the idea of weight in opposition to Sabina, giving form to Kundera's binary mode of speculation, yet never resorting to simplistic and deceptive identity of person and position. For Kundera contends that the human condition is determined by the co-existence of the two opposite impulses. He describes how our perpetual dilemma is caused by the absence of 'eternal return'. Our existence is linear, each moment of time unrepeated, which, in theory, has a remarkable mitigating effect. If an event is transient it can be of only passing significance: there is no logical reason why we should feel borne down. But whilst this knowledge may be liberating, it also threatens to be totally undermining: 'the absolute absence of a burden causes man to be lighter than air, to soar into the heights', but also to 'take leave of the earth and his earthly being, and become only half real, his movements as free as they are insignificant'. Even though weight is habitually associated with suffering -- 'the heaviest of burdens crushes us, we sink beneath it, it pins us to the ground' -- it remains the case, Kundera asserts, that 'in the love poetry of every age, the woman longs to be weighed down by the man's body. The heaviest of burdens is therefore simultaneously an image of life's most intense fulfillment. The heavier the burden, the closer our lives come to the earth, the more real and truthful they become.'[7]

It was in the light of these reflections, says Kundera's narrator, that he first saw Tomas clearly, 'I saw him standing at the window of his flat and looking across the courtyard at the opposite walls, not knowing what to do'.[8] The image is exactly replicated in the film by the first shot of Tomas' return to Prague after his encounter with Tereza at the spa town. His back is turned to Sabina, intransigent and heavy, and as such unprecedentedly human, or 'real', to use Kundera's term. It is a revealing endorsement of Kundera's vision of lightness and weight, that when Tereza makes her entrance it feels as though we have been waiting for her. She seems like an anchor in a film which floats. Her plunge into the glassy water of the hospital pool, where Tomas is idling after having performed the operation he came to do, is a symbolic *tour de force*. As a pool-side chess game is thrown into confusion by the impact of her dive, and as the players turn on one another, there is an enormous sense of relief, but also the intimation of the price to be paid for probing beneath surface shufflings. Relief is also the effect in the subsequent scene when, lip-reading Tomas' silent order in the bar, Tereza's 'Ah, cognac' cuts into the amorphous murmurings of the customers and into Tomas' silent game-playing on a note which is distinctly down to earth. Her interrogating gaze initiates a quest for meaning that shapes the film. As the camera pans around the other opaque bodies in the bar, it discovers Tomas pretending to be invulnerable to what she represents. She is at once faintly ridiculous and uniquely compelling.

The effect of rearranging events in chronological order would seem to reverse the impact of the novel. Seeing two physically compatible individuals presented within the conventions of screen romance, both caressed by the camera, we expect them to come together in due course and be the centre of the action. But this is just the kind of comfortable scenario which Kundera's oscillating, *in media res* approach will not allow us. His structure questions just these kind of assumptions, for, as his narrator explains, any event is just one of an infinite number of possibilities. Any action is undertaken on the flimsiest basis because one can never know the outcome. The issue, central to the novel, as to whether or not the absence of eternal return robs what actually takes place of any value, cannot be asked if the film allows us to take things for granted. But Kaufman *does* communicate the precariousness of our assumptions by subtly undermining the fairy-tale he is building. Like her counterpart in the novel, the screen Tereza's 'coincidences' are distinctly forced, arbitrary, drawing attention to human agency: 'Ah, you are in room six! That's funny, my shift ends at six'. Tomas waits for Tereza on 'her' bench, but instead of initiating anything he promptly leaves, temporarily cheating our expectations and drawing attention to them. Information is omitted – how does Tereza arrive at Tomas' door in Prague? As actors and spectators we are constantly making great assuming leaps. Kaufman has made an even bigger one to emphasise that fact. As Kundera explains, there is nothing unlifelike about the elliptical and contrived structure of the novel, the artefact: 'human lives are composed in precisely such a fashion'. 'Guided by his sense of beauty, an individual transforms a fortuitous occurrence . . . into a motif, which then assumes a permanent place in the composition of the individual's life'.[9] In binding their collection of fragments into a coherent and meaningful whole with arbitrary patternings, film-makers are simply exploiting an essential impulse.

Kaufman's film is given beauty and aesthetic coherence by waves of return; recurrent images and motifs lace it together. Yet any continuity of meaning is pointedly denied. For example, when Tomas first confronts Tereza it is to ask her for a cognac. The incident is repeated almost exactly with another waitress after Tereza has left Geneva, and as such denies any inherent value for the exchange. Finally, after the return to Prague, Tereza's precious moment becomes polluted when the request of an obnoxious drunk for a cognac precipitates her nightmare affair with the so-called 'engineer' who comes to her rescue but is in all probability a secret policeman. The recurrences in the film show the significance that individuals attach to particular images, but also the way in which, dependent for the appeal of the present upon our memories, we are constantly disappointed by the lack of connection between images and their original connotation.

In the novel, both Tereza and Sabina are 'obsessed by beauty'. For Sabina the charm of beauty lies in its inscrutability. Her paintings delight in constructing surface meanings and then exploding them to disclose 'the unintelligible truth'; always elsewhere, and only ever intimated, never made explicit. For this reason, Franz, her Swiss lover's, desire 'to live in a glass house' is as repellent to her as it is futile, and his inability to respond to her iconic bowler hat or to her very presence when his wife is in towns, fills her with frustration. The heavy irony of her dislike of novels where characters reveal their innermost secrets is spared her in the film. It expresses her point of view by luxuriating in the beauty of the image at the same time as emphasising its enigmatic qualities. Insights which in the novel are attributed to Sabina alone become apparent in the process of film narration itself, and specifically in the way characters are constructed on screen.

In contrast to the novel, which offers a deep account of its characters, the film's characters are 'light'. No past is offered to ground them, few musings or motives to explain them. Verbal exchanges are kept to a minimum: the currency is visual. More than anything, they just 'are'; they exist powerfully in the present through their physical presence. We cannot forget them, file them or explain them away. They force us to reassess our processes of inference, to challenge the assumption that the kind of information we usually look for is inherent, rather than construed. Lack of a sense of past in the film, unlike the novel, actually allows it to convey an important cognitive point. Characters construct themselves on screen, gesture by gesture, not through past operating in the present, or memory, 'the shooting acting on them like a revelation, each advancement of the film allowing them a new development in their behaviour, their own duration very precisely coinciding with that of the film.'[10]

Paradoxically, in her attempts to infuse the physical with 'something higher', Tereza finds herself more hopelessly grounded than Sabina. Her outlook on life is expressed almost exclusively in visual terms by Kundera, a strategy which facilitates the effectiveness of the film. On arrival at Tomas' apartment in Prague, Tereza's attempts to control her body only emphasise her dependence upon it, as Kaufman has her trying to deflect Tomas' proposition with a cough. She ends up having her face distorted by his 'medical probings', and breathing with a deliberation in stark contrast to the sensuous rhythms of Sabina in the preceding scene. Even as she lunges for Tomas, it is as though she wishes to fly at him unencumbered, an implication added to as they lurch and crash around the room as some improbable single entity. Tereza would surely sympathise with Virginia Woolf's objection that 'the brain knows Anna [Karenina] almost entirely by the inside of her mind – her charm, her passion, her despair. All the emphasis is laid by cinema upon her teeth, her pearls, and her velvet'.[11] The novel is therefore superior to life, whereas film is true to it. Kaufman's film works so well precisely because the novel dwells upon the dominance of physical perception in everyday experience.

The scene where Tomas brings Tereza to Sabina's flat to discuss photography is Kaufman's own – in the novel Sabina advises Tereza about her career in a café and Tomas is not mentioned. It demonstrates the potential of the medium for presenting complex ideas about perception with astonishing clarity. Tereza, young and devoted, has recently moved in with Tomas: Sabina, his long-standing lover, is seeing a kindred free spirit capitulate. As the two women study the photographs before them, and study each others' faces apparently aware of Tomas' presence, Sabina's apartment is heavy with latent emotion. Yet because the camera lingers slightly longer than is normal upon their faces, we are confronted with the infinite ambiguity, or rather the actual muteness of the image. The apartment is empty: what is 'there' is their looking and ours, no more. The faces of the three actors could not be more expressive, but there is no fixed signified to which they or we can gain access by simply staring. There are only the fragments of other past images which we have to mould into some kind of context.

Tereza's role as a photographer highlights the importance of the visual in Kundera's observations about perception. But it is in the context of the moving images of the film that her art acquires central significance. During her first experiments in spring-time Prague, moving colour scenes freeze into black and white through her lens. Her images of animated faces and everyday activities are powerful precisely because they are fragments, because they suggest a context but are still ineffable, enigmatic. They invite us to ask questions, but are incapable of disclosing anything. It is only when colour movement is re-established that the interaction of a perceiver is re-introduced, that the possibility of meaning is opened up. The emphasis shifts from the mute, isolated object frozen by the still camera back to the scene as narrative, and by implication Tereza's point of view. This becomes more explicit as Tereza literally brings her pictures to life in her darkroom, then pastes them onto the mirror around her own reflection. Even the benevolent surveillance of the peeping Tomas threatens the autonomy of her vision. With a whisk of the curtain, the shot cuts to black, the hopeful strains of 'Hey Jude' on the sound-track are abruptly silenced and the illusion is gone.

This sequence had started with an idealised postcard scene of central Prague, and then cut to a very close shot of Tereza with the camera over her face, a transition which anticipates the ingenious 'moment of truth' after Tereza's frenetic recording of the Soviet invasion. In this later sequence, her activity builds up to a climax of false confidence as she continues to shoot pictures courageously in the face of a gun. As the reality she sees through the camera lens fades to the imprint of a photographic image which drops in turn to reveal the leering face of a Communist interrogator, it becomes clear that taking pictures is no way to establish control over events. In fact by fixing arbitrary moments of interaction, the photographer is not able to secure their meaning but only to rob them of their relativity. The contrast between Tereza's face framed by her photo-images and that of the accused ciné-cameraman 'framed' by her picture of him and denying his own identity, could not be more marked. Yet the film emphasises these are two sides of the same coin.

Another scene in which Kaufman skilfully amalgamates several elements into a new whole, is that of the pre-invasion dance: the jubilant atmosphere of Tereza's photographic foray is retained as Sabina presents her with her pictures in print, and in the background young couples are dancing with the exhilaration of the Prague spring. A nearby table of Party officials is scrutinised by Sabina's group of doctors and artists: in answer to the question 'Does it [the fact that he is a scoundrel] show in a man's face?', we are challenged with close-ups of fat, complacent bureaucratic faces and with the repeated whispering of 'scoundrel, scoundrel'. It is a dangerous moment of confidence, based on the overwhelming clarity of the context, and later to be reversed by Tereza's meeting with the 'engineer' after her return to occupied Prague. Even here, as Sabina and Tereza interrogate Tomas' face – 'the mouth? the sly eyes?' – assumptions which are encouraged by cinematic stereotyping about the correlation between looks and character, are brought into question.

This is also the scene in which Tomas introduces his analogy with the Oedipus myth. He observes that whereas those in authority in Czechoslovakia before 1968 claim to be innocent because they were unaware of any wrong-doing, King Oedipus, who was unaware of his parentage, could not bear the sight of the suffering he had inadvertently

caused. In the novel the haphazard birth of Tomas' analogy is in inverse
proportion to its subsequent role in Tomas' downfall. He falls foul of the
new regime and loses his job because of his refusal to recant. Day-
Lewis's naturalistic, understated performance conveys Tomas' relative
detachment about what he is saying. In the face of Sabina's wry smile,
he is content just to shrug and not finish explaining. But like
photography, the Oedipus myth assumes a much more precise
importance in the context of the film. Oedipus has been deceived by
appearances – there is no way he could have 'read' his relationship to
events from what unfolded before his eyes. But whereas the Czech
politicians Tomas is accusing protest innocence because they did not
'see', as though events or sequences of images were autonomous and
inevitable, in blinding himself Oedipus literally denies that significance
is inherent in the visible world. In accepting responsibility for something
over which he had no control, he, paradoxically, asserts human potency
and stresses the fact that history, as well as meaning, is a human
construction.

The film's treatment of the invasion – tanks crashing through the
streets of Prague to the outrage and shock of its citizens – makes
pointed use of the anomalies of the medium to extend the novel's
insights. Typically, it materialises the details of Kundera's brief
evocation: 'when she went too far and took a close-up of an officer
pointing his revolver at a group of people, she was arrested . . .'[12] 'The
days she walked through the streets of Prague taking pictures of
Russian soldiers and looking danger in the face were the best of her
life'.[13] It conveys the euphoria of the time, and of Tereza in particular,
as she finds an outlet for her frustrated commitment. It creates a
sequence of events which allows a fruitful juxtaposition of the couple's
private problems and the public scenario over which they have even less
control. As Tomas and Tereza are reunited under the dazzling white
headlights of the Russian tank lurching towards them, the film
prefigures the ambiguity of its own conclusion where the two of them
will be heading in their truck towards their fatal accident and the white-
out of oblivion.

The bright white light of the tank and the nocturnal setting also have
a practical function, facilitating the blend of black and white archive
footage and the film's simulated reconstruction. The fact that the
archive material happens to be in monochrome has fortunate
implications. We see protagonists who have been grappling with
personal intricacies becoming absorbed in a far greater story, that of
human history in the making. They are revealed to be active composers
of the general significance. Here Kundera's notion of the fictitious
nature of experience is underlined by a contrary movement: we see
documentation of historical reality becoming integrated into an
indubitable fiction and being indistinguishable from it. There is a

definite change in direction in the film at this point, the highly relative earlier scenes giving way to those charged with historical significance. Suddenly, under the surveillance of the state, personal activities acquire public consequences. It is no longer possible to be the detached observer, or adventurer, when you are observed in turn.

A further achievement of the invasion sequence is the breakdown of the clear narrative structure up to this point. The confusion created by the camera as it lurches both within sequences and from one sequence to another not only simulates the chaos of the events depicted, but undermines the viewers' means of piecing things together. It reinforces the idea of what has gone before as an imposed structure. As our eyes dart after glimpses of Tomas and Tereza, we are holding out for them as we might cling to friends in a riot, but also, like the readers of Kundera's text we are clinging to the fragments of the 'story' against the constant dissuasion of the author's narrative structure. Because Kaufman's invasion sequence is infused with the emotion of Tereza and that associated with the documentary footage it uses, it is devoid of Kundera's cynicism about the 'Grand March'. It is only subsequently, when one is confronted with further crowd scenes thick with spies, or the fear of them, that we experience disillusion with the earlier apparent unanimity.

That question can be addressed more objectively by the film in a conversation between Sabina and Franz in Geneva. Franz's idealistic conception of mass endeavour – 'The Grand March ever onward to a better world' – is the opposite of Sabina's experience of false cheer and suppression of individuality: 'We were forced to march, everybody smiling . . . I could never keep in step'. Maybe the unsympathetic picture of Switzerland (and by implication Western democracy) which forms the backdrop for his arguments, weights things against Franz in a way in which the equivocation of Kundera's novel would not. In fact his actions after Sabina deserts him, wisely omitted in the film, threaten the coherence of the book. Again, film is able to express Franz and Sabina's complete failure to see eye to eye with an instantaneousness that eludes narrative writing. Likewise kitsch: we only need to glimpse Kaufman's typical Swiss restaurant, with its officious, pompous waiters, canned 'musak' and plastic flowers, to appreciate Kundera's conclusion that kitsch is the mis-application of signs, whether it be bird-song in a supermarket, or a benign smile on the face of an interrogator. The connection between the contrasting insincerities is made by the location of Franz and Sabina's discussion in this restaurant, not to mention the preceding scene in which the righteous indignation of Czech emigrés is undermined by the opulence of the Swiss setting.

The film exploits the potential offered by the novel's contrasting locations to the full. Kaufman's Geneva, bright and self-satisfied, is a different world from muted, poetic Prague. Even details such as the characters' dress speak volumes: Sabina herself has abandoned her soft, bohemian appearance for a distinctly cruel pair of Western jeans, which, whilst they are starkly revealing, allow her body to express none of its former grace. Appropriately enough, Sabina seems to undergo far more of a transformation than Tereza. The location of Tereza and Sabina's charged erotic duet in front of and behind Tereza's camera, is changed from Prague to Geneva and used by Kaufman to maximum effect. Certainly the scene invigorates the Geneva passage in the film without jeopardising the overall contrast in atmosphere. As time given to Franz is reduced, that bestowed upon Tereza, in her capacity as counter-weight to the levity of Sabina and Tomas, is increased.

Much more important however for the coherence of the film, is the occurrence of this cathartic and fulfilling moment for both women when Tereza is being forced to recognise her nature by her alien surroundings. It follows her disillusionment with the apathy and triviality of the West as she sees it: photography, which she has seen as an agent of great significance, is good for nothing but illustration and titillation here. A more complete impression of her despondent state of mind is conveyed by juxtaposing the image of her pointing the camera at an uninspiring cactus in the pristine Swiss flat, with that of the emotional reunion of Tomas and Sabina. The implication that their activities are present to her is substantiated by her asking Sabina if she has seen Tomas since their arrival in Geneva. Whether she actually knows is not the point. Rather his infidelity *per se* is continuing to preoccupy her and to contribute to her misery and self-doubt. She leaves Prague shortly after her adventure with Sabina. It is as if the encounter has given her the sense of self-purpose necessary for this act, and yet it is an act that she describes as an admission of defeat.

In both novel and film, Tereza's primary motive in photographing Sabina is to gain access to the area of Tomas' life from which she is excluded. Kundera writes: 'The camera served Tereza both as a mechanical eye through which to observe Tomas' mistress and a veil by which to conceal her face from her'. At the same time as beautifully depicting this combination of attack and defence, the film shows how the lens allows Tereza to subject Sabina to the same kind of objectification she suffers from Tomas. In the novel she is always trying to possess her body, to make it express her soul, and feels that Tomas has denied her this possibility by drawing an equal sign between her body and those of other women. Paradoxically, the film exposes her effort in Juliet Binoche's self-consciousness, gaucheness almost. But it is only in this scene with Sabina that the full implications of her position, and of, for example her visions of rows of naked women in the swimming pool, as depicted in the film, are fully explored in the adaptation. Through the camera, the two women see each other as

Tomas sees them, and exert the same power over one another as he does, but also see what they themselves look like to him. They experience one another as bodies, physical objects, as they are viewed by the male world, and yet from positions of equality. Both objects and subjects, they are ultimately able to achieve some kind of soul-body harmony in one another's company, and in the absence of both men and the camera. The sudden intrusion of Franz re-introduces the division which has been temporarily bridged, as Tereza dives to cover her nakedness, and Sabina's expression is totally misread by her hapless lover.

This is not a specifically feminist point. As seen earlier, the sequence of the two women together in Sabina's Prague studio shows the experience of the other-as-object to be a universal one, if more successfully exploited by men. However, the substitution of an unequivocally male narrrator by the androgynous eye of the camera does have implications for the material under scrutiny. In the film, Kundera's favourite character does not enjoy the protection afforded by his author. Tomas' promiscuity is dignified to an extent in the novel as the extension of a logical outlook on life, and in particular as a reaction against the hypocrisy of others. This association has further implications when the camera offers up the reaction of the women involved within the same sequence. The film exposes the weakness of Kundera's apparent obsession with the womaniser or Don Juan. If anything, the theoretical position that is supposed to explain it, is here threatened by it. The film has more credibility in human terms since the appeal of Sabina, as an individual and as the crystallisation of an alternative vision to that of Tereza, is obvious. It is the general compulsion of Tomas which is so unconvincing. It is presented in the novel as somehow inextricable from his identity:

> Was he genuinely incapable of abandoning his erotic friendships? He was. It would have torn him apart. He lacked the strength to control his taste for other women. Besides, he failed to see the need. No one knew better than he how little his exploits threatened Tereza.[14]

But it is hard to reconcile the *es muss sein* of his lust with his own appeal to the example of Oedipus, whose response was determined by the consequences of his actions upon others, not the question of his own guilt or the logic of the situation. One could say that in generating this contradiction, the novel anticipates such a reaction, but the account of Tomas' compulsion lacks credibility and reads more like authorial fantasy than anything else.

The film also exposes the extent to which Tomas is a victim of his own behaviour: 'He was caught in a trap: even on his way to see them, [the other women], he found them distasteful, but one day without them and he was back on the phone . . .'.[15] The risibility of his position is not overlooked by Kundera – it is his Sabina who first forces Tomas to pull on a fish-net stocking, she having hidden his sock as mild revenge for his distractedness during love-making. But it is when we can actually look at Day-Lewis from the perspective of Sabina and Tereza during the scene in which the women pore over photographs, that we can appreciate the real comedy of his position. Tomas is dispatched to the kitchen, and far from being the focus of attention is excluded from their conspiratorial whispering and laughter. When he re-enters the room, passing the mischievous sock dangling mockingly from a hook on the wall, he remarks, 'Here's the tea I made', a comic indignity to which Kundera would never have subjected his hero, though it seems a perfectly valid extension. Tomas is also a figure of fun after Tereza has abandoned him in the white empty flat in Geneva. (The proximity of the image of Sabina's evacuated flat with its mirrors to this one dominated by an anthropomorphic, white beanbag, prompts one to consider the fact that their apparently opposite motives have resulted in remarkably similar actions – a paradox that Kundera would surely relish.) As Tomas wades up to his ankles in the Swiss lake and awkwardly throws bread to a flock of swans, the contrived nature of this image of freedom undermines the idea that it is intended to convey. Each one of the characters refuses in one way or another to be expressed by the language of others, but in this scene it becomes apparent that while Tomas may have turned his back on some forms of convention, he has adopted a life-style which is equally constraining.

Once back in Prague, and stripped of his status as a doctor because he has refused to retract his Oedipus piece, Tomas' lust becomes even more problematic. His encounter with the wife of a communist dignitary is characterised by the same compulsion as pre-invasion seductions, despite its potentially disastrous outcome. The Janacek theme that accompanies the preceding scene, in which window-cleaner Tomas is hemmed in by criss-cross ladders and architectural verticals and horizontals, becomes an ironic anthem to his recklessness. Indeed the film, with its emphasis on the voluntary nature of Tereza's and then Tomas's return to Czechoslovakia, both relinquishing their passports to border guards, is true to Kundera's contention that 'the importance of [Eastern European] art does not lie in the fact that it pillories this or that political regime, but that, on the strength of social and human experience of a kind people in the West cannot even imagine, it offers new testimony about mankind'.[16] The regime is a powerful catalyst, but it only accelerates the realisation of destinies established long before the invasion.

In the film, Tomas' refusal to sign a retraction of his Oedipus piece is above all a refusal to the crippling and deceitful homogeneity that acts as the principal weapon of the Communist authorities. The film shows the claustrophobic pervasiveness of that official denial of discrepancy which is anathema to Tomas and Tereza; the former's existence predicated upon the infinitely varied nature of reality, Joyce's 'ineluctable modality of the visible', the latter haunted by the fear of anonymity and mediocrity. In crowd scenes laced with suspicious faces, in Tereza's bar, and in the hospital, there is a general feeling of uneasiness, distrust, the potential for betrayal. There is no room here for reliance on appearances, upon whether or not someone looks like a scoundrel. In the hospital, it is the very people so enthusiastic about the Prague Spring who are now prepared to comply with an authority which they apparently deplore, putting themselves at the mercy of that authority which is based on fear. In real terms, Tomas' action, his refusal to sign is mostly a protest against his colleagues' assumption that he will capitulate. The whole incident produces in him a contempt for society that destroys his desire to play any part in it.

Yet his exile is markedly different from that of Sabina: the contrast could hardly be conveyed more explicitly in the film. Her avoidance of the different hypocrisies she sees at the root of both Czechoslovakian and Swiss society, the latter personified by Franz, generates a mode of existence as problematic as that of Tomas. Not only is it impossible to live a life true to the logic of perception, it is potentially self-destructive. 'Do you want to see America, Tomas?' Her question is the nearest she can come to suggesting her chosen life is not fulfilling. At his evasive answer, she withdraws to her end of the big Swiss bed they are lying in: 'Maybe I'm seeing you for the last time.' The visual language of the film is strong: as we watch Sabina's endlessly reflected form we see her liberated from the sense of self that oppresses Tereza, but we also see her scattered, fragmented and finally effaced in the stark image of her evacuated flat. Her flight from Franz, and her indignant outbursts in Geneva combine to show that her effectiveness is limited: she does not like society and 'the uglification of the world' but she cannot change it because she can entertain no thoughts of commitment. Finally there is something sublime but sublimely empty about the Californian vistas, where her art is refined almost out of existence to impersonal sprayed lines. Sabina seems to have become a diversion in the lives of others rather than the subject-actor of her own. With a few deft strokes, the film has captured the essential paradox, the unbearable lightness of being: 'her drama was a drama not of heaviness but of lightness . . . Sabina felt emptiness all around her. What if emptiness was the goal of all betrayals?'.[17] As becomes clear in the depiction of country life which concludes both novel and film, the lie she is always in the process of rejecting can be a beautiful lie.

The final chapter of Kundera's novel, 'Karenin's Smile', is also the final chapter of Tomas and Tereza's story, and they are allowed to tell it almost uninterrupted. The dog's 'smile' is of course an illusion, as is Tereza's pastoral idyll on the collective farm. But the chapter title also alludes to the connection Kundera makes between animals and happiness. In effect, animals have never left Paradise, because they have never had to confront their own reflections, to experience the soul/body duality that has sent humans careering through time into the unknown. Animals ask for nothing more than repetition, a stable, circular existence: a state humans nostalgically long for, and call happiness, and yet which their nature could never be satisfied with. As film and novel demonstrate, we are constantly imposing patterns of repetition upon our lives, and constantly trying to escape them. And yet our tenuous links with Paradise are worth preserving, Kundera's typically categoric and evasive words would seem to say. The film is extremely sensitive to a complex and profoundly ambiguous exposition. On screen, the tentative optimism that hovers over the novel's final pages, like the 'large nocturnal butterfly' that circled Tomas and Tereza's last bedroom, grows more substantial, without in any way compromising the feeling of ephemerality.[18] An emotion can pervade an image, but its fullness can disappear in an instant, evoking the fleeting moments of happiness that words can only convey in an accumulation as sophisticated as Kundera's. But it is only in the context of the exploring of cognition which precedes this section of the film, that its full significance becomes apparent.

The film's depiction of the rural life of Tomas and Tereza is strikingly different from its earlier, philosophical, mood. There is a rhythm and a scale at once human and mythological. As we watch the couple herding cows on a screen framed by trees and mist, we could be looking at an old master: there is no mistaking this for 'objective reality'. As Tereza comforts her dying dog, Karenin, with tales of heaven 'It will be beautiful there. You won't feel any pain; don't be scared; you'll have cows to chase; Mephisto will be there . . .' we see her paint a picture very similar to the images in which she and Tomas are existing. This idyll is not a film-maker's easy way out, but a dream world which the protagonists make for themselves. The reality is starkly different, as the film illustrates by interrupting the couple's grief over Karenin with the screams of the farm worker who has dislocated his arm. And Tereza still has to confront the imperfections of her love for Tomas, even as she watches the death of the animal she loves 'in a better way'.

The difference between this and other myths is that it is archetypal. Testimony to that difference seems to be offered by the novel in its treatment of the death of Karenin. Throughout, the enemy has been kitsch, in its widest sinister sense. And yet here, the death of an animal, an event guaranteed to generate that indiscriminate communal surge of emotion exploited by East and West alike, is reinvested with genuine symbolic impact. That the film manages to pull this off is perhaps even more of an achievement than Kundera's original, when you consider the presence of the suffering dog. As implied by Kundera's observations about animals and Paradise referred to earlier, the significance of the death goes far deeper even than its subjective role as a cipher for the couple's relationship.

The penultimate sequence of the film conveys a sense of human action and its potential unequalled elsewhere. The screen is dominated by the growing of crops, the care of livestock, the preparation of meals, the healing of the injured arm, by dancing and spontaneity. Maybe here is the centuries-old narrative framework in which human need is most successfully accommodated; in which the lightness of being is made bearable by the weight of time; in which even death can be accommodated.

And yet, there is something ineluctable about Tomas and Tereza's fatal truck accident after their night of revelry at the inn. It is as hard to imagine the continuation of the story of Tomas and Tereza as it is to imagine the endless continuation of the film: these visual sequences can no more sustain themselves than they can sustain the lives of their protagonists – as the striking final white-out at the end makes plain. Like more conventional movies that abandon their characters to the sunset, it underlines the fact that human happiness is, in essence, momentary, the state of paradise of which we dream a fiction. Perhaps the film's greatest achievement, even with so archetypal an ending, is to preserve the novel's lack of closure. As Kundera puts it: 'My obsession as a novelist is to transform all answers into questions.'[19]

Notes

1. Quoted in 'The light stuff – An 'unfilmable' erotic epic', *Listener* 213, 24 March 1988. It should be noted that when I call the picture Kaufman's film, I include the collaborative efforts not only of Kundera but also of scriptwriter Jean-Claude Carrière and Ingmar Bergman's outstanding cinematographer, Sven Nykvist.
2. *Film and Fiction: The Dynamics of Exchange*, New Haven: Yale University Press, 1979, p. 10.
3. Milan Kundera 'The legacy of the sleepwalkers', *Partisan Review*, vol. LI, 1984, p. 728.
4. The phrase is Kaufman's. Quoted in Fuller 'The light stuff', *op. cit.*
5. 'Last looks' *Sight and Sound*, Summer, 1988.
6. Quoted in M. Beja *Film and Literature*, New York: Longman, 1976, p. 75.
7. *The Unbearable Lightness of Being*, London: Faber and Faber, 1985, p. 5.
8. *ibid.*, p. 6.
9. *ibid.*, p. 52.

10. Jean-Louis Comolli *Cahiers du Cinema* no. 205 October 1968: quoted in Gilles Deleuze *Cinema 2*, London: The Athlone Press, 1989, p. 193.
11. 'The movies and reality' *New Republic*, XLVII 4 August, 1926, p. 306.
12. *The Unbearable Lightness of Being*, p. 25.
13. *ibid.*, p. 26.
14. *ibid.*, p. 21.
15. *ibid.*, p. 22.
16. Milan Kundera: 'Comedy is elsewhere', *Index on Censorship*, vol. 6, no. 6, Nov–Dec 1977, p. 6.
17. *ibid.*, p. 122.
18. *ibid.*, p. 314.
19. Quoted in Fuller, *op. cit.*

Filmography

The Unbearable Lightness of Being (A Saul Zaentz Production US 1987.) Starring Daniel Day-Lewis, Juliette Binoche, Lena Olin, Erland Josephson, Daniel Olbrychski; Production Designer, Pierre Guffroy; Cinematography by Sven Nykvist: Music by Leon Janacek; Screenplay by Jean-Claude Carrière and Philip Kaufman from the novel by Milan Kundera; Directed by Philip Kaufman.

Part II

Hollywood and the literary property

8

Words selling pictures

JOHN IZOD

In the capitalist world the adaptation of literature into film is almost always a commercial enterprise. The American film industry provides a convenient place to examine the development of this practice because from its early days it was large and it grew into the most powerful and soiphisticated sector of the communications market. Adaptation has to be commercial for the sufficient reason that film production is costly and requires the investment of capital. Those who put money into the business do so in the hope not only of recovering it, but also of taking a profit. However, it has long been commonplace knowledge that, even at those times when the cinema industry as a whole is thriving, investment in any single motion picture is a risky matter.

From very early days the businessmen who ran the various arms of the American industry worked hard at finding methods of reducing that risk. Eventually they developed a number of highly effective means of spreading risks across a number of films. For example, among the best known and most powerful of these was block booking, a system which obliged cinema operators to take from the distributors weak attractions along with likely bestsellers. But long before the block-booking system was first extensively enforced (from 1916 onwards), they had discovered that the adaptation to cinema of written fiction was a reliable method (re-making successful theatrical productions and using popular music were others) of improving the chances of an individual film doing well.

From the period about 1906–8, by which time the standard length of a film was one reel (something in the order of twelve minutes), American film production companies began to satisfy their need for fresh story ideas by drawing upon literature – both popular and 'classic'. Although some film-makers began by simply stealing what they needed, they quickly found that they were under a legal obligation to purchase the rights to material they wanted to use: as Lewis Jacobs shows, the makers of *Ben Hur* (1907) were fined $15,000 for violation of the copyright on that story.[1] However, even denied the liberty to pirate other people's ideas, the film companies found it often worth their while to buy the screen rights to stories.

At this period few writers in the industry had managed to work out ways of writing efficiently for the screen (though this skill was soon to develop). Often the availability of a ready-made story to some extent simplified matters for them. The adaptation of published fiction had, of course, one other great potential advantage, as Robert Sklar argues – it promised to deliver a ready-made advance audience of people who had read the book and others who had heard of it.[2] Bestselling novels by Rex Beach and Zane Grey, by O'Henry and Upton Sinclair all were made into screen versions. Their popularity must have been apparent to the nickelodeon operators who screened them: both Westerns and dramas dealing with contemporary city life swiftly became familiar themes on the American screen.

While for its part the so-called dime novel was improving business in the nickelodeon, 'classic' literature was not being ignored by the industry. It had a double role. Firstly it was used as a weapon to resist pressures exerted on the film business by those middle-class reformers who held the cinema to be an evil influence on society. In 1908 they had succeeded for a time in closing the cinemas of New York, and had generated a fairly successful campaign in favour of censorship. Secondly, as an extension of the strategy directed at reformers, it was hoped that adaptations of 'good' literature would do more than reassure the middle classes that cinema was not a dangerous new social disease, and would actually entice them through the turnstiles. Thus, adapting literary classics was part of the industry's strategy to gain for itself both a clean reputation and new business.[3]

There were, however, two significant constraints arising from the shortness of films which limited the potential of adaptation in these early years. Firstly, and rather obviously, the twelve-minute film is far too short to cover in anything more than outline a few episodes of a novel. And secondly, the very way in which nickelodeons programmed the short films they screened made it difficult for any particular movie to build up a following. For in order to keep their patrons coming back, they changed their programmes frequently – in many cases daily, and seldom less than three times a week. Typically a film had finished playing at any given venue before word-of-mouth report had built the desire to see among those who had missed it.

The advent of the feature film changed both these factors. With a running time of anything from an hour upwards, it provided the scriptwriter with the space to develop more of the themes of the novel being adapted. Equally significantly, for inescapable commercial reasons features had to play longer runs in cinemas: in effect, since they cost more than a programme of short films, they had to take more money at the box office to return their investment. This factor had a further consequence in that the new, longer film had to draw its potential audience with identifiable and sure attractions to make certain that, when word-of-mouth report did get out, it would be good. Those attractions might include not only glamorous film stars, sensuous images, and expensive production values, but also the story itself. In turn this might be made more attractive if it had been taken from a well-known novel.

From its beginnings the feature film was associated with literary and dramatic classics – for much the same reasons that short films had attached themselves to similar literary properties in about 1908. However, there was one other factor to be considered. Since feature films were expensive, production companies exerted pressure on the distribution side of the film business, which was required to pass on a higher return from rentals. These rising costs forced distributors to put up their rental charges, and in turn caused cinemas to put up their ticket prices. Soon those cinemas that got films first (they became known as first-run houses) began to charge higher prices than cinemas taking later runs. In a relatively short time this arrangement became organised into a hierarchical system which had the effect that the first-run exhibition of any given film came to return the major part of its profits. Most of the film companies now made a practice of thinking of the patrons that attended those first-run houses as their target audience. And through most of the rest of the silent era, this audience seems to have been predominantly middle-class. Middle-class values and tastes, together with the plots and themes enjoyed by such an audience, came to occupy a substantial sector of the production schedules of most American companies.

For these reasons the classic novel became one of the kinds of artistic property with the aid of which the film industry sought to pre-sell its product. However, the industry did not limit itself merely to buying up the rights to published novels. As David Bordwell, Janet Staiger and Kristin Thompson show, as early as 1911 it had begun to turn film plots back into literature.[4] In the first instance production companies exploited the residual value of stories which had been featured on the screen by having writers rework them into the appropriate literary style for publication in movie magazines intended for sale in cinema foyers. Such tie ins (as they are called) rapidly advanced. The release of film serials was accompanied by newspaper publication of printed versions of the same stories. And by 1914 book publishers were promoting limited editions of novels based on films, illustrated with stills taken from them.

Nor did the film industry restrict its activities to preying on literature.

It had also developed a particular interest in Broadway theatrical productions. For the Hollywood companies realised from an early date that comparable marketing advantages attached to successful productions on the legitimate stage in that they too were pre-sold to a substantial audience. The studios kept in close touch with Broadway in the same way as they had established contacts with literary agencies. As early as 1915 according to Robert McLaughlin, competition between film companies for theatrical properties was so intense that screen rights were bought to many plays that had little or no potential film value.[5] Since theatrical plays could be fairly readily adapted to the screen, the movie companies did all they could to develop the relationship. And wherever they could they directly financed Broadway shows. This manoeuvre had the advantage for the film company that it could bid privately for screen rights, which made it possible to acquire them less expensively than on the open market. The theatrical impresario for his part gained all, or some of the backing necessary to set up his stage show. But in return for the advance sale of screen rights, he made less from them than he would expect if the production turned out to be a box-office success. The earliest known venture of this type was undertaken in the 1919/20 season when Paramount's Famous Players-Lasky bought up Charles Frohman, Inc. (a leading theatrical firm) and provided finance for its stage productions. Over the next five years an increasing amount of movie money found its way into Broadway productions.

For the purposes of publicity departments, stories could be treated a little like stars – whether they came from the legitimate stage, pulp novels, or literature of recognised standing. Those that had cost a lot to buy in could be shouted up in the market place. On the other hand if a studio found a little known book that it thought would conveniently adapt for the screen, it would attempt to pay no more than a small sum for the rights, and the publicity department would concentrate on other values (dramatic action or vivid characterisation, for instance) in its marketing campaign.

Thus far we have tended to concentrate on the benefits to the studios of adaptation. And they were very real. For example, some observers have noticed that in the early twenties the popularity of run-of-the-mill Western movies slumped. Audiences did not turn out for them unless they had some special quality. A celebrated epic such as *The Covered Wagon* (1923), or a movie boasting a number of star players would do well. So too would pictures based on dime novels by Zane Grey and a few other authors. Other Westerns would fail. However, if adaptations had these commercial advantages, they were not an unqualified benefit to the studios. The difficulties they caused arose in connection with the increasingly industrial organisation of the film studios. For with the advent of the feature film, scriptwriters found themselves firmly bound into the ordered process of producing to a regular schedule screenplays which could routinely be rendered into film. It was by no means always the case that every novel to which the studios had bought the screen rights converted easily into filmable material. Thus in a complex way, the issues of expense and organisation arise.[6]

In the first instance the pre-sold story cost more than an original screenplay. As Staiger reports, *Variety* reckoned in 1916 that royalties for the purchase of screen rights would start at a minimum of $1,000 plus 10 per cent of the producer's gross, whereas a screenplay based on a story written by a scenario department would cost no more than $250 to $500. The studio in any eventuality had to keep its own scenario department, not least because it could not be sure of a regular supply of bought-in stories. With the increasing sophistication of film production in the feature era, adaptation became a skilled task – and again only a script department could undertake the process reliably. At a minimum it required the writing (or rewriting) of a story whose plot and character logic it was possible to film; and the provision of a blueprint (that is a continuity script) which told technicians and actors what they had to do. Thus scenario departments had to produce material both routinely and so drafted as to facilitate the smooth operation of the factory system of studio production. This at least was the ideal from the management point of view.

In fact a system of production as detailed in its control as that which the studios developed towards the end of the first and second decades of the century put it within their power to govern rigorously both shooting schedules and costs. And indeed some studios concentrated on exercising this kind of control. Warner Brothers were to win themselves a reputation for doing so. However, the desire of studio accounting departments to exercise efficient cost control was frequently at odds with the wish of publicity departments to sell films which showed that expense had been lavished on them. As we have hinted, it was often advantageous to shout up the costliness of a pre-sold story, and to add to its attraction by giving it glamorous and extravagant treatment. Indeed it became a commonplace belief in Hollywood, a belief which still holds sway, that the extravagance of a film directly correlates with its profitability. When this ethos prevails, it makes the expensively acquired bestselling novel or smash-hit theatrical production an attractive property for a studio to own.

It would be wrong to give the impression that adaptations were always equally popular with movie executives. In fact their output fluctuated widely in response to economic and market conditions. For example, it seems reasonable to assume that with the advent of sound systems of acceptable quality, interest in the adaptation of literary properties increased. For the first time cinema possessed a technology which enabled film-makers to register the psychological complexity of fictional characters. Working without dialogue, directors had been hard pushed in the silent era to individuate their protagonists precisely, for which reason they tended to fall into types, or broadly marked classes of (usually two-dimensional) character. Now at last screen people could speak out of distinct and finely nuanced personalities, and thus could register individuality. Figures provided by Leo A. Handel confirm the popularity at that period of the pre-sold screenplay.[7] In 1935 some 35 per cent of feature films had a literary source, with 8 per cent deriving from the stage, and 47 per cent having been written as original screenplays specifically for the screen.

However, a decade later only about 18 per cent of screenplays derived from literature, 5 or 6 per cent from the theatre, and about 65 per cent were original screenplays. In part this shift towards the original screenplay can be explained by a pair of linked economic factors. Firstly, the cinema business in America prospered during the war, with large audiences attending routinely. The studios did not need to market special attractions to bring people in through the turnstiles, for a large part of the audience would go to the movies no matter what was showing. Secondly (and as we already know), having established script departments, the studios naturally wanted to keep them busy and to take advantage of the opportunities they offered for inexpensive and routine story production.

This tendency continued until the early fifties; but then the studios found they had no choice but to react to a number of unfavourable pressures that had come to bear on their activities since the end of the Second World War. Anti-trust litigation which had been rumbling through the courts for about a decade came to final judgement in 1948 with the decision of the US Supreme Court that the major companies had in effect conspired to take a virtual monopoly hold on the American film market, and that they had worked together to exclude competition. To rectify a trading arrangement which was contrary to American law, the Court required that the studios must divorce themselves from their cinema chains. From the early fifties, as the studios moved to comply with this judgement, they lost the profits generated by their cinemas, and had to look for the main source of their income to rentals from the hire of their films – whether to the cinemas, or in later years to television.

To make matters worse for the Hollywood companies, audiences were beginning to stay away from cinemas. To some degree this could be attributed to the new enemy of the cinema, television; but in part it seems to have been caused by a shift in social behaviour as people chose to spend more money and time enjoying life around the home. For these and other reasons film production declined. As a consequence almost all the studios found they could no longer afford to keep permanent staff on contract. By far the greater part of their permanent labour force (from stars to lighting assistants) was fired. Along with the rest, scenario departments were disbanded, and since there was no longer any need to keep employed writers fully occupied, the lifting of the pressure formerly exerted on the industry by this overhead removed one inhibition on the purchase of literary and dramatic properties.

If this was a negative reason for the return to favour of such properties, there were positive causes of it too. Many film producers decided they had a better chance of drawing an audience if they had something special on offer. In particular, given that most patrons were now understood to be selective in their cinema-going, a movie's potential was thought to be much improved if the audience already knew something about it. Accordingly, the concept of the pre-sold movie found favour again; but now not only novels and hit theatrical shows, but occasionally successful television plays provided the original text for adaptation (*Marty* (1954) was an early example of a film which had its origins in televised drama). As McLaughlin shows, the proportion of screenplays written originally for the cinema declined sharply during the period 1953–6 to less than 30 per cent of the total.[8]

Although the numbers of features made from original screenplays did recover from this low point in later years, Hollywood's interest in literary and theatrical properties had once again increased markedly from this period and on through the sixties. Inevitably the prices of desirable properties rose, and Hollywood companies redoubled their efforts to secure the rights to stage plays by making pre-production deals. On Broadway, advance payments for screen rights became an ever more significant investment, so that by the sixties theatrical producers (faced with the wildly rising cost of mounting theatrical spectaculars) made a regular practice of first seeking a sale for the rights to the movie before agreeing to back a stage production. It is not hard to see why from the mid-fifties, in circumstances in which its money was a prerequisite to launching new Broadway productions, the requirements of the American film industry came to have a profound influence on many theatrical productions intended for commercial success.

Similar pre-production deals began to be applied in some cases to literary sales. As Andrew Dowdy remarks, a public relations man called Ted Loeff set up a company, Literary Projects, to arrange tie ins between film producers and publishers.[9] His idea was to make possible the mutual exploitation of literary properties whose screen rights were sold before the novel was published. He began to arrange for the co-ordination of print publication and film release, and for the interrelation of the marketing campaigns of the two products so that advertisements for the film reminded people of the book, and vice-versa. Sometimes Hollywood was to pay out money (and this grew ever more common practice late in the sixties and on into the seventies) for the screen rights to a novel that hardly yet had shape in the mind of its author, let alone on paper.

As the sixties passed, these tendencies were to increase. They were pushed on by fundamental changes in the corporate structures of the giant media companies, and by significant changes in their trading patterns. To some extent it is possible to point to the way the movie companies were absorbed into massive conglomerates to explain their alertness to cross-media tie ins. So, to take the most striking example, when Paramount was taken over by the Gulf & Western group, it became part of a vast corporate empire which, according to James Monaco, in 1977 owned more than 300 subsidiaries.[10] One entire division was devoted to activities in the leisure field – in film, television, control of race tracks and boxing, ownership of hotels, electronic and coin games – and in publishing. In this last field alone they owned three important houses: Simon & Schuster, Pocket Books, and Monarch Books. Thus Paramount had ready-made connections with the book trade. And the same was true of Warners and Columbia, though their book imprints were less prestigious. It also was and still is the case that cognate media industries have strong publishing interests: this is, for instance, true of CBS, the tv network corporation. Sometimes a print-based corporation expanded into other media. Time Inc. did this. Originally a publishing house, in the mid-seventies it set up a massive subsidiary in the cable tv company HBO (Home Box Office). In turn HBO joined with Columbia Pictures and CBS in the mid-eighties and set up an entirely new film studio, Tri-Star, which released its first film in 1984. Each of the partners stood to gain from the enterprise, with print publication, cinema, cable and television release all tied together via the new production plant.

However, just as important as these and comparable structural changes in the pattern of corporate capitalisation was the change which they helped bring about in company executives' attitudes to marketing practice. It is now automatic (and on both sides of the Atlantic) for publishers, theatrical producers and film producers to think of release through each others' outlets. Furthermore, since the late sixties the interlocking of the media has extended way beyond these three channels. The consequence can be that, in many cases of co-ordinated exploitation, it may be more helpful to think of cross-media marketing of a *fiction*, rather than of the adaptation of a novel into film. For now the executives of media corporations will consider not only the exploitation of film, stage play and novel, but will also think of entering an array of co-ordinated markets with pre-recorded video-cassettes, cable television, the tv series, sound-track albums and audio cassette tapes, video and computer games, and a whole range of marketable tie ins from vests through shoelaces to ice-cream and horrible toys. Thus toy shops, newsagents and bookshops are implicated in the marketing programme for movie blockbusters. Cinemas sell books, record albums and video-cassettes.

Not infrequently the commercial activity surrounding a fiction marketed across several media may blur its outline: novel, film and all can be softened by relentless hype. Such softening may well be increased by the requirement that the fiction be produced with characters and plot delineated in broad and simple outlines so that it can be enjoyed by the largest possible audience. Some executives require that nothing difficult or thought-provoking should be permitted to disturb the pleasures of the mass audience they hope to win.

However, quite often something altogether more worthwhile may occur. For example, cross-media marketing may discover books that otherwise would have gone unnoticed. For many people Universal's simplistic blockbuster *Out of Africa* (1985), for all its regrettable seizure of an entire (black) continent as merely the backdrop to an ineffable affair between two (white) aristocrats, will have discovered the subtle lyricism and uncomfortable intelligence of the writer Karen Blixen (Isak Dinesen). First published some fifty years ago, her books will have been brought into existence for them only by the cinema.

Notes

1. Lewis Jacobs *The Rise of the American Film*, New York: College Teachers Press, 1975, pp. 122–3, 129–30.
2. Robert Sklar *Movie-Made America*, New York: Random House, 1975, pp. 29–30.
3. See Jacobs *op. cit.*, pp. 137–41: and Tom Gunning 'Weaving a narrative' *Quarterly Review of Film Studies*, 6, 1 (Winter 1981), pp. 15–16.
4. David Bordwell, Janet Staiger and Kirstin Thompson *The Classical Hollywood Cinema*, London: Routledge & Kegan Paul, 1985, p. 99.
5. Robert McLaughlin *Broadway and Hollywood*, Salem, NH: Ayer Co. Publishers, 1974, pp. 52–66.
6. These issues are well explored by Janet Staiger, '"Tame" Authors and the Corporate Laboratory' *Quarterly Review of Film Studies*, 8, 4 (Fall 1983), pp. 37–41: and 'Dividing labour for production control' in G. Kindem (ed.), *The American Movie Industry*, Carbondale: Southern Illinois Press, 1982, pp. 94–103.
7. Leo A. Handel *Hollywood Looks at its Audience*, Salem, NH: Ayers Co. Publishers, 1976, p. 22.
8. McLaughlin *op. cit.*, pp. 238–60.
9. Andrew Dowdy *Films of the Fifties*, New York: William Morrow & Co., 1975, p. 209.
10. 'Who owns the media?' *Take One*, November 1978, pp. 26–7.

9

The impossible object:
Reflections on *The Shining*

JOHN BROWN

Conclusions

I remember that when Stanley Kubrick's film of Stephen King's novel was first released in Britain (in November 1980) I was in no hurry to see it. A Kubrick horror movie was too intimidating and depressing a prospect.

There were two reasons for thinking this, and the first of them had to do with Kubrick's work in general. My responses to his films had varied widely over the years; I'd been strongly impressed by his early thriller *The Killing* (1956), about a perfect robbery, and by his anti-militarist fable *Paths of Glory* (1958), and I had admired enormously his spectacular Roman epic *Spartacus* (1960). But on the other hand I hadn't thought much of his film version of the controversial Vladimir Nabokov novel *Lolita* (1962), nor had I seen much point to his critically acclaimed anti-nuclear farce *Dr Strangelove* (1964). Up to this point in his career Kubrick seemed to me a very odd director, idiosyncratic to the point of perversity in his choice of material and elusive in his continuing artistic concerns. Then, in 1968, *2001: A Space Odyssey* appeared.

I was completely dazzled by *2001*. The sheer technical skill and stylistic virtuosity evident in the earlier films had been taken to new and astonishing heights, and the results (especially in 70 mm) were overwhelming. But not only that; the special effects were used less for their own sake (a recurrent fault, then as now, of much science-fiction cinema) than for exploring abstract ideas in a kind of hi-tech allegory. The film's strange narrative structure, from apes to spaceflight to a Louis XIV room at the end of the universe, turned out to form a meditation on the concept of God – an amazing demonstration that popular cinema could successfully accommodate difficult or abstruse subjects. It made me very eager to see what Kubrick would do next; and three years later along came *A Clockwork Orange*.

To my consternation, I loathed it; indeed, I could not recall ever having experienced such a powerful aversion to any other film. It was visually cheap and spatially claustrophobic; its ideas about social repression and adolescent rebellion seemed crass and snobbish; its pedantic illustration of conditioned-reflex psychology was simplistic and condescending to the audience. But what I hated most was its representation of acts of extreme violence. While all the critics were praising Kubrick's 'unflinching' staging of all the beatings, rapes and killings in the story, I thought the film secretly gloated over the violence, allowing, even encouraging the audience to revel in the mayhem on the excuse that this was a serious work of art. If *2001* was the product of a conscious philosopher, *A Clockwork Orange* was close to that of an unintentional pornographer.[1]

The shock made me look back at Kubrick's earlier work, and I began to see something I had not noticed before. There was scarcely a trace of emotional warmth or openness in his films. For all their apparent diversity, the stories all unfolded inexorably, beyond human control, and the characters in them were inevitably shown to be at best self-deluded and at worst malignant. Kubrick's cinema was essentially about failure and defeat, and there was a kind of nihilistic delight in the repeated representation of defeat, from the wind that sweeps away the banknotes from the robbery in *The Killing* to the nuclear holocaust that sweeps away humanity in *Dr Strangelove*. The only moment of positive triumph and celebration to be found in his work was the birth of the star-child in *2001*, where superior non-human intelligences have come to transform poor stupid mankind, which the film uniformly represents as a race of robots.

When I learned that Kubrick had disowned the one film which did not conform to this pattern – *Spartacus*, with its deeply moving climactic affirmation of human endurance[2] – I came to the conclusion that he was one of those strange artists whose creative impulses and energies stem purely from negative sources, from a systematic and destructive rejection of all human values and hopes.

My other reason for not wanting to see *The Shining* had to do with horror movies. They are meant by definition to frighten the audience, to make us afraid to keep on watching the screen, but I find it almost impossible to enjoy such a response or to get much benefit from it. This produces a catch-22 situation. If a horror film works (that is, makes me afraid to look) I dislike the experience, and if it does not work, I don't see the point. I would not deny that the genre of the horror movie is a significant one or that it has produced some major films. It is simply that for me, a horror film is bound to be a seriously limited emotional experience; and even the ones I like best (such as Hitchcock's *Psycho*, Tobe Hooper's *Texas Chainsaw Massacre*, William Friedkin's *The*

Exorcist or Brian de Palma's *The Fury*) are nowhere near as emotionally disturbing on later viewings as they are first time around.

So in November 1980 the idea of an artist as technically ambitious and as emotionally sterile as Kubrick working in my least preferred genre held little appeal – especially since he had been quoted as having long had the desire to make the cinema's most frightening ghost story. My response was thanks but no thanks. A few months went by, then by coincidence I finally caught up with *Barry Lyndon*, the adaptation of the minor Thackeray novel which Kubrick had made in 1975 (another example of his bewildering choice of material) and which had been a notable commercial and critical failure. I was pleasantly surprised to find that while it was yet another of Kubrick's obsessive exercises in defeat, it presented its characters, self-deluded or malignant, with some generosity and compassion.

So, my curiosity aroused by the unexpected experience of *Barry Lyndon* and by some peculiar reports of *The Shining*, I braced myself and went off to submit to Kubrick's new horror show. What I found in *The Shining* was even more remarkable in its way than *2001*: a great movie, endlessly fascinating, astonishing and exhilarating. What follows here is not an attempt to provide a conventional critical account of what seems to me Kubrick's masterpiece to date. What I want to do instead is to open up different ways of responding to *The Shining* and of thinking about it – to suggest starting points for several varied and even contradictory explanations and interpretations. Not the least tantalising aspect of Kubrick's ghost story is the way in which it subtly transforms itself, like a shape-shifter, with every viewing . . .

Texts

Stephen King's novel *The Shining* was published in 1977 and has since sold over three million copies. His fiction, which he produces in enormous quantity, has not been the subject of much serious critical study, so I want to offer a few observations on it here.

Since the success of his first novel *Carrie* (filmed by Brian de Palma) King has remained almost entirely within the parameters of the horror story, and as his collection of essays *Danse Macabre*[3] makes clear, King knows what he is doing: he understands and appreciates the complex traditions of American Gothic fiction. But the bulk of his fiction seems on closer inspection to contain two different and in a sense opposed impulses which give his work its curious and distinctive quality.

The most obvious impulse is, of course, the mythological and supernatural dimension which generates the horror elements; his novels and short stories are full of vampires, ghosts, zombies, werewolves, monsters and all the traditional apparatus of the Gothic mode from Mary Shelley and Edgar Allan Poe onwards. This is blended in several

books with the more modern (in a literary sense) phenomena of extra-
sensory perception, telekinesis and so on. But the second impulse in
King's fiction seems to me a more subtly important one, which is his
drive towards a detailed realistic rendering of small-town American life
and social experience from roughly the late forties to the present day.

There are various strands to this second impulse. One indirectly
confirmed by *Danse Macabre* is a strongly nostalgic and auto-
biographical strain, particularly in relation to childhood and early
adolescence; another is a recurrent concern with the experience of
growing up within an unstable family and of coming to terms painfully
with the realities of adult life – an Oedipal preoccupation shared by
King with an important parallel figure in contemporary American
popular culture, Steven Spielberg. A third strand, closely interwoven
with the others, is the continuing saving grace, as King consistently
portrays it, of sports, movies, junk food, comics, television and rock
music. All of these provide King's unhappy children with their only
escape route from the dark side of the nuclear family and its demons
into the wider community of adult life.

For me, *The Shining* is King's most accomplished work because it
mostly holds these two impulses in admirable balance. The simplicity of
the central situation – father, mother and child snowbound in an isolated
luxury hotel during winter – allows King to explore the three characters
in considerable depth and to trace the complexity of their relationships
in absorbing detail. Interestingly, long stretches of the book are devoid
of supernatural happenings, but the Gothic elements are skilfully
combined with a convincing account of the family's breakdown and
have a credible American root (as opposed to the overtly European
horror motifs in *Salem's Lot*, King's sprawling version of *Dracula* in an
American setting). The narrative construction of *The Shining* is also
extremely well-planned and executed. Adopting the position of an
implied narrator and using free indirect speech, King moves back in
time from the present tense of the story to provide the history of the
family from the cleverly interwoven viewpoints of each of the three
characters. Oddly enough, the novel is at its weakest in the last quarter
of the story, where the slow build-up of tension is replaced by slam-
bang action and a noticeable descent into the purple prose which is
King's main fault as a writer.

In an interview[4] Kubrick has claimed that he cannot say why a
particular book or novel appeals to him as the basis for a film, although
all his work from *The Killing* onwards has been based on pre-existing
material (very distantly in the case of *Dr Strangelove* and *2001*). But I
think two factors affected his choice of *The Shining*, one economic, one
artistic.

As far as the economics of film production are concerned, Kubrick has legendary status within the industry. He has been uniquely able to establish the freedom to select his own subjects, command very high budgets and take several years to script, shoot and edit his films – all without interference from the studio (Warners) which finances him. Having lived in Britain since the early 1960s, Kubrick keeps his distance from Hollywood in several senses, but just how he has established this much-envied position as a director is unclear; none of his films has attained the degree of commercial success (and comparable freedom) of a Spielberg. It has been suggested that Kubrick dominates his sources of finance by sheer steely intransigence.

It is tempting, therefore, to speculate that in the late seventies, Kubrick saw a threat to his freedom. *Barry Lyndon*, reputedly costing over thirty million dollars, had been a failure at the box office, while *Jaws* and *Star Wars*, the work of 'Movie Brats' half his age, had become the two most profitable movies in cinema history to date.[5] Perhaps Kubrick looked at the contemporary cinema and saw how successful this kind of fantasy film was with mass audiences. Perhaps he decided to steal a leaf from that book.

The Shining, as a highly popular novel, met that requirement and an artistic one into the bargain. Kubrick's films often deal with a situation in which someone tries to create an ideal (the perfect robbery, the ideology of nuclear deterrence, the dream woman/child, the cure for violence) only to find that the attempt to create perfection brings about its opposite. In *The Shining* Jack Torrance takes the job of caretaker at the Overlook Hotel to allow himself to re-build his life with his wife and son, to cure himself of alcoholism and take his shot at the Great American Novel – and all these elements conspire to destroy him. In King's book Kubrick found, ready-made, his favourite plot.

Apart from its credit sequence, *The Shining* was filmed entirely in Elstree Studios near London over a period of a year in 1978/79; the exterior of the Hotel was one of the largest and most elaborate ever built. The screenplay was written by Kubrick and his chosen collaborator, the American novelist Diane Johnson, herself the author of several Gothic novels. The film was first shown in America in June 1980, with a running time of 146 minutes; Kubrick later cut about 27 minutes from the version released in Europe some months afterwards.[6] Although it was not in the end as commercially successful as had been predicted, *The Shining* earned more than forty-seven million dollars in its first few weeks of American release, and is probably second only to *The Exorcist* in the list of top-grossing horror films.

Opinions

'The novel is by no means a serious literary work, but the plot is for the most part extremely well worked out, and for a film that is often all that really matters.' (Kubrick on King[7])

'There are, of course, some film-makers whose particular visions are so clear and fierce that such fear of failure never becomes a factor in the equation. This factor of vision is so real and apparent that even when a director such as Stanley Kubrick makes such a maddening, perverse and disappointing film as *The Shining*, it somehow retains a brilliance that is unarguable; it is simply there.' (King on Kubrick[8])

'The truly amazing question is why a director of Kubrick's stature would spend his time and effort on a novel which he changes so much that it's barely recognisable, taking away whatever originality it possessed and emphasising its banality.' (*Variety* reviewer[9])

'. . . its origin and purpose still a complete mystery.' (The last words spoken in *2001: A Space Odyssey*)

Metaphors I

Tales of fantasy and the supernatural raise some interesting philosophical and critical issues about the nature of fiction and our understanding of it. If you believe absolutely in the existence of ghosts and the reality of psychic phenomena, a ghost story can presumably be read as having the same relationship to real life as the novels, for example, of Jane Austen. But since relatively few readers appear to believe this, a novel like *The Shining* raises the question of how the majority of unbelieving readers can make sense of and accept 'impossible' events within a story, such as the intervention of a ghost.

Basically, I think, there are two critical strategies for dealing with such narrative events. One is to 'read' the ghost as existing only in the imagination of the character(s) in the story. Freud's theory about the way in which certain desires and emotions are suppressed into the unconscious and erupt into the conscious mind is used, for example, in relation to the Henry James story *The Turn of the Screw*, in which the apparitions seen by the central character of the governess are interpreted as the projections of her own (primarily sexual) neuroses. The second is to recognise the necessary 'reality' of the ghost within the facts of the story and interpret the impossible event as the symbolic expression of the author's conscious or unconscious vision of the world; thus Bram Stoker's *Dracula* becomes an allegory about the return of the repressed in Victorian sexuality, or Tolkien's *Lord of the Rings* becomes a fable about the rise of Fascism in pre-war Europe. In this way the literature of the fantastic (which would also include novels as different as William Golding's *The Inheritors* and Brian Moore's *Cold Heaven*) can still be directly related to the humanist concerns of realist fiction.

King's novel metaphorises its impossible events in various ways.

Firstly, *The Turn of the Screw* model: the character of Jack Torrance is presented in considerable psychological detail as a man in constant struggle with himself; in many ways a potentially decent man, his personality is made unstable by his desire for fame and wealth as a writer (a neurosis which King relates to Jack's childhood and his ambiguous attitude towards his father) and his assessment of himself as a failure – which reveals itself in alcoholism and a ferocious, barely restrainable temper at times of even minor stress. In the first three-quarters of the novel the supernatural presence in the Overlook Hotel can be interpreted as the projections of Jack's rage at himself and compensatory hostility towards his wife and son. At the end of the novel Jack recognises that he has in a sense summoned the ghosts by his psychological instability, and tries to fight against them long enough to save his son.

Secondly, the *Dracula* model of allegory: the gift of 'shining', of extra-sensory perception which the five-year-old Danny possesses, enabling him to read minds and foresee the future, can be taken as a metaphor for the perceived ability in children to understand intuitively matters which should be beyond them – 'out of the mouths of babes and sucklings comes wisdom'. Another example of this metaphorisation (which is foregrounded in the novel – an example of King's high degree of awareness about the conventions he is using) is the Overlook Hotel, the novel's haunted house, in this case high and remote in the Colorado mountains. Just as in non-fantastic literature a house can be made to stand for a whole society or culture (in E. M. Forster's *Howard's End*, in L. P. Hartley's *The Go-Between*, or most obviously in Margaret Mitchell's *Gone with the Wind*), so the Overlook is explicitly presented by King as a beautiful luxury hotel which has been spiritually corrupted by the ownership of a mysterious millionaire in direct descent from the robber barons of nineteenth-century American capitalism.

But, as the critics noted even if they could not explain it, something odd happens to these metaphors (and much else besides) in the transition from King's page to Kubrick's screen.

Critics

The British and American reviewers were virtually unanimous in their negative reaction to *The Shining*. Those with readerships likely to be interested in entertainment (that is, in horror movies *per se*) complained that it wasn't really frightening and that the special effects were poor in comparison to, say, *The Exorcist*. Those reviewers who were more interested in it as a Kubrick movie agreed and added another complaint of their own: they couldn't understand what Kubrick thought he was doing. I will try to summarise their responses:

• They noted that the story-line preserves the main events of the novel but compresses, transposes or simply omits scenes which would have been very effective in horror terms, such as the haunted lift or Danny's experience in Room 237.[10] And the climactic invention of Kubrick's – the final shot of the photograph of Jack at the 1921 Independence Day party in the hotel – does not, they complained, make sense.

• In Jack Nicholson, they observed, Kubrick had one of the most subtly gifted actors in contemporary cinema; yet he allows Nicholson to overact grotesquely, to play Jack as a smiling psychopath from the very start. Reviewers are particularly oriented towards questions of performance, and this was in most cases a sufficient objection to the film; but they might have gone on to argue that Nicholson's acting makes nonsense of a central theme of the novel, in which Jack fights against his demons. Equally, they added, Shelley Duvall turns Wendy, Jack's wife, from the intelligent, capable woman of the novel into a shallow, dumb hysteric.

• Only one or two commented on technical competence, so most of the following, I confess, is my putting words into their mouths. But the attention to detail *is* astonishingly lax. The intertitles of date and time are so sporadic as to be meaningless. The character of Grady is given two different names (the manager refers to him as Charles, Grady calls himself Delbert) and his children are played by obvious twins when they are said by the manager to have been eight and ten respectively. There's one extraordinary lapse in camera-placement and cutting which has Danny and his mother entering the store cupboard on one side of a corridor and coming out on the other – which produces a weird, inexplicable sense of momentary disorientation for the viewer. And most peculiar of all, the maze which stands in front of the studio set is absent from the aerial shots of the actual hotel to which Kubrick frequently cuts in the first half of the film.

All these things work together, I think, to produce *The Shining*'s greatest problem and most curious feature: its weirdness, its unsettling qualities. Long before the ghosts appear to take it formally into the horror genre, it is a very odd film to watch. It seems to me that it actually defies the audience not to sense this weirdness. The *Variety* review got it right.

I think that the reviewers' reaction to these problems, however, stemmed from two assumptions. The first was that Kubrick could not have made 'just a horror movie'; his perceived status as a great director obliged reviewers to presume and search for meanings below the surface of the film. Secondly, since Kubrick is known to spend so much time, effort and money on his films without studio interference, the problems in *The Shining* could not be the result of accident, carelessness or incompetence; what was on the screen must be what Kubrick intended to put there.

The reviewers retired from the field, bewildered, but in due course the film's defenders began to appear, writing in critical magazines rather than newspapers. The most ambitious rescue attempt came from P. L. Titterington,[11] who argued that we have to decode the Overlook as the master symbol of the film. According to this, the hotel is America the Haunted House, an embodiment of privilege and luxury which depends for its existence on the violent repression of the past ('built on the Indian burial grounds,' the manager cheerfully explains) and on the exclusion of all the present dilemmas of American society:

> At the centre of *The Shining*'s portrayal of the American experience, and a major theme in its own right, is the key notion of communication. We are presented with a situation in human life where the entire middle range of what is customarily thought of as communication has broken down.

So the break-down of communication – between husband and wife, father and child, individual and society – becomes the thread which Titterington pursues, often with great ingenuity, through the labyrinth of *The Shining*, down those endless hotel corridors.

It is a rigorously detailed, carefully argued account of the film, but what struck me most forcibly when I read it is that Titterington has written the equivalent of an essay on Hamlet which never mentions the Prince: the Prince being all the problems I described above. For Titterington the weirdness is simply not there. He is analysing a conventional Hollywood movie.

What is happening here, I think, is that Titterington is trying to render *The Shining* as a classically coherent work of art, seamlessly integrating its content and form. You could say that his approach is to look down on the maze from above and trace the one correct route to its centre, and there is a special sense, as I will try to show later, in which his reading of the film is justified. But if you go through the maze on foot, that is, follow the narrative scene by scene, sequence by sequence, the process results in one dead end after another. Titterington (who writes at one point, 'Within hours of the screening, it can happen that *the sequences and experiences begin to re-arrange themselves'* – my italics) gives us a map of a possible maze, and one that tantalisingly resembles *The Shining*. But it is not the specific maze which Kubrick has constructed for us, the specific order and structure of celluloid images which runs through the projector and is cast on the screen.

For example, what about those ghosts?

Metaphors II

Wendy is the last to see the ghosts. They form the casual witness of her

climactic hysteria as she gallops round the hotel: the couple in the
bedroom, one in fancy dress that looks like a pig and a bear, who are
interrupted during sex, and the genial man with the cracked head who
lifts his glass in a toast. She is also granted a single vision: the blood
cascading from the elevator which has previously haunted Danny.

In other words, Wendy's ghosts have no metaphorical significance
for her or, by this time, for us; what they 'mean' is that she does a
double-take and screams, as we laugh at her – she's only just found out
she's in a horror movie, and we knew all along.

Danny is the first to see the ghosts. He already has, before he arrives
at the Overlook, an imaginary companion called Tony, who warns him
not to go to the Hotel with his parents: it suggests *The Turn of the
Screw* model. Then he has visions of the blood from the elevator and a
couple of visitations from Grady's dead children: more problematic, but
he might have picked these up from his telepathy act with Hallorann
the chef – Hallorann knows the history of the Hotel.

We would know a lot more about the metaphors of Danny's ghosts if
we saw what happened to him in Room 237, but it occurs off-screen and
he himself gives no direct account of events there. Presumably he tells
Wendy (again off-screen) since later she comes looking for Jack in the
bar with the news that there's 'a crazy woman' in the empty hotel and
could only have got this information from Danny. What we do see of
Danny and his ghosts is inconclusive. He is almost the equivalent of the
twist in the tale, in that while other characters might theorise away
apparitions, the child whose sense of reality is not yet fixed can accept
that there are more things in heaven and earth, and says so. But oddly
the Overlook's ghosts never threaten him directly, just warn him. They
are, after all, his father's ghosts, his father's metaphors.

Jack Torrance's ghosts are a real problem, however. Let's take them
in order of appearance.

After dreaming (yet again, off-screen – why does Kubrick refuse us
so many scenes of the genre's *raison d'etre*?) that he has slaughtered
Wendy and Danny as Grady did his family, and having been accused
by Wendy of hurting Danny on his spectral re-entry from Room 237,
Jack storms into the empty bar for a drink. Delightedly, he conjures up
his first prosaic, mildly contemptuous demon in the shape of Lloyd the
barman. The staging of the scene – Jack speaking mockingly direct to
camera in his manic high persona, with Lloyd replying equally straight
to camera – and the hinge line of Jack's dialogue about giving his soul
for a glass of beer encourage, indeed practically force us, to read the
scene in classic Freudian terms: Lloyd is the projection of Jack's desires
for both satisfaction and punishment. Then, after Wendy finds him in
the empty bar – no Lloyd – Jack goes off to Room 237. Lloyd hasn't
bothered him, but now he starts acting, for the only time in the film,
like the conventional hero of a horror movie. He is determined but

fearful, then lascivious at the sight of the naked girl and finally horrified to find he's embracing an old woman with skin disease.

What is most striking about Jack in Room 237 (apart from the scene's sheer derivativeness and explicit nods to the shower scene in *Psycho* and the corpse rising from the bath in *Les Diaboliques*) is the way it is sealed off in narrative terms from what happens before and after. Jack does not tell Wendy or Danny what happened there, nor do they ask him, and it is never referred to again, by Jack or anyone else. The scene seems to have no purpose, and when Jack returns for his second encounter with Lloyd, it is as if it never happened. Why Jack is at ease with one ghost and baffled/terrified by another is a question the film will never answer.

In Jack's next visit to the bar, however, the projection of his desires has become more powerful and elaborate: he is now able to populate the bar and the ballroom with several hundred extras in twenties costumes and an orchestra. Then one small shift occurs. Lloyd tells Jack that the drinks are free ('orders from the house') and Jack then encounters the waiter whom he gradually identifies as Grady the dead caretaker. But the scene in the washroom (where the waiter/Grady tells Jack that Danny is attempting telepathically to summon help from Hallorann) begins to pull the rug out from under the 'it's all Jack's secret desires' explanation.

Firstly, the waiter (puzzlingly) denies he is Grady, and says that Jack himself has 'always' been the caretaker. Secondly he gives Jack information about Danny and Hallorann which we know is true but which Jack has no way of knowing, even subconsciously. And thirdly, Nicholson plays the scene in the spaces of his (fairly neutral) dialogue in a very complex way, moving from being jovially at ease with the situation through dawning suspicion and surprise to half-appalled delight at the instruction of 'the house' to correct the ways of his errant family. It is as though Jack is perfectly prepared to be in one kind of ghost story, but is warily fascinated and pleased to find he is in a different one. The metaphor of Jack's ghosts is shifting; from being the projections of his desires they are becoming the personification of abstract forces of evil. They are bringing out the bad in Jack, not the other way round.

This implication is apparently confirmed when the ghosts release Jack from the store cupboard – yet again off-screen, in the sense that we hear them talking to Jack but don't see them – to make another attempt to kill Wendy and Danny. But then something odd happens: Jack's ghosts play no further part in the story – like the reviewers, they retire from the field, leaving Jack to pursue Wendy and Danny unaided. Only at the end does the supernatural reappear, in the relevatory track and zoom towards the photograph, which seems to be both a confirmation and a denial of the waiter's statement that Jack has 'always' been here – where or who or what was Jack before 1921? What does reincarnation have to do with all this?

The result of this absence, I think, is that whatever interpretation is adopted – the ghosts as Jack's own suppressed desires or the ghosts as impersonal forces of evil – there is a major thematic problem. Not only is it difficult to argue conclusively for one theory of the ghosts or the other. They actually and actively collide with each other, leaving both in pieces. Jack's suppressed desires cannot release him from the store cupboard by pulling the bolt on the outside, but impersonal forces of evil are ridiculous if they cannot achieve something as simple as the killing of a woman and child or stand by while Jack fails.

My conclusion from all this is that the supernatural elements in *The Shining* are deliberately and subtly organised to *prevent* a single consistent interpretation of the ghosts and visions. The film in effect teases anyone who wants to practise this kind of critical analysis, by setting up various possible interpretations and then making them contradict one another. The process of decoding produces an unintelligible message, partly through conflicting evidence and partly through a lack of evidence, that artful series of gaps and off-screen events which we fail to register consciously or question while watching the film. This dead-end structure is one of the major sources of the film's unnerving quality, its downright weirdness. In other words, *The Shining* does not construct metaphors, it deconstructs them. And the principle of deconstruction does not stop with the ghosts.

Readings

How do we set out to establish the meaning of a text?[12] Contemporary literary theory tells us, I think rightly, that the text does not 'possess' a single meaning which exists independently of the reader or viewer. Instead, meaning consists of a complicated process of production which occurs through a specific interaction of forces within and upon the text – forces such as the formal organisation of the text, the skills of the reader/viewer and the social and ideological context in which the act of reading/viewing, as well as the act of writing/film-making, takes place.

Part of this argument is that the reader/viewer does not experience the text from a position of ignorance; he or she will inevitably have some kinds of pre-knowledge. In the case of *The Shining* these will include (a) for virtually everyone, the knowledge that the film is in a particular genre, the horror genre which has a set of familiar motifs and conventions; (b) for many, a familiarity with the story through reading the book; and (c) for some, a familiarity with the themes and style of Kubrick's previous work.

To a greater or lesser extent therefore, anyone watching *The Shining* begins the process of 'understanding' it from a basis of preconceptions.

As in the case of all texts, we speculate to ourselves as we watch or read about what is going to happen next – we form working hypotheses about the characters and the narrative which are then continuously tested out against the actual experience of the film or novel. Setting aside the Titterington hypothesis (that the film is a relatively unproblematic fable), I want to bring forward here three other hypotheses or readings which might be applied to the film.

The first is one which rests partly on the concept of the Jack Torrance character and partly on some information external to the film itself. This reading argues that the film is a self-portrait of Kubrick as an artist.

The external information is that Kubrick lives in some isolation in a large country house where, it is said, he has installed everything necessary for living and working except for going to the studio to shoot his films. As a glance at any recent photograph will show, there's some resemblance between Kubrick himself and Nicholson as he appears in the film. But much more significant for this reading is the status of Jack as a 'writer', a would-be artist who is 'outlining a new project' as he rather oddly describes it to the manager during the interview. His efforts to find an idea ('plenty of 'em,' he tells Wendy, 'all bad') echo what Kubrick has said about the immense difficulty of finding the right subject for a film.

This reading would propose that *The Shining* can be understood as Kubrick's bitter allegory of the problems of the artist/film-maker, haunted by the ghosts of the characters he is struggling to create/control, searching for a story-line which will make sense and constantly changing it, attempting to produce a particular artistic statement only to find (Jack in the washroom with the waiter/Grady) that his material is forcing him to go in a different direction. On this hypothesis, *The Shining* also dramatises the way in which the artist's pre-occupations with his demons are destructive of normal family life and relationships while being at the same time parasitical upon them. In this perspective some otherwise baffling but striking details in the film make sense. Jack stares down at the model of the maze, studying it much as Kubrick himself must have studied models of the sets, and sees/projects his wife and son at the centre of it. At another point, when Danny enters the lounge after his encounter in Room 237 and Wendy rushes forward to comfort him, Jack remains in his chair, watching, in a pose oddly reminiscent of the director observing the action he has staged for the camera.

This reading can be pushed further. In this allegorical self-portrait Danny – with his gift of 'shining' that enables him to conjure up images and visions and to communicate effortlessly and magically with Hallorann, the ordinary man and like Danny but unlike Jack, a television viewer – may represent a different kind of artist: the generation of

Movie Brats such as Spielberg and George Lucas, whose work was proving so astoundingly popular while *Barry Lyndon* was failing at the box office. Interestingly, Danny wears a Mickey Mouse sweatshirt and an Apollo mission sweater, and what is *Star Wars* (in contrast to *2001*) if not a comic book space opera? Is that why Jack comes, otherwise inexplicably, to hate Danny so much?

The problem with this reading is that nothing within the film prompts it; you have to know about Kubrick to make the leap. Nor does it account for the weirdness, the playfulness, the *humour* of the film. A second hypothesis does, however, offer an account of this, by taking as its point of departure the status of *The Shining* as a horror movie.

The genre itself offers a paradox, namely that we can derive pleasure from being frightened, and as everyone who sees horror movies in the cinema knows from experience, this paradox produces complex audience reactions, such as defensive laughter at moments of extreme suspense or gruesome imagery. It is also the case that the horror film often boasts the most inept and unconvincing acting to be found in cinema – a factor which has made old horror films into a late night comedy cult and which forms a major element in spoofs such as *The Rocky Horror Picture Show*.

This reading suggests that *The Shining* is a kind of critical parody of the genre, which deliberately exposes and undercuts all the stock motifs of the genre while keeping within its general domain and maintaining a straight face. The result is what we could call an anti-horror film. There are analogies in such movies as Monte Hellman's *The Shooting*, an anti-Western also starring Jack Nicholson, Robert Altman's *The Long Goodbye*, an anti-private eye film and Martin Scorsese's *New York, New York*, an anti-musical; all of these are genre movies which end up deliberately denying the audience the specific pleasures of the genre and thus subvert themselves.

In this perspective those problematic performances from Nicholson and Duvall finally make sense. Duvall delivers a perfectly judged pastiche of the traditional heroine in forties and fifties horror movies, swinging from bland and blind 'normality' to complete hysteria and never at a loss for clichéd dialogue in either mode. And Nicholson's performance could be his finest and most subtle work because he presents Jack Torrance almost exclusively as a compulsive bad actor, responding to every circumstance by reaching at random into his repertory of B-movie portrayals: the perfect interviewee, the regular guy in the bar, the loving father, the stern father, the weary husband, the serious artist, the man of responsibilities, the black humorist ('Wendy, I'm home!' and 'Heeere's Johnny!'), the fearful hero of the horror movie in Room 237, the raging monster of the genre as he chases Danny through the icy-white maze.

Only twice, I think, do the masks slip. There is the brief glimpse of

Jack typing, calm and intent, just before Wendy comes in to break his concentration. But that is overshadowed by the eerie, haunting image of him standing hunched in the lounge, transfixed by God knows what thoughts and dreams as the camera moves slowly in and his eyes rise slowly upward to gaze at – who? what? It takes a great actor to create, as dazzlingly as Nicholson does here, a character who refuses to exist.

To see *The Shining* as an anti-horror movie, an inexplicit critique of the genre, is also to grasp most satisfactorily its relationship to King's novel. Think of the procedure in contemporary avant-garde art known as bricolage,[13] in which fragments of existing artefacts are re-worked and placed together to form a new artefact in itself, and you can see that Kubrick's film functions like a bricolage based upon King's novel.

For instance, a key moment occurs in the novel when Jack finds a mysterious scrapbook (itself a kind of bricolage) which contains the hotel's history. This doesn't happen in the film, but Kubrick places the scrapbook open on the table beside Jack's typewriter; it can only just be seen in the corner of the screen and no reference is made to it. Similarly, Danny's vision of the word 'redrum' which occurs in the novel, building up a small mystery of its own, is omitted from the film, except for Danny's sudden (and in terms of the film inexplicable) scrawling of the word on the bathroom door, the reflection of which Wendy sees ('murder') as Jack's axe comes crashing through the outside door. These moments serve as fleeting memories of the book, as if they were glimpses of an alternative version made by another director.

I argued earlier, specifically in relation to the ghosts, that *The Shining* denies us the possibility of constructing a single consistent metaphorical framework in which to interpret them. Something of the same is true, I think, of these two readings. They are both partially valid, and they both carry us some distance towards a coherent account of the film; but neither is sufficient in itself to form the essential key which unlocks the film and converts it to an integrated whole.

Like Titterington's hypothesis, they are potential solutions to the mystery, each unable on its own to make straight the film's studied contradictions, inconsistencies and discontinuities. Like that old trick drawing of the steps which appear to rise until they join up with the bottom flight, *The Shining* is an impossible object.

Yet there is a third reading, one which preserves those contradictions and discontinuities, indeed one which locates them at the centre of the extraordinary experience the film offers. Here is David Lodge on the modern novel:

> [it is] the novel which exploits one or more of these modes without committing itself to any, the novel-about-itself, the trick-novel, the game-novel, the puzzle-novel, the novel that leads the reader (who wishes naively only to be told what to believe) through a fairground

of illusions and deceptions, distorting mirrors and trapdoors that open disconcertingly beneath his feet, leaving him ultimately not with any simple or reassuring message or meaning but with a paradox about the relationship of art to life.[14]

And Philip Stevick on the same subject:

[such fiction] permits itself a great degree of latitude from the illusionist tradition . . . it presents its texture as devoid as possible of aesthetic and philosophical depth . . . it contains and often intensifies the tendency to assimilate and transform the bad art of its own time . . . it seeks to represent the act of writing as an act of play.[15]

Writing in 1971 and 1973 respectively, Lodge and Stevick are describing the essential characteristics of what we call post-modernist fiction: fiction which forces the reader to question the assumptions we make in reading fiction, the work of Thomas Pynchon, Donald Barthelme, Richard Brautigan and John Barth in America, that of John Fowles (whose 1968 novel *The French Lieutenant's Woman* is perhaps the most famous example), Julian Barnes and Martin Amis in Britain. Lodge and Stevick argue that the roots of post-modernist practice lie in a post-war sense of both social and artistic crisis, that the traditional forms of prose fiction have collapsed and that the novel has turned in on itself to define a new rationale for continuing.

Hence the way in which the artist in crisis becomes a central recurrent figure; hence the desire to experiment, to play with accepted forms and genres; hence the imitation or parody of other media -- films, radio, television; hence the desire to break the illusion of reality which the nineteenth-century novel sought so strenuously to create; hence, above all, the revolt against providing a simple, paraphraseable 'meaning' to be disinterred from the text.

What is fascinating about these accounts of post-modernism in the novel is that if you substitute film-making for writing, film for novel and viewer for reader, you have an almost uncannily precise prediction of Kubrick's movie. All the elements cited by both Lodge and Stevick are there: the 'writer' in crisis and his alter-ego/enemy the almost mute child with the gift of shining that becomes a metaphor for the rival medium, cinema; the relishing of banalities in characterisation, acting and dialogue; the multiple references to other movies, including Kubrick's own; the playful use of conventionally-read symbols such as the hotel; the displaced black humour and the flat anti-logic of the plot; the lapses and 'mistakes' in detail and continuity that break the illusion of the illusionism; and the remorseless teasing of every narrative assumption we make, and of any hypothesis or reading which we might try to construct.

A fable about communication and the American experience, a portrait of the artist as sociopath, an anti-horror movie – the great achievement, post-modernist or otherwise, of *The Shining* is that it is all of these things, some of these things and none of these things. Like the black monolith to which the last words spoken in *2001* refer, there's a sense in which *The Shining* will always remain a mystery. Like no other movie I know, it both necessitates and defies the critical act.

Beginnings

The Shining has an extraordinary opening shot. It jolted me in my seat the first time I saw the film, and I still find it unnerving after repeated viewings. It's a shot of a huge glassy lake surrounded by high cliffs, deep in the Rocky Mountains. In the middle of the lake there is an island and in the first split-second of the shot you think you are flying across the lake towards the island. But then, suddenly, your brain tells you that the perspective of the camera is fixed, and that you are *not* moving in relation to the cliffs at either edge of the frame. Which means that, even though it's an impossible event, the island is skimming across the lake, moving towards you. A moment later, the island passes beneath you and the perspective is no longer fixed. It's you who are flying. Normality has been restored.

I don't know how this spectacular and electrifying effect was achieved by the camera; my guess is that the helicopter with the camera on board flew away from the island while the camera simultaneously zoomed in on it, and that the film was then reversed for running through the projector. But I think I do know why this remarkable shot – which has apparently no possible connection with what follows – forms the gateway to Kubrick's ghost story. It demonstrates the power of the moving image to represent the unreal, to enforce the impossible. It declares that things are not what they seem nor mean what they say. It tells a lie in order to problematise 'truth'. It's a trick, a confession, a warning, a joke. It's the first, and only the first, false step on our journey to the Overlook Hotel and what waits for us there . . .
 . . . shining.

Notes

1. The representation of violence in films is a complicated issue, as can be seen from the fact that many of the reviewers who praised Kubrick's handling of violence had reviled Sam Peckinpah's *Straw Dogs* a few weeks earlier for its alleged savagery. Charles Barr's article on the critical reaction to these two movies (in *Screen* Spring 1972) is very acute in its analysis of the issues involved.
2. *Spartacus* was initiated as a project and produced by its star Kirk Douglas, who quarrelled with its director Anthony Mann after the first few days' shooting. Douglas fired Mann and

brought in Kubrick, with whom he had worked on *Paths of Glory.*

3. Macdonald (London 1981) in hardback and Futura (London 1982) in paperback.
4. In Michel Ciment, *Kubrick*, London: Collins, 1983.
5. A huge box-office gross measures audience popularity, but not necessarily profitability. *The Shining's* gross receipts have to be measured against the film's cost (18 million dollars, according to *Variety*) and the costs of distribution and promotion, which in the Hollywood system are often twice the film's actual cost.
6. The cut material consists of one complete scene near the start, where a doctor played by Anne Jackson (who is still listed in the credits of the British version) examines Danny. Full details can be found in the November 1980 issue of the *Monthly Film Bulletin* (British Film Institute, London).
7. Ciment, *op. cit.*, p. 181.
8. Stephen King, *Danse Macabre*, London: Macdonald and Co. (Futura), 1981, p. 244.
9. *Variety*, unsigned review, 28 May 1980.
10. In the Ciment interview cited earlier, Kubrick explains that the owners of the real hotel used for the credit sequence (the Timberline Lodge, near Mount Hood in Oregon) asked for the room number to be changed from the novel's 217 to 237, because they thought that no one would want to stay in the actual 217 after seeing the film. The Timberline Lodge has no room 237.
11. 'Kubrick and *The Shining*', in *Sight and Sound*, London: British Film Institute, Spring 1981.
12. You cannot ask authors about intention because they might not remember, might refuse to answer, might claim never to have carried them out, or might never have formulated intentions in the first place; John Haffenden's *Novelists in Interview*, London: Methuen, 1985, is the best confirmation I know that the intentionalist fallacy is exactly that.
13. Terence Hawkes, *Structuralism and Semiotics*, London: Methuen, 1977, p. 121.
14. *The Novelist at the Crossroads*, London: Routledge & Kegan Paul, 1971, p. 22.
15. *Scheherezade Runs Out of Plots, Goes on Talking; the King, Puzzled, Listens: an essay on the new fiction*, reprinted in Malcolm Bradbury (editor), *The Novel Today*, London: Fontana, 1977, pp. 209-15.

And finally, my thanks to Kevin Cowle and other former colleagues for the benefit of several lengthy conversations about *The Shining* which they have now almost certainly forgotten.

Filmography

The Shining (A Warner/Stanley Kubrick Production GB 1980.) Starring Jack Nicholson, Shelley Duvall, Danny Lloyd, Barry Nelson, Scatman Crothers, Philip Stone; Production Design by Roy Walker; Cinematography by John Alcott; Screenplay by Stanley Kubrick and Diane Johnson from the novel by Stephen King; Directed by Stanley Kubrick.

10

Dune: A tale of two texts

ELISABETH and MICHAEL LIDDELL

I

David Lynch's 1984 film of Frank Herbert's 1965 cult science-fiction novel *Dune* presents us with an interesting situation: an acclaimed and innovative director whose earlier work had captured the contemporary imagination and who in his immediately preceding film had been nominated for two Academy Awards (best director and best screenplay adaptation for *The Elephant Man* in 1980 – which film convinced the De Laurentiis family that Lynch was the director for their *Dune* project), engaging with a text even more acclaimed as one of the great genre achievements of the last twenty years, winner of the Hugo and Nebula Awards, and never out of print since first published. Surely, this was a combination to guarantee major success.

Instead, it produced one of the major failures in the history of the film industry – 'a disaster of the very first order', as we are succinctly informed in *Halliwell's Film Guide 7*.[1] This essay attempts to establish a line of argument that might clarify some of the reasons for that failure.

Film is another country: they do things differently there. As Ferdinand de Saussure would remind us immediately, they also use a different language. This fundamental concept underpins a number of related perspectives that help position us with regard to the two texts: that the relationship between them has to do with the complexities of translation, of finding filmic referents for written expression; that there are different constraints on the creative process and the creative imagination between the two; that there are different relationships with the audience, as well as different audiences; and that a body of critical theory exists which casts light on the foregoing items, offering a set of effective analytical tools which can be applied directly. Details of these perspectives will emerge in the course of deconstructing the texts, but it might be helpful to focus on two general conclusions that have particular relevance to the shaping of our approach.

Firstly, because a film text, despite its techniques for creating moments of intimacy, is necessarily a *mass* experience framed within a set time and place for completing the action, it deals inevitably in broader representations of situations and themes than an equivalent print text. *In this sense, film is a simplifying medium.*

Secondly, because film is also a collaborative medium and its text the product of negotiation within primarily budgetary and technical considerations rather than artistic ones, *the film text is driven by commercial imperatives.*

It may well be that these were major obstacles to making the film earlier. The history of false starts by other directors and script-writers (including Herbert himself) also helps place into context the fact that Lynch was attempting something so problematic that it had defeated several of his peers; and so it might also help offset some of the more hostile and dismissive comments which greeted the film's appearance – for Lynch's text is by no means a *simple* failure. (It ought to be noted at this point that the term usually applied – disaster – relates more to the fact that the film failed to recoup its massive costs (estimated variously at between \$40-\$50 million dollars) at the box-office: it has little critical validity as a response to the film *qua* film.)

II

Herbert's *Dune* has become a seminal text of that school of science-fiction (SF) which, through its more extended range of discourse, moves beyond Hugo Gernsback's description of the stories published in the first SF magazines as 'charming romance intermingled with scientific fact and prophetic vision'[2] and challenges the view that:

> Science Fiction has mostly settled for a pseudo-objective listing of marvels and wonders and horrors which illuminate nothing beyond themselves and are without real moral resonance; daydreams, wishful thinking and nightmares. The invention is superb, but self-enclosed and sterile.[3]

Herbert's text, in its political, sociological, ecological, philosophical and spiritual concerns presents a vision both complex and coherent, its conceptual richness and imaginative density embedded in a narrative facility which is impressive and satisfying. It is, without question, a major achievement.

Part of its appeal is the simplicity of its construction: within a framing outer story expressed essentially in mythic terms Herbert establishes a range of imbricated or overlapping discourses, from the personal-to-the-author (the messianic impulse and the ecology of planets), through the genre-related (the political opposition between totalitarian and liberal regimes, and the ethics of imperialism/colonisation), to the universal (love, family, personal identity and the individuation process) – a brief and far from exhaustive list.

'Mythic' is used here not in Barthes's sense, but more in terms of the basic element in fairy-tales and romances – Herbert's text moves beyond Gernsback but assimilates many of his ideas. Indeed, the use of a mythic outer story creates dynamic tension within the text, in that it sets up an opposition between the story and the discourses already noted. Darko Suvin shows how this can be so:

> The use of estrangement both as an underlying attitude and dominant formal device is found also in *myth*, a 'timeless' and religious approach looking in its own way beneath (or above) the empiric surface. However, SF sees the norms of any age, including emphatically its own, as unique, changeable, and therefore subject to a *cognitive* view. The myth is diametrically opposed to the cognitive approach since it conceives human relationships as fixed and supernaturally determined . . . Where the myth claims to explain once and for all the essence of phenomena, SF first posits them as problems and then explores where they lead; it sees the mythical static identity as an illusion, usually as fraud, at best only as a temporary realization of potentially limitless contingencies.[4]

To follow just one strand from Herbert's text, Paul Atreides is always fighting against the *mythic* construction of who he is and what is his destiny as the Lisan-al-Gaib and the Kwisatz Haderach, trying to establish instead his own sense of his identity so that he can find his way among the 'limitless contingencies' of the future as the *actual* Kwisatz Haderach.

Further to this, mythic stories have ideological implications in that they are formulated out of the author's cultural context. Herbert's text was produced in 1965 after a gestation period of some six years: throughout the Cold War, the Cuban Crisis, the Kennedy Presidency and assassination. This background clearly informs the way in which aspects of the text and its discourses develop: House Atreides mirrors the contemporary romantic glamour of the Kennedy Presidency, the physical characteristics of Baron Harkonnen (interestingly named Vladimir) echo the Russian leader Kruschev, and the Emperor's Sardaukar troops are perhaps symbolic of the nuclear deterrent in the way they ensure the Emperor's supremacy over the Houses of the Landsraad.

Mythic stories have other ideological implications. They deal in archetypal concepts and so lend themselves directly to the kind of formalist analysis associated with Vladimir Propp, whose main immediate concern was the classification of Russian folk-tales. He identified as many as thirty-one separate narrative elements (or functions) which can make up the plot, arguing that each element can be varied without distorting the narrative drive: so that in the motif 'dragon kidnaps king's daughter' it is possible to replace each element yet preserve the plot (dragon = any villanous force; kidnaps = any form of disappearance/violence; king = any form of possessor; daughter = anything beloved or precious). Clearly, Herbert's outer story fits this pattern very well: the Harkonnen/Emperor betray/rob Paul of his rightful inheritance/Dukedom.

But Propp offers a more detailed survey of possible patterns that also has relevance for Herbert's text: stories begin with two elements, injury to the victim or the lack of some important object(s); they end with the pattern of retribution for the injury and the acquisition of the lacked object(s); the hero is called forth and two key events follow -- he meets the donor, who, after testing him supplies him with a magical agent; he meets the villain in decisive combat/is given a series of labours -- in either case the magical agent enables him to triumph; and usually within stories there are a series of retarding devices used before the final transfiguration of marriage or coronation. Despite the simplification of this summary it is clearly directly applicable -- in only marginally modified form -- to Herbert's outer story; which means that that story must share some of the ideological aspects of fairy-tales: the mystical appeal of Royalty or nobility, and the consequent sense that individuals are more important in effecting change in the world than other agencies, such as economic social or political systems; the idea of predestined unproblematic romantic love; the brotherhood of noble warriors; the necessity of rites of passage or initiation into full manhood; leadership as a quality of heredity; the essential passivity of women, who wait to be acted upon -- or female activity seen as malevolent, 'witch-like'; the undoubted unimportance of ordinary people and ordinary life.

Such things have resonance because they come from a deep cultural and psychological reservoir so familiar that it can pass unnoticed -- and which is framed by the long dominance of the patriarchy in Western thought. Herbert himself, as we have seen, is constructed by this: the Kwisatz Haderach can only be male; the common term of abuse for the Bene Gesserit (so common as to be something of an unconditioned reflex) is 'witch'; House Atreides is a band of noble warriors -- and so on.

None the less, one of the attractions of Herbert's text as an author denied the benefit of a developed feminist critique at the time of writing his novel is the way in which his range of discourses actively try to engage with some of these limiting ideas. The effort of the Fremen to alter the ecology of Dune/Arrakis by building secret reservoirs of water deep within the hidden sietches is founded on collective action by ordinary people who work towards a common purpose. Women exercise power through the mind-body disciplines of the Bene Gesserit sorority -- and the Lady Jessica is a major narrative consciousness within the text.

Paul's leadership qualities come not merely from heredity but from rigorous training by both his military mentors and his mother's instruction in the Bene Gesserit techniques – and from the necessary habitual exercise of caution. The strength of the Landsraad derives largely from the commercial relationships within CHOAM, the economic grouping which, alongside the Bene Gesserit and the Spacing Guild, underpins the Empire – and it is made very clear that the move of House Atreides to Dune/Arrakis is prompted as much by commercial advantage as by Imperial Edict. Paul struggles against the easy dictates of destiny, attempting to construct an independent identity for himself outside the ones imposed upon him – from Ducal heir to Usul to Muad'dib to Lisan-al-Gaib to Kwisatz Haderach; and there is finally no simple dichotomy between good and evil, for in the last battle Paul breaks all conventions of 'civilised' behaviour by using the House atomics to break through the Emperor's shield wall. Even more significantly, he discovers that his sworn enemy the Baron Harkonnen is his maternal grandfather.

A further aspect is worth noting here: Herbert attempts to project ideas about our present society far into the future (Darko Suvin's 'estrangement'), to create for them a sense of possible development and application so that they are then presented as trace cultural memories within the text, part of the mythic pool shared and tapped by the characters in the novel. They are the sad remnants of our contemporary ideologies – the Orange Catholic Bible, a Jihad (then as now the name for a holy war) – and there are references to a time in the far past when humans were enslaved by or dependent on computers, which are now forbidden. Human potential has been actively encouraged, producing Mentats, humans able to compute and process information and to predict possibilities – and, in different developments, both the Bene Gesserit and the Navigators of the Spacing Guild.

One of the deep and abiding fascinations of Herbert's text is how the universe he has created seems so far away in time from our own lives that little in it can be traced back to today – and yet our present gently washes as half-remembered reverberations upon that other shore. But recognition of this textual richness and complexity cannot disguise a potential weakness in the simplicity of its construction that carries with it serious ideological consequences for any intending film-maker.

Strcuturalist theories on narrative offer a means of foregrounding this potentiality.[5] Barthes suggests a four-way analysis of the linguistic categories of narrative through the concepts of functions (relating to the sequential movement of narrative) and indices (which operate vertically, detaching the reader from the flow of events to build up a structure of meaning which informs that flow – helping create atmosphere or character, or pointing up implications in the flow of events). Barthes goes on to suggest that functions and indices can be sub-divided thus: functions are either cardinal (narrative 'nuclei' which carry the main sequence of events) or catalysers (which facilitate progress from one cardinal function to another and can be altered without affecting the narrative sequence); and indices are either indices in the sense already described, or informants or realist operators (which are details which 'index' fictional events in place and time, thus creating the illusion of 'realism'). These categories do not operate in isolation nor separately, neither are their operations mutually exclusive.

As regards Herbert's text, it is clear that the oppositional discourses mentioned cannot be cardinal functions, but are at best catalysers and indices: it is the outer mythic story which provides the main sequential movement of the narrative, and it is therefore that outer story that will dominate the structure of any film version, because film is a visual medium. *The film-maker stands in immediate danger of losing the richness and complexity of Herbert's text because the discourses which provide that richness are not essential to the main narrative flow.*

We can see this process at work to a limited extent in Herbert's text itself. There are three 'Books' in the novel, each dealing with a particular stage of the story: the introduction of House Atreides, the move to Dune/Arrakis, the betrayal by Yueh, death of Duke Leto, and the escape into the desert of Paul and Jessica; the meeting with the Fremen, the acceptance into the tribe, the delineation of the communal life of the sietches, Paul's developing mental powers under the influence of the spice environment, his developing relationship with Chani, Jessica's translation into the tribe's Reverend Mother; the destruction of effective spice production, Paul's mastery of a Worm, meeting Gurney Halleck once more, drinking the Water of Life to become the Kwisatz Haderach, defeating the Emperor and then Feyd-Rautha, and in effect taking over control of the Empire. The first two Books cover a time-period measured more in months than years, and take 332 pages; there is a gap of two years between the end of Book Two and the beginning of Book Three; and Book Three covers a matter of weeks, taking 117 pages.

In other words, the narrative pace of the outer story quickens into a headlong rush towards resolution, and the oppositional discourses of the text are increasingly swallowed up in the mythic impulse for revenge and retribution followed by Paul's transfiguration into the substantive Emperor – in the classic progression of Propp's analysis.

It is possible to argue that at the end of the novel the flywheel of the myth has managed to escape the containment of the more serious delineations of family and communal life and the central exploration of the spiritual dimension to human existence which have been a feature of the first two Books. It becomes questionable whether Herbert's text after all manages to escape from the tendency of the genre towards simplification and away from serious exploration of serious issues – a question posed by Ursula Le Guin in some comments on the nature of the SF genre, where she addresses the genre's tendency to male elitism very precisely:

> The women's movement has made most of us conscious of the fact that SF has either totally ignored women, or presented them as squeaking dolls subject to instant rape by monsters – or old-maid scientists de-sexed by hypertrophy of the intellectual organs – or, at best, loyal little wives or mistresses of accomplished heroes . . . Isn't the 'subjection of women' in SF merely a symptom of a whole which is authoritarian, power-worshipping, and intensely parochial? . . . From a social point of view most SF has been incredibly regressive and unimaginative. All those Galactic Empires, taken straight from the British Empire of 1880. All those planets – with 80 trillion miles between them! – conceived of as warring nation-states, or as colonies to be exploited, or to be nudged by the benevolent Imperium of Earth towards self-development – the White Man's Burden all over again. The Rotary Club on Alpha Centauri, that's the size of it.[6]

The relevance of these remarks to Herbert's text is obvious, but it is possible to claim that in the final analysis he moves far enough beyond them to escape whipping.

Actually, one of the satisfactions of the novel, perhaps one of the reasons for its gigantic success, is the fact that several 'readings' need to be made simultaneously for its full textural quality to be fully appreciated. This places it firmly within Umberto Eco's useful definition of an 'open' text, in that it does not impose nor move towards a preferred reading but instead encourages participation and negotiation. Most mass media texts, including most films, tend to promote a particular reading – perhaps because of the nature of their processes of production. In Lynch's adaptation of Herbert's novel the needful simplification (for Lynch must primarily ensure the commercial viability of his film, encompassing it within the benchmark duration of 150 minutes that seems to apply for most American distributors) will inevitably close down some of the alternative readings available in the original.

The important point to be made here is that Lynch can select to a large extent which reading(s) he prefers for his film. It may well be that, depending on the decisions he finally makes, Le Guin's analysis impacts more directly on his text than on Frank Herbert's.

III

The film opens with the face of a beautiful woman, hair ornately braided, seen against a background starfield. She speaks directly to camera, her tone measured and certain, establishing the pace and emphasis of someone accustomed to the exercise of power:

A beginning is a very difficult time. Know, then, that it is the year ten thousand and one ninety one. The Universe is ruled by the Padishah Emperor Shaddam the Fourth – my father. In this time the most precious substance in the Universe is the spice *melange*. The spice extends life. The spice expands consciousness.

(fades in and out)

The spice is vital to space travel. The Spacing Guild and its Navigators, whom the spice has mutated over four thousand years, use the orange spice gas, which gives them the ability to fold space. That is, travel to any part of the Universe without moving.

(fades in and out)

Oh yes, I forgot to tell you: the spice exists on only one planet in the entire Universe – a desolate dry planet with vast deserts. Hidden away within the rocks of these deserts are a people known as the Fremen, who have long held a prophecy that a man would come – a Messiah – who would lead them to true freedom. The planet is called Arrakis – also known as . . . Dune.

This use of language is very impressive (despite the rather clumsy beginning to the third paragraph): personal, yet maintaining a formality of address underpinning the speaker's claim to be the daughter of an Emperor; informative and functional in the clipped sentences that effectively summarise the nucleus of Herbert's outer story without distorting or reducing it.

The rest of the opening credits are shown against a backdrop of huge sand-dunes, the choral effects of wind amidst the music helping create an eerie unsettling atmosphere, causing the audience unease. We are then shown immediately a snatch of 'A Secret Report Within The Guild' which projects the planet Dune/Arrakis alongside the planets Caladan (House Atreides), Giedi Prime (House Harkonnen) and Kaitain (Home Planet of the Emperor), and a voice-over talking of a secret plot only recently uncovered, the need to send a Third Grade Navigator to interview the Emperor. 'The spice must flow!'

The first scene proper of the film shows that interview, and the Emperor's acknowledgement of his plot with the Harkonnen to destroy

House Atreides. The Spacing Guild want Paul Atreides killed, thus awakening interest in him on the part of the Bene Gesserit Reverend Mother Gaius Helen Mohiam, who is the Emperor's 'truth-sayer' because of her telepathic powers – and who has plans of her own.

From this point on it is clear that the main thrust of the film should be to develop the main outline already delineated with impressive professional economy: the flow of information is nicely judged as to pace and detail, with a good mix of narrative devices – direct address to camera outside the diegesis of the film, computer-generated graphics, voice-over, dramatic interplay within the diegesis.

Lynch is here revealed as a master craftsman, this opening sequence displaying his powers at their best: innovative, interesting, imaginative. It augurs well for the rest of the film. For those familiar with Herbert's text the use of Princess Irulan as the initial narrator is a firm nod in the direction of the novel, for Herbert introduces each narrative sequence in the three Books of his novel with a quotation from one or other of the books on Paul Atreides/Muad'dib written by the Princess, thus prefacing each piece of present action with an historical perspective allowing an extensive system of internal nuances and reverberations and ironic cross-references.

The readiness to use such a range of techniques to progress the narrative is also encouraging, especially the use of voice-over to express the inner thoughts of characters and reveal their telepathic linkages, because much of the range of discourse in Herbert's text operates on the internal unvoiced level, deep in the minds of the characters.

The brief example of special effects in this opening sequence is likewise positive: the mutated form of the Third Grade Navigator floating in his orange spice gas is a serious attempt to suggest what mutations or adaptations might have taken place in this kind of future. This is crucial to one of the major areas of difficulty facing Lynch: how to make this imagined world credible and comprehensible to the audience, how to imply relationships within the social system, to establish patterns of power, to develop psychological and atmospheric characteristics, to draw the audience into the 'reality' of the text – to create, in Barthes's resonant term, the 'scientific vulgate' for this epoch. Barthes's theories on how certain processes of coding work within narrative to make the constructed 'reality' of textual diegesis appear natural offer a further window onto the quality of Lynch's achievement here.[7] Lynch engages succinctly with those three codes which not only provide the narrative with the connotations which make it intelligible but which centre the text within the frame of cultural negotiation: the semic, cultural and symbolic codes.

Semes are connotations which gradually coalesce around a character or structure an atmosphere or psychology within a text – as through the ornate braided hair and linguistic usage of the Princess. The cultural code uses the reader's competence and understanding of how, say, notions of character are constructed within a text by using the reader's pre-existing knowledge of how society works – as through the positioning of characters within the interview scene, where the Emperor is physically below the Navigator and shown as defensive by his stance, expression, intonation and gesture in a complex but immediately graspable set of signals.

The symbolic code uses cultural positioning of the reader – male/female, black/white, homo-/heterosexual, and so on – to use their commonsense knowledge of what things mean or infer. It operates here in the use of costume to indicate rank or wealth or privilege or power – the Bene Gesserit tonsure and robes, for example, speak of the spiritual/religious dimension of the order as well as its wealth and power at exactly the same moment that the tonsure itself implies the *apartness* of the members of the order. Especially fascinating about this opening sequence is how it carries the seeds of a wider failure of narration in the film within the excellence of its own function. Indeed, this is true of much of the rest of the film, in that its various aspects taken individually (visual style, special effects, actors' performances, use of camera, and so on) are very good and successful, if not at times excellent – but the film as a *whole* collapses. For example, using Irulan as the initial narrator (and she is used in voice-over at several other points in the film, especially to gloss over the sudden abyss of two years which opens up before the final battle) sets up certain valid expectations in the audience concerning this character: that she will play an important if not prominent part in what follows; that she will be also involved in the resolution of the film, establishing a symmetry of narration; that she offers a particular perspective on the action and characters within the film. All of these things hold true for Herbert's text, where at the end Paul enters a political marriage with Irulan but offers her no love, and where she finds her fulfilment in writing books about him – a powerful irony that reverberates back through the text and her 'introductions' to the narrative sections. There is nothing of this in the film as it stands.

Indeed, in the next scene in which we meet Irulan – moments before the entry of the Third Grade Navigator – she is just one of the many minor figures in the Emperor's Court who is hustled away. This extreme passivity marks all her appearances, contexting her within the marginalisation of female characters which is a constant effect in Lynch's vision. Using her as the initial and repeated narrator must be incomprehensible to that part of the film audience unfamiliar with the novel.

A second example from this opening sequence is the massive golden Court itself. This is obviously seen as one of the major sets in the film,

intended to impress with its spectacle and space – and to a limited
extent it does so. But it points up the question of *scale* in the film, the
overt attempt to produce an 'epic'. There are several such massive sets:
the Great Hall of the palace at Arrakeen; the Hall of Rites in the
Fremen sietch; Giedi Prime. They are beautifully constructed (indeed,
they caused tremendous complications for the camera-crew because
some were solid), and it is clear that a lot of time and effort and
imagination went into their design, as part of the conscious technique
used to establish the separate planetary locations and their visual
styles. In the film that we see, however, these sets have a somewhat deactivated impact. The reason for this is by no means clear or simple, but
is has something to do with a lack of *human reference*: the camera-
angles tend to be from above, or within a fairly tight set of close-up
positions. We do not really see these sets from the eye-level viewpoint
of an ordinary person (visual shades of fairy-tale ideology?), and so
have no *involvement* with what we see. The camera tends to pan
quickly across the various surfaces of the sets without lingering lovingly
on a particular detail of design that we can appreciate with awe. It is
irrelevant, for example, that the Emperor's Court had a jade floor, or
that the pattern of the floor of the Great Hall at Arrakeen is based on
the actual tiles in the cathedral at St. Mark's, because in the film they
are not highlighted in any meaningful way.

Seventy-five sets were created on eight sound stages, and taken
individually they work brilliantly in establishing the background
'reality' of the film – but the operative word is background. It is possible
to develop this further. When talking on set to the journalist Ed Naha,[8]
Lynch made a passing reference to David Lean's preparedness to comb
the world for 'the picture-perfect location' – an option unavailable to
Lynch and one which he implies is alien to his methodology anyway.
Lean, of course, directed that other great desert picture about a
messianic figure, *Lawrence of Arabia*. It suggests that deep in Lynch's
thinking was the need to create something different from that earlier
picture – a natural response. But Lean's film offers a possible
explanation for the failure of Lynch's epic effects: the fact that Lynch,
because of the physical constraints of his location, had to rely on the
sets for his epic grandeur, supplemented by optical effects and skilful
miniaturisation. The desert world of Dune/Arrakis – and it is this
element which gives the two texts their title, remember – has none of
the scale and sweep of the desert in *Lawrence of Arabia*, and no sense of
meaningful human interaction with it (as in the glorious scene in Lean's
film when Sherif Ali comes out of the desert on his horse in a wonderful
slow long shot, appearing first as a shimmering blur of lines in the far
distance, and slowly resolving into the cloaked figure who causes

Lawrence's guide to react with horror when he realises who it is – rightly, as the Sherif kills him for drinking from the water-hole without permission). There are no slow long shots in Lynch's film, and only the dust exists in his desert, and the odd mountainous dunes that have no other reference-point, no sweep of horizon behind and beyond them. To mask the fact that much of the desert in his film was shot in a rubbish dump, Lynch resorts to tight angles and close shots, with little swirls of dust thrown up in front of the camera lens to emphasise the desert 'feel'. Within these constraints his achievement is very praiseworthy – but they severely impair the epic quality everyone was aiming for. Dune/Arrakis is confined to a rubbish dump, enhanced with optical effects. In a very important way, despite all the other ways in which Lynch does successfully create a credible comprehensible world for each of his major locations, the planet at the heart of his film remains lifeless, unlocalised, without identity.

Writers have the luxury of following only the dictates of their imagination: if something does not quite work, then another sheet of paper goes into the typewriter or the word processor and the only thing that's lost is time and effort. Directors work within more absolute limits: films cost money. In order to save money – the budget would perhaps have doubled anywhere else – the film was shot in the Churubusco Studios in Mexico City, despite a lack of experience in handling such major projects and an equipment-level well below the state-of-the-art to be found in other centres of production. Added to this was a very obstructive Mexican Customs Service, which created manifold problems of getting material and people in and out; illness was a constant problem; power supply was intermittent at times, as were the telephone connections; the solid sets created major difficulties for the director of photography, Freddie Francis, in terms of lighting, and camera placement and movement; temperatures were oppressive; the live shooting schedule was only some twenty-three weeks. Much of this was beyond Lynch's control.

Underpinning all of this was the other major technical problem of the project: the script. Simplifying Herbert's text is a formidable and crucial task: how does one achieve a balanced reduction of the richness of the novel whilst preserving its spirit? Earlier attempts to produce a filmscript ran into this very difficulty: in 1975 Alejandro Jodorowsky produced one that would have filmed in some eleven or twelve hours; in 1981 Ridley Scott (who directed *Alien*) attempted a script with Rudy Wurlitzer, but it was decided that the book's plot-line was too unwieldy for a conventional script. So the fact that Lynch was able to come up with a workable script – and one that Herbert approved of – is further testament to his determination and ability. Unfortunately, Lynch regards a script as merely a starting point, as not complete. This complicates matters dreadfully on such a complex production, however much it freed up his other films. His attitude is clear:

> The script is like a skeleton. You can rely on it. If it works in the script, then you have a certain leeway to play with things. I don't practise what they call 'cinema verite'. I like things under control, but I still realise – maybe now more than ever – that I cannot work being locked into a script or a story. I hate storyboards now more than anything. I would hate to do what Hitchcock did and storyboard everything and stick exactly to that. All the fun of making a movie would be gone, for me.[9]

This certainly explains the eclectic eccentric nature of his output, and his success in creating freewheeling imaginative effects; but it is very much at odds with the discipline required to adapt Herbert's text. The use of Princess Irulan as narrator might well have benefited from a more rigorous storyboarding of the main threads of narrative significance, enabling them to be more integrated into the fabric of the film and to be resolved in an organised coherent way at the end.

One motif which shows a lack of control over narrative in the film we see is the beautifully constructed 'prescient vision' sequence(s) that punctuate the action, underlining Paul's basic telepathic and prophetic competence and how it is developed in the spice environment of Dune/Arrakis. Lynch uses simple repeated images that reveal how the humanly intimate moment is always more effective and involving than the grand set. In the first such sequence, as Paul lies sleeping before meeting Gaius Helen Mohiam's black box and gom jabbar, there are five elements: a single drop of water falling into a dark pool, the laughing insanity of Feyd-Rautha (whom we have not yet met), the second moon of Dune/Arrakis with the shape of the kangaroo-mouse which gives Paul his name of Muad'dib, another drop of water into the pool, and Chani (whom again, we have not yet met) saying 'Tell me of your home world, Usul'. The second sequence, after Paul has nibbled his first spice on Dune/Arrakis, the fabric of time rips apart to reveal four elements: the cackle of Gaius Helen Mohiam, the familiar drop of water into the pool, the second moon once again, and finally a hand, palm outward against a vague waving background, coming out of the void towards the camera as a voice intones 'The sleeper must awaken'. As filmic referents for written expression they are excellent: evocative, arresting, alluring – Lynch at his best.

More importantly, they are signalled very carefully as significant moments, part of the film's hermeneutic code, posing and reposing the central enigma of the text and regulating the pace of disclosure of information in such a way as to arouse and sustain the audience's interest in how the situation will be resolved. But what these images signify is not at all developed in the film that we see. This failure eventually causes the wider failure of the film itself.

The drop of water falling into a mystic dark pool signals the secret purpose of the Fremen to 'awaken' their planet, so it opens up the ecological theme in the text and emphasises the process as the slow distillation of effort and intention within an essentially spiritual frame. It is the most repeated of the images, which suggests that this theme is major to the film. Within the film we see, however, the ecological dimension apart from this image consists of one brief scene when Jessica and Paul enter the Fremen sietch after their escape from the Harkonnen guards sent to kill them and leave their bodies in the desert and after they have met with Stilgar and his tribe. There is the stretch of a dark lake of water and Stilgar's terse comment that the Fremen have many thousands of these. There is no other sustained reference at all, and the character of Dr Kynes (who as the Fremen leader Liet is the driving force behind the ecological imperative) is effectively excised from any real or implied relationship with this theme – unless his prayer to Shai-Hulud when the worm attacks the spice factory that Duke Leto is overflying after arriving on the planet is intended to encapsulate his involvement.

Feyd-Rautha is clearly indicated here as an oppositional force to Paul. He is nicely characterised in the film as an evil presence, but he is not seriously counterweighted against Paul at all – they are both heirs to a Ducal House. Their duel at the end of the film is gratuitous and sterile, because it has no context nor any real expectation that Paul can be in any danger. In Herbert's original novel, Feyd-Rautha was a potential Kwisatz Haderach himself, and a worthy adversary. His skill in fighting was highlighted in the scene where he kills his hundredth gladiator – which counterpoints Paul's first such deadly struggle against the Fremen Jamis. None of this emerges in the film as it stands.

Chani represents Paul's emotional life within the sietch, as well as fulfilling the mythic function of the predestined romantic love of the hero. We see her several times in the film, but always in a subservient relationship to Paul, a nurse-figure who declares that he is her life or something equally fatuous; at the end she briefly appears as a warrior riding one of the worms in the final battle against the Emperor -- but it is without resonance. She is little more than a convenience. For Herbert, she was a much more central figure, for in addition to her mythic function she bears Paul a son, is the daughter of Liet-Kynes and therefore a powerful symbol for the Fremen in her own right, and she is closely linked with Jessica both in terms of their marriage-position (both are concubines rather than wives) and the religious emphasis within the text, for Chani is a sayyadina within the sietch, a female acolyte within the Fremen religious system. In the film she is deactivated and marginalised – a fate which, as already noted, she shares with the other female characters.

Gaius Helen Mohiam represents many strands in the text, pointing up not only the political dimension through her relationship to the Emperor but also indicating the separate genetic plans of the Bene Gesserit, who have laboured over many long years to build blood lines that might produce the Kwisatz Haderach. She seeks to exercise control over Paul, and hers is the first major challenge with which he has to deal. Despite Sian Phillip's arresting performance, this too is a character who is eventually given little structure in the film: the sense of the Bene Gesserit as one leg of the tripod which controls the Empire is never foregrounded in the way that Lynch's text does bring out the fact of the power of the Spacing Guild.

The hand moving irresistibly towards the camera represents the force unleashed by Paul Muad'dib when he organises the Fremen and is accepted as their Messiah, the Lisan-al-Gaib – what in Herbert's text is the Jihad that will rampage through the Galaxy destroying everything in the name of Muad'dib. But the only narrative link to the hand in the film is when Stilgar introduces Paul to the group of Fremen warriors who will henceforth act as a bodyguard, and raises a bloodstained hand from the shoulder of the Fedaykin still-suit stained in red as a sign that these are the fearsome death commandoes. This link is so fragile as to be unnoticed in the flow of action: this reading alone does not justify the use of the image because it is not weighty enough. Of course, the Fremen themselves are merely convenient ciphers in the film as it stands, part of the weaponry Paul uses in his quest for revenge. The exploration of the messianic impulse which was one of Herbert's motivating forces to produce the original text just does not exist in the film, because Paul really has no coherent people to lead.

All these images in the 'prescient vision' sequences examined here will carry meaning for that part of the film audience that knows Herbert's novel – but for those unfamiliar with the novel these images need careful placing into context if they are not simply to become part of a narrative confusion and lack of clarity. Signalling them as significant but then not developing the details of how they are significant destroys any trust between the audience and the film. It is increasingly apparent that the necessary compression of Herbert's text has resulted in some serious distortions of the structure of the film text and an underrepresentation of the primary interests of Herbert's text – the messianic impulse and the ecology of the planet Dune/Arrakis. The messianic is diminished because the Fremen are diminished; and the Fremen are diminished because of a conscious decision taken long before the final edit – to excise the whole strand of the script that dealt with Paul's fight with the Fremen Jamis and his new 'inheritance' of

Jamis's family. Lynch apparently felt that this strand seriously compromised the pace of the film – although it would clearly more directly affect its length. This excision completely obliterates a direct route into the communal and spiritual life of the sietch, however, and removes a major opportunity of detailing the social and value systems of this 'hidden' people. If it is possible to claim a single reason for the failure of the film to captivate its audience it would be something along the lines of this blankness at its very centre. The void creates problems of narration, pace and ideology far more important than the ones it seeks to avoid. What has happened to the crucial importance of the symbolic significance of the Fremen and their relationship with their planet?

Epic films require time as well as space: *Lawrence of Arabia* succeeds where *Dune* fails as much because of its greater length as of anything else. The suspicion has to be that Lynch finally fell foul of the commercial pressures to make his film conform to a fairly rigid time-scale.

The selections Lynch chooses to make are therefore of overriding import for the final effectiveness of his text, and it is not surprising that the aspect of the film as it stands which is a sustained and coherent success – the exploration of the House Harkonnen – is the one which, throughout the shoot, Lynch was seeking to expand and develop and in which he clearly invests his emotional as well as intellectual effort.

His films are all, in one way or another, investigations of the grotesque. In House Harkonnen he presents a definitive grotesquerie that in typical Lynch fashion teeters daringly on the edge of caricature. Giedi Prime and its inhabitants engage with his creative imagination in a way which is not particularly evident in any other area of the film. The sets are stunning, a nightmare confusion of skeletal steel girders, black and oily, the industrial wasteland turned manic, a society founded on coercion and medical tyranny. The Harkonnen are the great enemies of taste, decency and moderation, their physical appetites as gross as their behaviour. The Baron is so fat that he requires a suspensor (anti-gravity) device to help him move – and tends to float upwards in depraved ecstasy at any given moment. His face is covered with warts and pustules, symbolic of the corrupt psyche within. His two nephews dress in a ribbed black uniform reminiscent of a spacesuit (unless Feyd-Rautha is taking a shower, when he wears a glorified jockstrap for his uncle's delight and edification), and they delight in drinking the life-juices of little animals squashed inside a version of a cafetiere – the deliciously-named 'squoods'. House Harkonnen is the personification of perverse evil, the antithesis of House Atreides, which is a symbol of decency, humanity and moderation. It is vital that the different visual styles of the two Houses imply the moral differences: the human against the inhuman, decency against perversion, the values of the past (for House Atreides are costumed out of Ruritania, and human lives are more important to Duke Leto than spice production) opposed by the totalitarianism of a possible future, where individual life does not matter and the only levers of action are lust and lust for power.

Lynch achieves this brilliantly, and at the same time instinctively redresses a possible imbalance in Herbert's text, where only eight of the forty-eight narrative sections focus on the Harkonnen.

Against this is the fact that the time-constraints increasingly squeezing Lynch's text mean that redressing one imbalance creates another. The pace of the film becomes frenetic, because the deliberately swift cutting between scenes (which heightens the excitement and danger of intrigue) allows less and less time for the moments of personal introspection that mark the first sections of the film, especially before the Atreides take over Dune/Arrakis. Lynch increasingly opts for the grand visual effects, capturing a gigantic worm, destroying a palace, staging a battle. More and more, the dual processes of textual simplification and compressing the action into too short a time, pull Lynch's text further and further into the external actions of Herbert's mythic outer story. This is at the expense of involving those other discourses which raise Herbert's text as a whole beyond the normal limits of the genre. External action in this case means more battles; and what battles do, however brilliantly they are handled, however splendid the special effects, is to emphasise the impersonal. Men die on vast scales, surrounded by bright lights and smoke bombs and explosions. It is not possible to identify with them in the way we were invited to identify with those characters who died earlier in the film – Leto, Yueh, the terrified slave boy whom the Baron kills in the first scene on Giedi Prime.

Wholesale slaughter is finally emptied of meaning. This might well be one of the ideological points Lynch is seeking to make within the frame of his text's central discourse about political power, but it has consequences for the effectiveness of his film, which itself stands in great danger of being emptied of meaning. Sadly, the film finally becomes little more than a puerile revenge melodrama sentimentalised by the worst type of 'happy' Hollywood ending, where Paul is said to bring peace and then, to show the wonder of his new powers, causes rain to fall as garish green searchlights light up the skies above the planet.

Or is this Lynch's final ironic comment on what the various pressures circumscribing his effort have forced him to do?

Notes

1. Leslie Halliwell *Halliwell's Film Guide 7*, St Albans: Paladin, 1989, p. 301.

2. P. Nicholls (ed.) *Encyclopedia of Science Fiction*, New York: Doubleday, 1979, p. 159.
3. P. Nicholls (ed.) *Explorations of the Marvellous*, London: Fontana, 1976, pp. 32–3.
4. Darko Suvin *Metamorphoses of Science Fiction*, New Haven: Yale University Press, 1979, p. 7.
5. Roland Barthes *Image-Music-Text*, London: Fontana, 1977, pp. 79–124.
6. See R. D. Mullen and D. Suvin *Science Fiction Studies: Selected Articles on Science Fiction 1973–1975*, Boston: Gregg Press, 1976.
7. See Roland Barthes *S/Z*, London: Jonathan Cape, 1975.
8. Ed Naha *The Making of Dune*, London: MCA/Target, 1984, p. 233.
9. *ibid.*, p. 232.

Filmography

Dune (A Dino de Laurentiis Production US 1984.) Starring Francesca Annis, José Ferrer, Sian Phillips, Brad Dourif, Dean Stockwell, Freddie Jones, Linda Hunt, Richard Jordan, Kyle MacLachlan, Silvana Mangano, Jürgen Prochnow, Max Von Sydow, Sting: Production Design by Anthony Masters: Cinematography by Freddie Francis: Music by Toto; Screenplay by David Lynch from the novel by Frank Herbert; Directed by David Lynch.

11

Ballard's nightmares/Spielberg's dreams:
Empire of the Sun

FRANK GORMLIE

In the film adaptation of J. G. Ballard's *Empire of the Sun*, the same joke is played three times. The first time is in the American hut in the camp at Lunghua. 'Hey kid, want a Hershey Bar?', an American prisoner asks Shanghai Jim, the protagonist. 'Yes please,' he replies, always the polite well-brought up English child. 'So do I kid,' the American quips.[1] The second shows Jim after his victorious excursion outside the wire, marching to the hut. He plays the same joke on a little girl watching him go. The third occasion is near the end of the film when Basie, Jim's American mentor in the art of survival, asks the question and this time actually throws a Hershey bar to Jim.

These small incidents, absent from the novel, serve to demonstrate some of the difficulties involved in the interpretation of film adaptations. The traditional analysis of a novel finds it easy to ascribe the elements within it to one particular mind or consciousness. We know that there may be certain features which are the product of the editor or publisher but in general we believe that what is in the novel is the intention of the author. There are difficulties with such an approach to film, not simply because film production is a more collective process, but also because it is a more industrial and commercial one. While it may not really matter if we call the film of *Empire of the Sun*, Steven Spielberg's (or for that matter Tom Stoppard's who wrote the screenplay) – we have problems if we are to speculate about the commercial and financial considerations involved in the production.

Although hidden for a long time, Hollywood is now openly admitting that product placement is a valid way of helping to finance a film production. We can speculate about the amount of money Spielberg may have received for the three endorsements of Hershey bar – the product is actually mentioned by the two main characters and given a close up 'pack shot' at the end – but we are unlikely actually to know whether the Hershey bar is there as a piece of disguised advertising or whether it was intended by the director or screenwriter as a significant, symbolic item contributing to the overall meaning of the film.

In fact, as readers of the film we have no alternative but to accept the Hershey bar as significant. How do we interpret? If it were not for our suspicions of the commercial reasons for its inclusion we would think that it had a very meaningful place in the narrative. As it does not appear in the novel, we think the screenwriter or director must have deliberately chosen to place it in the film. It is not simply a throwaway joke, designed to add a bit of colour or flesh out a character. Its repetition makes it a motif and suggests significance.

When the joke is first played on Jim he is trying to be accepted by the Americans around Basie. It is a cruel joke but one which Jim takes as a lesson in realism. When he does it to the little girl, it is a sign of his acceptance into the American group. When it happens near the end of the film it is a symbol of a return to normality, and a parting gift from Basie, weakening the final split between him and Jim, recuperating Basie once again, making him a likable rogue. The Hershey bar then points to one of the main alterations the film makes, the shifted emphasis onto the role of the Americans. To recoup its investment, an English language film must appeal to the biggest English speaking audience, the United States, which it does in this case by making the American presence much stronger than in the novel and by changing the character of Basie. Hollywood production values demand stars to sell movies and stars need starring roles. The shifts in the characters of Basie and Mrs. Vincent, played by John Malkovich and Miranda Richardson, to accommodate this also alter the meanings of the text.

Ballard's concerns are more aesthetic and ideological than commercial. In the Introduction to the French edition of his 1974 novel, *Crash*, Ballard writes of his concern about the modern world and about the role of the writer.

> the balance between fiction and reality has changed significantly in the past decade. Increasingly their roles are reversed. We live in a world ruled by fictions of every kind – mass merchandising, advertising, politics conducted as a branch of advertising, the instant translation of science and technology into popular imagery, the increasing blurring and intermingling of identities within the realm of consumer goods, the pre-empting of any free or original imaginative response to experience by the television screen. We live inside an enormous novel. For the writer in particular it is less and less necessary for him to invent the fictional content of his novel. The fiction is already there. The writer's task is to invent the reality.[2]

The reality that Ballard invents in *Empire of the Sun* is a representation of the Second World War, different from the normal Euro/American perceptions, themselves partly created by cinema as history is rewritten by the victors in endless fictional replays. Jim's illusions about war, and his gradual disillusionment, form the novel's core but a sense of unreality is at the heart of the book: a sense expressed in a nightmarish vision of bodies and death, which would not be out of place in a modern 'visceral' horror movie.

The film adaptation of the novel avoids this sense of nightmare, replacing it with dream-like surrealist sequences serving to show how attractive the war is to Jim, a great adventure, and thus avoiding the novel's critical edge.

Although *Empire* is the closest Ballard has come to a conventional novel, it retains elements of the science fiction and horror which mark his other work. In the preface to *Crash* – at the time of writing the next film project of David Cronenberg, master of body horror and director of *The Fly*, and *Videodrome* – Ballard claims that science fiction 'represents the main literary tradition of the 20th century'. He attacks the mainstream modern novel, identifying its dominant characteristic as: 'its sense of individual isolation, its mood of introspection and alienation, a state of mind always assumed to be the hallmark of 20th century consciousness.'[3]

Ballard denies that this is a true picture of twentieth-century consciousness, suggesting instead that the real subject matter of the mainstream novel is a rationalisation of guilt and estrangement. But, he claims: 'if anything befits the 20th century it is optimism, the iconography of mass merchandising, naivete and a guilt free enjoyment of all the mind's possibilities.'[4]

Ballard writes horrifically (in *Crash* he also writes pornographically) about the modern world as a warning to his readers. We have appropriated both the past and the future into our present, rewriting them, recreating them, trying out possible futures.

Towards the end of *Empire of the Sun* as print-text, the hero, Jim, walks out into the streets of Shanghai and sees three gigantic cinema screens endlessly replaying propaganda movies of battles fought and won in the Second World War. Cinema is one of the recurring motifs in the book. We first encounter Jim at the start of his war watching the same kinds of newsreels in the crypt of the Shanghai Anglican cathedral. Such images pervade Jim's dreams. References to films and cinema form a grotesque and ironic comment on the action in the novel; from the honour guard of fifty hunchbacks in medieval costume outside the cinema showing *The Hunchback of Notre Dame*, to the ironic giant poster showing the ransacking of Atlanta and Gable/Leigh from *Gone with the Wind*. Jim is imprisoned in an open air cinema and his chauffeur is an actor in locally-made films. Ballard's style, indeed, reveals many cinematic techniques, from long slow tracks through the streets of Shanghai, to dramatic cuts at the ends of chapters or sections.

The film makes some use of these references, at one point showing Jim, a tiny figure in his school uniform, against the giant poster of *Gone with the Wind*. Long, slow tracks follow Jim through the streets of Shanghai and around the house. But the film fails to draw out the full significance of the metaphor. Ballard's references are reflections on the ways in which modern communications systems represent and create the realities we inhabit in the twentieth century.

Narrative

Another recurring image in the novel is of coffins floating in the water of the Yangtse, surrounded by flowers, borne backwards and forwards on the tide. The novel begins and ends with this image. In the Ballard text, the meanings of the opening and closing passages cluster around the circularity of time. It is one of the main philosophical themes connecting with such images as Jim's attempts at resurrecting the dead Belgian woman and the Japanese airman. It connects also to Jim's perception that when one war ends another is beginning. Eastern conceptions of time are more cyclical, producing attitudes which the West, with its linear notions of time and progress, consider to be pessimistic. Jim's experience of life and death and war teach him to experience life in this way as a means of coping with the horror which surrounds him.

Part of its strength is its narrative drive and rapid pacing and this is likely to pose problems for the adaptor of any novel. On the whole Stoppard/Spielberg's version is excellent in its pacing, and the resulting loss of complexity, particularly in characterisation, seems inevitable and perhaps not too much of a price to pay for narrative tautness and tension. The cropping of much of the middle section with Jim and Basie in the detention centre and their trip to Lunghua, adds to the shift in power relations between Jim and Basie. Jim is a much stronger character in the novel, Basie a much weaker one, with Jim keeping Basie alive. When they drive around looking for a prison camp, it is Jim who liaises with the Japanese, who gets them water and food.

Jim assumes responsibility for the survival of many people in the novel, a process foreshadowed in his belief that his game with the flashlight and the Japanese destroyer started the war. Jim's childish assumption of guilt is a reflection of the personal guilt which the twentieth century individual accepts and Ballard's narrative technique, where the point of view is almost exclusively the child's, lets us reflect ironically on that.

Jim is confused about war. He was a spectator of the Japanese/Chinese war from the age of six. He recalls driving out to the battlefield at Hungjao with the other Europeans dressed in their Sunday best.

> All around were the corpses of the dead Chinese soldiers, they lined the verges of the roads and floated in the canals, jammed together around the pillars of the bridges. In the trenches, beneath the burial mounds, hundreds of dead soldiers sat side by side with their heads against the torn earth, as if they had fallen asleep together in a deep dream of war.[5]

He is unsure when the war begins and when it ends. The European war which he sees on the newsreels and in his dreams began in 1939. It ends before his war ends. The armed gangs which roam the countryside after the defeat of the Japanese tell of other wars to come and the flash of the atomic bomb on Nagasaki, which Jim thinks he sees, is the beginning of a Cold War lasting more than forty years – a war which has only recently ended.

Ballard's point is a political as well as a philosophical one. Those who write the histories may tell us the dates of the wars but the struggles for power and for survival are continuous. Time is cyclical for which the Western notion of linear progess is demonstrably inadequate. Ballard's may be a more pessimistic message, but it is a truer one. The war did not end. We just changed enemies and friends.

The film cannot deal with such a fatalistic philosophy. It satisfies Hollywood's demand for a happy ending by inventing a scene where Jim is reunited with his parents. The meaning of the print-text is reversed and the film becomes a celebration of individualism. Narrative closure suggests that the problems can be solved, the disruption of normality which began with the Japanese invasion, is over. Everything is back in its place and Jim has managed to survive and reap the reward of the return to family. The final shot of the film, Jim's box floating among the coffins and garlands is a neat narrative rhyme but the meaning is entirely different from Ballard's ending. Jim's war life floats away in this coffin. His war personality is dead. He is once again Jamie, safe in his mother's arms.

The film makes the loss and search for parents a major theme, foregrounding a psychological strand. Jim's relationships with Dr Ransome, Basie and with Mr and Mrs Vincent are presented this way. His voyeurism becomes a kind of Freudian moment, another step in his adolescent growth towards manhood. While such relationships are there in the novel they are of minor importance.

The film also avoids the visual horror of the book. In the novel the countryside is dotted with burial mounds – corpses rise from earth washed away by the rains. Rats eat holes in the shallow mounds which cover the dead in Lunghua. Jim witnesses the beheading of Chinese peasants with the same disinterest with which he watches the newsreels. If Spielberg were to reflect this, the film would resemble a George Romero zombie movie. So Ballard's nightmare vision is softened to a slightly disturbing but interesting dream.

But by avoiding references to the corpse-filled earth, the film also unbalances another major theme, Jim's desire to fly. In the novel it can be read as a contrast to the reality of the earth in which he digs graves and buries the dead of the camp. It becomes symbolic of the human desire to rise above the material and the gross, to become god-like in a sense. That spiritual sense is linked to technology, both a bearer of death and a means of escape and it offers one of the main optimistic notes of the novel. Despite the horror of life we have the capacity to transcend. Spielberg's treatment of the theme, apart from Jim's conversation with his mother early in the film where he asks if god lives in the sky, makes of it a more mundane symbol; a boy's interest in aeroplanes, a link with his lost past which drives him over the edge during the Mustang attack on Lunghua airfield.

Representation and Character

As earlier noted, Hollywood's demands for stars requires the alteration of characters. Film's economy of narrative makes similar demands. Mrs Vincent takes on the actions and roles of a number of other characters in the novel. Mrs Phillips on the walk from Nantao, Mr Maxted, dying in Jim's arms in the stadium. Spielberg has collapsed a number of different novel characters into the role of the young kamikaze pilot and in doing so has again shifted meaning. For Jim the Japanese are not enemies, their depiction in the novel is very far from the stereotyped ideas we have gained from war films like *Bridge on the River Kwai*. Jim admires their bravery and skill as pilots. He admires their codes of honour. It is the Japanese who feed him when he is wandering around Shanghai at the start of the war. He knows how to talk and act with them.

What is lost by the amalgamation of characters is a sense of the individualism and complexity of the Japanese. The film's Sergeant Nagata becomes a stereotyped figure whom Jim can sometimes appease because he understands strange Japanese concepts like 'face'. The boy pilot becomes much more closely identified with Jim. His friendship becomes part of the psychological theme of the film. He is like Jim in many ways, caught up in the horrors of war, with a boy's desire to fly. Their similarity is emphasised in the opening shot of the second section when we see the silhouette of a figure running and flying a toy plane and we only gradually come to realise that it is not Jim. That identity is reinforced when Jim tries to pump life back into the shot pilot and in an hallucinatory point of view shot we see him working on his own younger body. Jim's resurrective powers in the film are thus directed inwardly to try to recreate the happy state of lost childhood. In the novel they are directed outward. Jim wishes to resurrect everyone. In the novel the incident fits into a wider theme that life is more than the personal. Earlier Jim knew that inmates of Lunghua were dead though they remained on their feet and walking. Now he knows that they can be brought back to life. There are cycles of return rather than linear beginnings and ends.

If the representation of the Japanese suffers because of the demands of film and the representation of the Americans is more positive because of the demands of audience, what happens to the other nationalities in translation? Ballard's description of Shangai is historically accurate when he describes the pre-war international community. Many other Europeans are present in the novel, but the film only concentrates on the British presence.

One scene shows the alteration particularly well. Again there is a masterly economy of narrative and again it shifts meanings in important ways. There is an almost surrealist sequence when Jim and his parents drive through the market on the way to a fancy dress Christmas party and from the 'screen' of the car we see strange images of fascists and bar girls and sailors and a nun and the boy 'No mama, no papa, no whisky soda'. The parallels are drawn with thick lines. The English in their carriages, dressed up and on their way to the party through the teeming crowds of Chinese being beaten by the police, are shown as bewildered outsiders who cannot understand the reality of their situation. Jamie is in Sinbad costume – a stranger on a strange voyage in a strange and magical land; his mother in a white pierrot costume, his father rakish as a pirate – reminding us of the origins of the Tai Pans' wealth. In other cars we see someone dressed as a clown, someone as a Chinese mandarin, and the last shot is of powdered, bewigged French eighteenth-century aristocrats. Like Marie Antoinette, they do not understand how history is about to roll over them.

The scene is followed by one at the party in which the racism and complacency of the English are displayed. We meet the only real Chinese character in the film and see the ridiculous English 'gentleman' in grass skirt and dinner jacket making offensive remarks about 'Chinks'. The sequence is followed by one in which Jim confronts a Japanese soldier and we learn from the old hand, Mr Maxted, that you should not run when faced with the Japanese but be calm. Spielberg undercuts this display of knowledge. Maxted does not realise the threat from the Japanese. He talks of it being time to leave, time to go somewhere safe – 'like Singapore'. The irony of the remark, on the eve of Pearl Harbour as we have been told at the beginning, serves to reinforce a picture of the British as unrealistic, existing in a dream world.

The organisation of the novel's narrative, with Jim as the focaliser – where his perceptions and thoughts form a lens through which we see the world - allows for the development of an ironic perception in the reader. To take one example, when Jim thinks that the war is over and the Japanese have won after the takeover of Shanghai, we allow ourselves amusement at his naivete. At the same time we are invited to reflect on a main theme of the novel; when do wars begin and when do they end? Who writes the histories and allocates the dates and from whose point of view are the histories written?

Similar distancing processes happen in Jim's perceptions of other nationalities. Europeans are simply there, part of his natural life, their role only vaguely questioned by Jim, his eleven year old mind more concerned with the pattern the tyre makes running over the foot of the beggar who sits outside the door of his parents' house than in reflecting on relations of power and wealth.

For Jim, Basie's nationality is a minor aspect of his character. More important is his knowledge, skill and will to survive. For Jim too, the Chinese are not to be dismissed in stereotyped descriptions. They have an elemental and mysterious quality, a tide washing back and forth, their bodies sprouting out of the ground and floating down the river. The Chinese are a part of the landscape as inevitable as death. Nationality is another small illusion measured against the more vast truths of life and death and history. The players of this historical game are as circumscribed and rule governed as the Chinese peasant victims.

For Spielberg, the strangeness of the Japanese serves to connote all the problems of understanding Eastern culture and references to the Chinese are minimal. We see them in their thousands, but they are a mere backdrop to Jim's adventures, they have no effect on the narrative.

In the Spielberg/Stoppard version the discourses of national identity are not so much inflected as deflected. In Ballard's, when we again encounter Jim in Lunghua, the camp is in a much more desperate situation than in the film. All British community spirit has been dissipated by hunger and illness. Faced with the realities of life, British culture - Shakespeare readings, lecture programmes - has disintegrated proving no bastion against the basic realities of disease, hunger and death. It is the poverty of this explanation of the world, this British way of thought, the inability to cope with real life situations, to which Ballard draws our attention. Jim has to go elsewhere for his lessons in survival.

Naming the sewage stained paths between the rotting huts after a

vaguely remembered London allowed too many of the British
prisoners to shut out the reality of the camp, another excuse to sit
back when they should have been helping Dr Ransome to clear the
septic tanks . . . The years in Lunghua had not given Jim a high
opinion of the British.[6]

The film has to show the disintegration of the British stiff upper lip in a
more collapsed time than the novel. In the opening sequence to the
second part of the film we are introduced to the camp, major themes are
reiterated, characters reintroduced and developed. But – and here we
are tempted to speculate again about the commercial pressures which
shape the film's narrative – Jim's ultimate goal on his journey round
the camp is the American hut. The picture we get of the camp is
initially relatively pleasant. Prisoners are still practising amateur drama,
a vegetable garden is being tended, there is organisation – even, in the
American hut, a kind of escape committee making compasses from
needles, corks and bowls of water.

In the novel all optimism has long disappeared and what's left seems
much closer to the kind of passive acceptance of death which we were
earlier shown as a Chinese trait. It is Jim's will to survive and his belief
in his own miraculous resurrective powers which are the focus of the
narrative. In the film, Jim's hope rests on the pragmatism of the
Americans. The planned escape, Jim's scouting through the wire, its
dangers and the heroism mark a rite of passage, the reward being to
bunk with the big boys. The film does not present the Americans as
simplistically heroic. The sequence in which the whole American hut
watches Jim and bets on his life or death is chillingly satirical within
the narrative context of the film and read as a wider metaphor for
America's capitalist spirit.

Nevertheless, we are invited, with Jim the focaliser of discourse as
well as narrative, to admire the pragmatism of the Americans and to
contrast it with the illusions of the British with their insistence on
learning dead and useless knowledge, the Latin verbs which Jim rattles
off.

Towards the end of the film more ambiguous readings are invited.
The 'fridges from the sky' can be read as symbols. While American
consumerist abundance saves the day it also marks the kind of
intervention in Far Eastern (and world) politics which America was to
develop from the end of the war.

Such a political reading is correct in one sense. It points to the real
power relations which existed in the East after the war, but it is correct
from a narrow, historical perspective refused by Ballard. By avoiding
national stereotypes of British and Americans, certainly of Japanese
and perhaps less successfully of the Chinese who still seem a little
'inscrutable', Ballard takes us to a deeper historical truth about the

differences which exist between the philosophies and ideologies of the East and West. He suggests that the failure of understanding condemns us to the continuation of war. As indeed it did and does.

Contrast the final chapter of the novel again with the final scenes of the film. Spielberg's personalisation of the war, as Jim's psychological loss of his parents, his search for substitutes and his eventual tearful reunion with them, have nothing to do with Ballard's conclusion. Jim's parents don't actually reappear in the novel. He refers to them but they are 'off stage'. He is cool and dispassionate about them. The Jim of the final chapter is much more grown up than the shattered, broken child of the film. And what does he watch in the novel? American and British sailors urinating on Chinese.

> Fifty feet below them, the Chinese watched without comment as the arcs of urine formed a foaming stream that ran down to the street. When it reached the pavement the Chinese stepped back, their faces expressionless. Jim glanced at the people around him, the clerks and coolies and peasant women, well aware of what they were thinking. One day China would punish the rest of the world and take a frightening revenge.[7]

Spielberg's seventh cavalry intervention to save the crazy cycling Jim satisfies conventional audience demands and is more likely to provoke narrative relief than ideological questioning.

To some extent this indicates the problems and opportunities for the film-maker in the late twentieth century. We now live in a world where audiences are 'super-literate'. The community of shared knowledge of the sixteenth and seventeenth century was tiny compared to that of today and that community of knowledge is no longer restricted to a small, literate, educated class fragment. Film and television, mass publishing of novels and magazines mean that there are shared representations of events, peoples and histories. There are also shared narrative codes, expectations of how a story should be told. The liberating aspect of this is that an author, an artist, a director can now quote, through reference to shared cultural icons, a whole complex of ideas and feelings by the use of one reference. (In linguistic terms, a shift from the iconic to the symbolic.)

An image of Marilyn Monroe no longer merely represents a specific person, it is full of meanings. Her whole life history, her roles in films, her tragedy and public life, her value as a symbol for women can all, potentially, be invoked. Agglomerations of meaning can be manipulated through such a sign, given new contexts and thus new meanings. The problematic side is how to cope with the audience's sophisticated expectations of a text. In our context what does a writer do with the readers' expectations of the prison camp novel or film? You can ignore them and try to describe the camp in a way not tried before. But ignoring audience expectations not only threatens the popularity of the text but can also avoid ideological and political engagement. Past representations of the world are political constructions. To avoid confronting *Tenko* and *Colditz* and *The Great Escape* is to seal the text hermetically and is very unlikely to be successful. Ballard is successful in dealing with our prison camp narrative expectations. The failed attempts of the British to maintain their cultural identity are not given narrative precedence. Instead Jim's rapid disintegration is presented in non-nationalistic (as well as less Freudian) terms. He is a human being and his dsintegration holds a universal message. His thoughts and feelings are not simply those of an English boy, but those of us all in similar extremes.

Notes

1. *Empire of the Sun* - produced and directed by Steven Spielberg © 1987. Distributed by Warner Bros. Available on Warner Home Video.
2. J. G. Ballard *Crash*, London: Triad/Panther, 1985, p. 8.
3. *ibid.*, p. 6.
4. *ibid.*, p. 6.
5. J. G. Ballard *Empire of the Sun*, London: Grafton, 1985, p. 32.
6. *ibid.*, pp. 167-8.
7. *ibid.*, p. 351.

Filmography

Empire of the Sun (A Robert Shapiro/Amblin Production US 1987.) Starring Christian Bale, John Malkovich, Miranda Richardson, Nigel Havers, Joe Pantoliano; Production Design by Norman Reynolds; Cinematography by Allen Daviau; Music by John Williams; Screenplay by Tom Stoppard from the novel by J. G. Ballard; Directed by Steven Spielberg.

12

Hollywood and race:
To Kill a Mockingbird

COLIN NICHOLSON

Nothing, it would seem, could be much faster than the ability of the reader's eye to move across the printed page, processing linguistic information, absorbing it and 'staging' it in the imagination. Almost instantaneously, the mind decodes the words on the page, translating complex messages into images, into imagined events. On the cinema screen, however, things move even faster. The viewer encounters several sign systems at once. These include spoken language, musical accompaniment and pictorial event and the viewer is bombarded with additional modes of communication. Novel readers thus exercise much greater control over their responses, and over the time taken to digest and respond to them, than do film spectators.

In the case of the literary and filmic texts of *To Kill a Mockingbird*, these differences of pace and control are in some ways intensified. Harper Lee's celebrated novel of the American South is leisurely, reasoned and reflective. As directed by Robert Mulligan, the film of the book moves with considerable speed, selecting and compressing incidents into a relatively short running time, so that several themes developed in the narrative space of the novel are necessarily compressed in the film's option to concentrate upon the central theme of racial hostility towards blacks by Southern whites. In the novel there are repeated image-patterns and themes which provide a context and a sense of depth for this central concern of racial prejudice. The care with which a family history is integrated into a wider sense of the history of the Southern States: the theme of family relationships, of journeying both literal and metaphorical out of childhood, of religious hypocrisy; all these, if they survive in the film, survive only at fleeting moments, and not as fundamental parts of the fabric of the story as they indubitably are in Lee's novel.

The novel is narrated by Jean Louise Finch, one of the central characters, from the perspective of an adult remembering events from her own childhood. As a child she was known as 'Scout', and because she had lived through these experiences *before* she begins to record them as an adult in written form, Scout reports for us more than she properly realises she is seeing. It is a familiar literary technique in first-person narration, and here, in the tension between what Scout saw as a child and what she understands as a remembering adult, we are able to follow the steps of her development from innocence to maturity. Since the focus of the novel is on Scout's brother, Jem, he becomes the main character, with the reader observing Scout's changing awareness through the characterisation of Jem and through her own relationship to him. In such ways, the Finch children, together with Dill, remain the centre of attention throughout the book.

The obvious and frequent corollary in American film of a remembering first-person narrator in fiction is the use of the 'voice-over' technique. When Scout first comes into view on screen, her adult voice is already speaking words on the sound-track which closely approximate to those used in the novel. But the star system of the Hollywood studio productions of the sixties changed the focus of the novel in crucial ways. In the screen version, Scout's father, Atticus Finch (Gregory Peck), becomes the central character. The American white male, cast here in the heroic figure of a progressive liberal lawyer fighting for the civil rights of a black man falsely accused of raping a young white woman, dominates the action. This shifts our attention onto the campaigning for, and survival of, the rights and principles of racial justice which are denied to the accused African-American, Tom Robinson. The film's concentration on the father, stressed throughout by the camera's constant attention to Peck, is seen particularly in the sequence where Atticus shoots the mad dog. The camera lingers on Jem's open-mouthed admiration for his father's mastery with guns. Atticus may be an American liberal, but even though his spectacles slip symbolically from his eyes as he aims the gun, he shares, in both film and book, the masculine prowess which a wider American culture considers to be important. As the all-powerful father-figure, Atticus displaces the children as the source of developing awareness. Hence his dominance and authority on the screen narrow the film's scope and range.

The deeply ironic schoolroom discussion of American democracy and German fascism, which takes place in Chapter 26 of the novel, is only the most obvious case in point.[1] The smug complacency of Miss Gates does much to prepare the Finch children and the reader for the gap between Maycomb's opinion of itself as a town, and the stark actuality revealed by things which are to come. It contributes a considerable amount towards the experience and understanding of Jem and Scout, and provides a cutting counterpoint to their forthcoming live encounter with racism and persecution in the small Southern town. But all of this is omitted from the picture, as is the novel's extensive satire on religious hypocrisy. Another crucial omission is the novel's repeated reference to and detailed treatment of family structure and family life. From Dill's status as unwanted child to the repression in the Radley household and the Ewell poverty and violence, the greater narrative attention of the novel enables it to explore the often painful experience of family influences. In this respect the Finch family household proves the most interesting, with the black servant Calpurnia becoming accepted as a surrogate mother-figure, though there is no verbal reference in the film to the fact of her colour, and the children form relationships which cross over the immediate ties of blood-kinship.

In the film the viewer sees things immediately, through a camera which is always allied to Scout, the narrator's, perception. As a result there is an inevitable slackening of the narrative tension which generates some of the novel's most powerful effects. Conversely the immediacy of film enables Mulligan's picture to register the shock impact of unsettling experiences on the children. The novel, however, remains more powerful. Consideration of the image of the mockingbird might help us to understand the process whereby some things are lost in the transition to film mode. In the opening lines we read:

> When he was nearly thirteen, my brother Jem got his arm badly broken at the elbow. When it healed, and Jem's fears of never being able to play football were assuaged, he was seldom self-conscious about his injury. His left arm was somewhat shorter than his right; when he stood or walked, the back of his hand was at right-angles to his body, his thumb parallel to his thigh. He couldn't have cared less so long as he could pass and punt. (p. 9)

The careful attention to detail here suggests that this is a self-conscious piece of narrative foreshadowing, looking forward as it does to the vicious attack upon the Finch children by Bob Ewell, an attack which does not take place until the novel's penultimate chapter. Such things cast a shadow forward, as well as registering that this is, in fact, a discourse of memory, a personal history the outcome of which is known to the narrator, though not to the reader. But it is rather more than that, too.

Whereas in the film there is virtually only one mockingbird, that is to say only one victim, the accused Tom Robinson; in the novel several characters besides Jem Finch are at one time or another considered in that light. Much play is made, in the film's climactic court-room scene, with the fact that Tom Robinson's left arm hung dead at his side, the result of an accident with a cotton-gin which meant that it was anyway impossible for him to have raped anyone in the way his supposed victim had described it. The novelistic foreshadowing, which suggests that Jem Finch is also in some sense a mockingbird and that his experiences of racism have damaged him and, in his transition from childhood to adulthood, left him permanently scarred, is passed over in the film. Images which give the novel a kind of depth and range, are omitted, leaving Atticus's court-room remark to echo reductively in the film version: 'This case is as simple as black and white' (p. 207).

Nor can this be attributed solely to the inevitable selection and compression which must take place in the translation of a novel into film, since this film demonstrates an ability to find correlatives for the novel's backward-looking narrative structure. Quite apart from the voice-over technique of Jean-Louise's adult voice, the film makes suggestive and subtle uses of childhood images in its opening sequence as the credits roll and before the film narrative proper begins. As a visual equivalent to the novel's adult narrator re-creating the world of her own childhood beginnings, we watch a child's hands shaping the letters of the film's title – a kind of writing – and we see a child's hands drawing an image of a mockingbird. While this image is being made, the camera pans across a watch, symbol of time passing, and itself an image which recurs in the film. Then, the child drawing the bird tears the paper, 'killing' the mockingbird and leaving a jagged image of white on black; the camera continues to pan across the different toys and objects left by Boo Radley for the children to collect from the tree-knot outside the Radley house. Spilled from the toy-box which normally contains all of these items, we see a penknife, which foreshadows two subsequent events in Boo Radley's life: the attack upon his father, and much more significantly, his slaying of Bob Ewell at the time of the latter's attack upon Scout and Jem. We also see two carved figures, perhaps representing the two Finch children.

That toy-box forms a part of the film's own reference back upon itself in much the same way that the novel's narrative is a return to time past. On the evening of the day when Nathan Radley cements up the knot-hole in the tree, Jem shows Scout all of the objects which have been left for them by Boo. 'It was to be a long time before Jem and I talked about Boo again,' says the adult voice-over. Then a hand closes the toy-box which takes us back to the film's opening sequence. Such use of images suggests several possible ways in which film can find its own equivalents and correlatives for techniques of continuity, recall and foreshadowing used in narrative fiction.

Perhaps one of the most striking of these connects the small-town atmosphere of Maycomb ('a tired old town'), static and enclosed, with a particular tendency in the film's camera-work. On page 11 of the novel we read words which are remarkably close to the opening sentences of the film's screenplay: 'A day was twenty-four hours long but seemed longer. There was no hurry, for there was nowhere to go; nothing to buy and no money to buy it with'. This is taken almost word-perfect into the screenplay. The end of the novel's sentence – 'nothing to see outside the boundaries of Maycomb County' – is omitted, perhaps because Hollywood sought a wider American audience for the film's narrowing of focus onto the theme of racial prejudice. But that oppressive, self-regarding community is explored in a variety of ways in the novel's leisurely space. Given the more intense demands of unity in film-time, such space is not available.

From the opening camera-shot, a shift from looking upwards to trees and outwards to the sky beyond, down onto the practically deserted streets of Maycomb, we gradually become aware that the severely restricted camera-movement throughout the film is having particular effects. When the children peer over the fence into the Radley house, the camera slides conspiratorially up behind them: as they move around the side of the house, the camera arcs upwards, to look down on them. In the courtroom scene the camera moves into close-up on Tom Robinson's face as he gives his evidence. Clever editing during the moment of Ewell's assault upon the children gives the impression of rapidity and confusion. And for the final shot, in a sense reversing the open movement down onto the streets of Maycomb, the camera tracks away from Jem's bedroom, and away from the Finch household. With the exception of these shaping movements, the camera is remarkably static during the film narrative; sometimes tracking slightly to the left or right, but more predominantly remaining fixed, unmoving. Even when Atticus drives from Maycomb proper to where Tom Robinson's wife Helen and the rest of the segregated Negro community live, we see only the car's departure and arrival. In all these ways, any sense of movement is kept to minimal levels, and the overall atmosphere of statis and enclosure reinforced.

Both novel and film suffer from being sentimentalised narratives. One reviewer of the film commented:

> Harper Lee's *To Kill a Mockingbird* is one of the best recent examples of the sentimental novel: the book designed principally to create warmth, which doesn't exclude ugliness but views it through generally optimistic eyes . . . is not vigorous enough to celebrate life, but does enjoy it.[2]

The scene early in the film, where Jem and Scout discuss their dead mother while the camera lingers on Gregory Peck's listening expression out on the front-porch is a case in point. Or, perhaps to more obviously engineered effect, when, at the conclusion of the court scene, Scout tells us, 'I looked around. They were standing. All around us and in the balcony on the opposite wall, the Negroes were getting to their feet' (pp. 215–16). With Reverend Sykes's comment, film and novel indulge in the creation of sentimental emotion towards the idealising of Atticus Finch: 'Miss Jean Louise, stand up. Your Father's passin'.'

Moreover, both versions veer at other times – and frequently – towards the melodramatic, and on at least one occasion the film seems better able to keep a sense of greater realism, even at a moment of high melodrama. In the novel, during the scene when Jem, Scout and Dill arrive at the jailhouse where a lynch-mob has gathered, the staginess of the affair is accentuated: 'I sought once more for a familiar face, and at the centre of the semi-circle, I found one' (p. 156). It is Mr Cunningham, and Scout proceeds to address him on the matter of his entailment and concerning their family relationships in the closed community of Maycomb, reminding Mr Cunningham to say 'hey' to his son Walter on Scout's behalf. The unreality of the scene is further conveyed:

> when I slowly awoke to the fact that I was addressing the entire aggregation. The men were all looking at me, some had their mouths half-open. Atticus had stopped poking Jem: they were standing together beside Dill. Their attention amounted to fascination. (p. 157)

In the silence which follows Scout's speech, the novel records that she:

> looked around and up at Mr Cunningham, whose face was equally impassive. Then he did a peculiar thing. He squatted down and took me by both shoulders. 'I'll tell him you said hey, little lady,' he said (p. 158) before leading the mob away.

Both film and novel wish to stress the creative goodness of childhood, even in such extremes of situation. Perhaps realising that when translated into visual terms such a transformation of Cunningham from angry potential lyncher into softened and caring father might stretch the bounds of credibility, the film opts for registering the acute embarrassment of Cunningham's sideways glance – he is obviously too disconcerted to face Scout directly while she is talking – before he mutters the response included in both versions. Within the margins of a highly melodramatic and unlikely resolution of the scene, the film is slightly more satisfying than the novel.

When, however, melodrama passes over into a more gothic mode, when aspects of mystery and of terror at the unknown form part of the narrative – the film often seems better able to convey a sense of threat, of suspense and of shadowy uncertainty. For the children involved, the figure of Boo Radley is one such gothic dimension, a character who in many ways typifies an identifiable strand in American fiction from the Southern States. Again, for the children, the Radley household figures as the equivalent of a gothic mansion:

> Inside the house lived a malevolent phantom. People said he

existed, but Jem and I had never seen him. People said he went out at night when the moon was high, and peeped in windows . . . A Negro would not pass the Radley place at night, he would cut across to the sidewalk opposite and whistle as he walked. (pp. 14–15)
Although this provides Harper Lee with ample opportunity for comic insight into the workings of childhood imagination and superstition, we also realise that the bogey figure of Boo Radley serves as a symbolic figure of more serious dimensions. Not only is he both sign and representative of an oppressive and inhibited society which, rather than face up to them, is far happier suppressing home truths that are shaming, he is also by that same token a mark of embarrassment to his own family as well as a signal of the repressive intolerance in a wider community.

Aided by Elmer Bernstein's musical score, the film's judicious use of light and shadow, and in particular its presentation of night sequences as the children pursue Dill's idea of 'making Boo Radley come out' (p. 14), catches this mood and feeling of the uncanny and the mysterious. When Jem stays at home on guard, while Atticus takes the black servant Calpurnia home (Calpurnia, of course, sitting on the back seat of the car), Jem sits in the swing chair on the front porch, hearing a screech-owl as shadows of leaves cast black and white patterns on his face. Frightened, he runs down the street after his father's car, shouting 'Atticus.' Outside the Radley house he hears their swing-chair creaking in the wind, and knocking against the woodwork. At this moment he finds the first of the objects left in the tree-knot by Boo. Hearing the sound of the screech-owl again, he takes to his heels and heads for home. The camera repeatedly plays upon that creaking swing-chair on the Radley porch, but even so, this whole aspect of the story is expertly condensed into that cinematic moment when in order to 'get a look at Boo Radley,' Jem, watched fearfully by Scout and Dill, crawls one evening onto the Radley porch. As he peeps through the window, he is approached by a figure casting a looming, threatening shadow which is seen first by the viewer watching the film, then by Scout and Dill, then again by the viewer. When a shadowy hand reaches out to touch Jem, all three children crouch in terror; the figure, starkly stage-lit to register black upon white, withdraws and the three children run for their lives. Symbolic overtone, as well as melodramatic event are registered together. And towards the film's close, Boo Radley, at Scout's invitation, does touch the unconscious Jem's forehead, bringing to the surface, and out into the open a relationship that had hitherto remained unclear and incomplete.

Boo Radley ends by helping the children at a decisive moment, and anyway makes them presents during the progress of the story, those presents with which the film opens. But the way in which Boo saves the children, and more importantly the reaction of the authorities to his intervention, brings us into an area where both texts appear to be complicit in the very values they seek to reform. Much more so than in the novel, the film makes great play with the court scene, devoting to it a disproportionate amount of playing time. It is the scene in which the central values of democratic justice and common decency come into conflict with racial prejudice so deeply rooted that it overturns utterly convincing evidence of Tom Robinson's innocence. But although there may be dramatic reasons for Atticus Finch's defence and celebration of America's legal procedures - after all, he is concerned primarily to sway the opinions of a jury whose biases he knows only too well - none the less the words he uses stand in sharp opposition to the actual practices of the court and its jurors.

In the major summing-up speech for the defence, some passages from the novel are altered in their sequence, but with minor exceptions the language is the same. Atticus Finch, played with style and conviction by Gregory Peck, asserts that 'there is one institution in which all men are created equal,' and he continues, 'in this country our courts are the great levellers' (p. 209). Then, of the integrity of the jury system, he claims 'that is no ideal to me, it is a living working reality. Gentlemen, a court is no better than any man of you sitting before me on this jury. A court is only as sound as its jury, and a jury is only as sound as the men who make it up' (pp. 209-10). The first irony which strikes us is the obvious one that no women could serve on juries in Alabama at that time (p. 225). To have black men serve was unthinkable. But the film makes a telling point in this respect. Although the three children, symbols of warmth, light and innocence, sit next to Reverend Sykes, the court is otherwise rigidly segregated. This is dramatically focused for us when the pronouncement is made: 'will the defendant please rise and face the jury.' What happens is that the camera does not turn to the jury, but to the people who are in fact Tom Robinson's peers and equals - the black community sitting up in the courtroom gallery. It is a brief shot, but it carries considerable cinematic weight in terms of its irony and social comment.

Given the horrors that overtake Tom Robinson after a guilty verdict is returned, the whole of the court scene creates serious problems for the readers' and viewers' attitudes towards the sentimental warmth with which much of the story unfolds. Overall, both novel and film serve to vindicate the liberal values of domestic and civic virtue which the Finch household represents. The reviewer for *Newsweek* makes the appropriate comment on this problem:

> In a seemingly leisurely way, the novel drifted through 121 pages of youthful adventure, and, only then, with the children solidly established did it turn into a rape case. The two discrete parts of

the novel are telescoped in the film, however, and the result is to
bring the trial out of the blurry background and into sharp focus.
The trial weighed upon the novel, and in the film, where it is
heavier, it is unsupportable. The narrator's voice returns at the
end, full of warmth and love . . . but we do not pay her the same
kind of attention any more. We have seen that outrageous trial,
and we can no longer share the warmth of her love.[3]

That sentimental warmth helps to create the conditions for a tidily
'happy' ending, an ending that further suggests that problems have
been raised which the authoress, and following her the director Robert
Mulligan, cannot finally resolve. Brendon Gill writing in *The New
Yorker* makes the point:

In the last few minutes of the picture, whatever intellectual and
moral content it may be said to have contained is crudely tossed
away in order to provide a 'happy' ending. Peck . . . and the sheriff
agree to pretend that a wicked white man who has been killed will
be reported to have fallen on his own knife, thus sparing the man
who killed him - admittedly a mental case, but the saviour of the
lawyer's children - the humiliation of a public arraignment. The
moral of this can only be that while ignorant rednecks mustn't take
the law into their own hands, it's all right for *nice* people to do so.[4]

If Boo Radley has cast a shadow upon the development of the children
throughout the unfolding story, the way in which his killing of Bob
Ewell is covered up by those in authority leaves the unavoidable
impression that for Maycomb, and by extension for Alabama more
generally, 'Law' and its 'Order' are to be manipulated by those who, it is
presumed, know best. *To Kill a Mockingbird* generates serious moral
and social issues. But in order to bring them to a satisfying conclusion,
film and book take refuge in the very suppression of truth and deception
of a community which the assumed story has attempted to expose.

Notes

1. All page references are to the *Pan* edition of the novel, and are
given paranthetically in the text.
2. Stanley Kauffmann, *New Republic*, 2 February 1963, p. 30.
3. *Newsweek*, 18 February 1963, p. 93.
4. Brendan Gill, *The New Yorker*, 23 February 1963, p. 126.

Filmography

To Kill a Mockingbird (An Alan Pakula/Universal-International
Production US 1962.) Starring Gregory Peck, Mary Badham, Philip
Alford, John Megna, Frank Overton, Rosemary Murphy, Ruth
White, Brock Peters: Narrated by Kim Stanley; Cinematography
by Russell Harlan; Music by Elmer Bernstein; Screenplay by
Horton Foote from the novel by Harper Lee; Directed by Robert
Mulligan.

13

Blade Runner:
The economic shaping of a film

RICK INSTRELL

The setting: Hollywood in the 1980s

The structure of Hollywood film production has undergone profound changes over the last forty years. Following Anti-Trust legislation in 1948 which ruled that production and distribution had to be separated from exhibition, the major studios could no longer guarantee screens for their films. Combined with the rise of television ownership, this led to the break-up of the assembly-line system of production with waged workers. Instead Hollywood shifted to a system of freelance piece-workers working for independent production companies whose products were and are distributed and marketed by the major studios. In the 1960s, as studios faced serious financial problems, they were incorporated into giant conglomerates with interests in and out of the entertainment business.

Warner, the studio with the distribution rights on *Blade Runner*, grew at the end of the sixties from Warner Brothers into Warner Communications Incorporated (WCI). According to Gustafson, Warner was 'organised according to the principle of multiple profit centres which reinforce each other in an interlocking and financially conservative pattern that is designed not only to generate revenue and profits, but to keep such monies in the corporation.'[1] Warner became financially stable because of its capacity to divert money from profit-making to loss-making divisions of its enterprises, but also by turning its movie products into multi-media products through tie-ins such as videos, music, toys, clothing, books and computer games. *Blade Runner*'s eventual producers were The Ladd Company, a powerful independent group of the early eighties who also produced *Body Heat*. The dilemma for a group like The Ladd Company in its production strategy was whether to use Warner's existing structures for multi-media exploitation or set up their own deals and ancillary profits. The former was likely to be more effective but more designed to profit Warner, the latter less effective but likely to give them a greater share of the profits. Similarly

160

Warner themselves would look carefully at whether or not tie-ins in movies like *Blade Runner* are likely to be profitable, based among other things on their consideration of likely demographic appeal.

It should be noted, however, that the studio structure in the eighties changed further when studios started buying their way back into exhibition. In 1985, Columbia bought up a small group of New York cinemas and since then Universal/MCA, Paramount, Warner's, the Cannon Group and Tri-Star have all acquired or opened cinemas with the tacit approval of the US justice department. By 1988, the majors had acquired nearly a fifth of movie houses in North America, creating what many see as the beginning of an impenetrable vertical and horizontal monopoly. The advantages of vertical integration are that the corporation 'sells' products to itself and need not worry about being excluded from key markets.

This shift from the old studio to the new conglomerate structure has led to a concomitant shift from product to profit – and hence market-orientation. Production is funded by the studio but carried out by the independent company and in order to obtain funding, studio executives must be presented or 'pitched' with a 'package'. Desirable characteristics of a package would normally include:

1. The concept, preferably a 'high concept' or 'jingle' which reduces the story to a readily understandable – and hence marketable – phrase: for example Alien as '*Jaws* on a spaceship', or *Top Gun* as '*Star Wars* on Earth'.
2. A good title and a positive ending.
3. A blend of novelty and familiarity using heroes with whom an audience could easily identify.
4. An appeal to teenagers as the most frequent filmgoers as well as mass appeal to a wider audience, both male and female.
5. A bankable star and a big director.
6. Tie-in potential and previous success for the project in another medium such as stage or fiction.[2]

According to Murdock and Golding, the overall effect of this packaging means that 'the determining context of production is always that of the market. In seeking to maximise the market, products must draw on the most widely legitimated core values while rejecting the dissenting voice or the incompatible objection to a ruling myth.'[3] In this context, we may move on now to consider the vexed production history of Ridley Scott's *Blade Runner*.

The film's main literary source was the 1968 science fiction novel of Philip K. Dick, *Do Androids Dream of Electric Sheep?* In Dick's novel a world is depicted where animal life has almost completely been wiped out because of nuclear war. Human status and self-esteem are measured by the ownership of the few remaining animals, and if real animals are not available then people have to settle for surrogate models such as electric sheep. Early in the seventies, Herb Jaffe optioned the novel and gave it to his brother to adapt for the screen, but, according to Dick, the resulting screenplay was dire. In 1974, a further source for the movie emerged. Alan E. Nourse, a little-known writer, produced a science fiction thriller called *Blade Runner* in which illegal doctors help their sick patients by using surgical instruments supplied by so-called blade runners. The celebrated novelist William Burroughs was later to write a screenplay based on Nourse's book. In the same year Hampton Fancher, a screenwriter, approached Dick regarding the rights to *his* novel and in 1978, when the Jaffes allowed their option to lapse, Fancher and his collaborator, Brian Kelly, immediately bought them up. They produced an eight page outline which was shown to Michael Deeley, the producer of Michael Cimino's Oscar-winning *The Deer Hunter*. Deeley then approached several production companies all of whom showed interest but requested changes, including a happy ending. The script went through several more drafts before 1980, when Deeley approached the British director Ridley Scott whose science fiction feature *Alien* was a top-grossing film of that year.

Before becoming a film director, Scott had made his name as a prolific director of television commercials in Britain and the United States, his most acclaimed successes being advertisements for Hovis, Strongbow Cider and Levi Jeans. At that time he was scheduled to direct an adaptation of Frank Herbert's *Dune* novels, but production delays gave him a chance to work with Deeley instead and *Dune* was eventually directed by David Lynch. Scott's involvement clinched a financing and distribution deal with Filmways, an independent production company, and Dick's original title was changed to *The Android*. The project was budgeted at between twelve and thirteen million dollars but quickly escalated to over twenty million. Scott added to the cost by bringing in the renowned industrial designer Syd Mead at a fee of $1150 a day and a budget of one and a half million dollars over eighteen months.

The production encountered further difficulties. Shooting was originally planned for London but Harrison Ford, eventually to play the central character, Deckard, a private investigator or 'blade runner' of the future, refused the location because five out of six of his previous films had been made in London. Meanwhile Dustin Hoffman turned down the part because he was uninterested in the macho role of the central character. In 1981, moreover, Filmways found themselves in financial difficulty and the escalating budget of the movie too burdensome. The film went into turnaround and was picked up by The Ladd Company in association with Tandem Production. Meanwhile

Ford accepted the lead when the location was changed to Hollywood and negotiated a 20 per cent profit sharing deal. A start was made on creating a Los Angeles of the year 2019 on the Warner studio lot where Cagney and Bogart had shot many of their celebrated movies.

Script development also became more complicated. Scott and The Ladd Company suggested a major revision of the script, now titled *Dangerous Days*. As co-owner of the property, Fancher at first resisted but eventually agreed to another writer, David Peoples, being brought in to incorporate Scott's desired changes. Peoples introduced a new term 'replicant' to replace the more hackneyed 'android' and dispensed with the idea of Deckard's hunt for rebel androids being motivated by a desire for live animals. Other scenes dropped included Deckard's past exploits as a bounty hunter in days when it was easier to eliminate primitive and less humanoid androids. These scenes were excluded partly because of cost and partly because of Scott's feeling that the plot lines were already complicated enough. After the start of pre-production, Peoples took out of the script items such as a futuristic ambulance which had already been built at considerable expense. The movie title was now changed to *Blade Runner*, a term which had little to do with the story, but was felt to be more appealing and more bankable. This change, of course, necessitated the producers buying the rights to use the title of Nourse's novel on which Burroughs had already worked, and to which their own project had little relevance.

Another troublesome area of production was special effects. The special effects team, headed by Douglas Trumbull and Richard Yuricich, who had worked on *2001: A Space Odyssey* and *Close Encounters of the Third Kind*, originally estimated the script's effects at five and a half million dollars while only two million dollars had been budgeted in production. The script had to be altered to reduce the number of effects and their eventual cost, covering 85 shots, was three and a half million dollars.[4] In March 1981, *Blade Runner* went into full production but Peoples was still changing the script, occasionally writing scenes that were to be shot that day. Each revision also took the script further and further away from the original novel. As Robin Wood remarked:

> *Blade Runner* is not really an adaptation . . . Gone or played down are most of the novel's structuring premises: the nuclear war that has rendered the earth unsafe for the support of life and health; the use of animals as rare, expensive, coveted status symbols: the pseudoreligion of Mercerism.[5]

It could be argued then, that although the film was built on motifs selected from the novel, it had become so different that it is best regarded, as Wood claims, as an autonomous work. Finally with relations between Ford and Scott strained over the director's demands for endless retakes, shooting was completed over-budget and over-schedule with two endings, a downbeat ending and an alternative happy ending. In his initial cut, Scott opted for the former.

The choice turned out to be a preview disaster. A rough cut was shown in Dallas and Denver, but the audience was unhappy with the downbeat ending and angry Ford fans threw cans and popcorn packets at the screen. Ladd Company executives ordered a hasty recut, concerned that they had an expensive flop on their hands. According to Alan Mackenzie, one crucial scene excised from the final cut attempted to eliminate the element of despair in Deckard's character.[6] Returning to his apartment, having just revealed to Rachael that she is a replicant, Deckard sits idly tinkling piano keys, surrounded by photographs. Into this scene Scott had cut now-absent flashes of a unicorn running through woodland. The motivation of this unicorn sequence became clear in the final scenes. Gaff leaves behind an origami unicorn, indicating that he knows Deckard's private memories, and the only way this could possibly happen would be if Deckard was a replicant with all his memories nothing more than artificial transplants. The original version ended with a despairing look of realisation on Deckard's face and a final shot of a lift door slamming shut. Scott accepted this crucial omission of his original ending but objected to others which attempted to give added pace to the film, including Ford's voice-over which was added to clarify the story-line. Out-takes from the opening helicopter shots of Kubrick's *The Shining* were also added to give the film an upbeat ending. At this point, relations between Scott and The Ladd Company were understandably strained.

With release pending, tie-ins proliferated Dick's original novel was now retitled *Blade Runner*, with a publisher's reassuring note that 'though the novel's characters and background differ in some respects from those of the film, readers who enjoy the movie will discover an added dimension on encountering the original work.' The book was promoted by Granada Publishing as 'the action-packed tie-in of the year' with display bins, counter packs and posters. However in June 1982, the picture opened to unfavourable reviews. After a first week box-office gross of nine and a half million dollars, Warner quickly initiated 'rapid pullback', withdrawing the film from US theatrical distribution and releasing it on pay television through its Warner Amex Satellite Entertainment Network on the Movie Channel, as well as on hire or purchase video through its Home Video outlets. This restricted its US-Canada domestic rental to fourteen and a half million dollars as compared with production costs of twenty-seven million dollars.[7] The rule of thumb used in Hollywood is that for a film to break even, the domestic rentals must match the production budget with the marketing costs being offset by overseas and ancillary income. With

Blade Runner this had clearly not happened.

The tortuous production history of the picture has shown many inputs at work – both enabling and constraining its final shape. Conceived as the popular picture of a commodified and anonymous literary property, it ended up as a compromised filmic text and yet became a darling of the art-house circuit, a cult movie revered by critics who often felt safe in its apparent mass appeal while ignoring its commercial failure.

Blade Runner: The question of meaning

The picture has a narrative typical of many mainstream American movies. Deckard, the white enforcer hero, restores order to society and is rewarded by the love of a beautiful princess, Rachael (Sean Young). In a science fiction variation of this traditional theme, Rachael is, of course, a replicant. Yet the film presents some very puzzling features. The opening is a special effects *tour de force* with magnificent yet oppressive shots of a future industrial landscape reminiscent of Fritz Lang's *Metropolis*. Throughout the film, the city is perpetually dark and rain-soaked at street level with the sun only hazily apparent from the mile-high Tyrell building. The film ends with a shot of Deckard and Rachael escaping in his car (which has wheels and cannot fly). This shot then dissolves in helicopter shots, out-takes from Kubrick's *The Shining*, of a sunlit countryside with snow-topped mountains. Compared with the spectacular beginning, the ending seems artificial, an unsatisfying conclusion.

One way of trying to read the beginning of a film involves employing the formalist concept of the 'dominant'. Kristin Thompson argues that through the dominant 'the stylistic, narrative and thematic levels will relate to each other . . . The work cues us to its dominant by *foregrounding* certain devices and placing others less prominently'.[8] The dominant can usually be identified in the opening sequences of a film. In Scott's opening sequence, the stunning night shots of the vast industrial landscape are intercut with giant close-ups of an eye reflecting the golden tongues of flame shooting out of huge towers. The sequence ends with shots of twin neo-Mayan pyramids suggesting human sacrifice to the God, or Moloch, of capitalism. This encapsulates a major theme of the film as a whole: the individual trapped in a world dominated by conglomerates. At the same time Scott cues the spectator into what will be a recurrent motif essential to the understanding of the narrative – the 'golden eye'.

This motif is re-engaged immediately in the next sequence when Leon undergoes the replicant test, and throughout the film all replicants, that is to say genetically-engineered humanoid robots, are seen with glowing eyes. One specific shot, however, also shows Rachael *and* the supposedly human Deckard with illuminated eyes, suggesting that Deckard too is a replicant. The enigma of the shot is then reinforced when Rachael asks Deckard if he has ever subjected himself to the replicant test. A further recurring motif is the fixation of the replicants with the photographs which reflect their artificially implanted memories. At the same time Deckard and Captain Bryant, who has coerced Deckard into hunting down replicants in the first place, are both visually framed surrounded by photographs. One of the main puzzles for the audience, therefore, is to decide exactly who is a replicant and who is not.

Perhaps the most puzzling motif of all, however, is that of the three origami figures which police officer Gaff constructs. Early in the film when Deckard is unwilling to take on Bryant's assignment, Gaff makes a tiny chicken from scrap paper and the meaning is obvious. Later when Deckard searches Leon's hotel room, Gaff makes a tiny figure of a man with either a tail or a penis. Here the meaning is more ambiguous. It could be that Gaff knows that Deckard is not a real man but an android. Near the end, as Rachael and Deckard flee from his apartment, Rachael steps on something which Deckard picks up. It is the small silver paper figure of a unicorn, and Deckard shakes his head despairingly at the memory of Gaff's last words as they come through in voice-over: 'It's too bad she won't live, but then again who does?' Without a knowledge of Scott's original cut, the connotations of the unicorn remain obstinately mystifying.

The mysteries of *Blade Runner* highlight what is the case with any film: pure textual analysis which ignores the institutional context can never lead to full understanding. In what follows I wish to examine further the general and particular production contexts of the picture which shaped its meanings. David Bordwell, a leading American critic, has argued that when viewers or critics interpret a film, the constructed meanings are of four possible types:

- referential meanings
- explicit meanings
- implicit meanings
- symptomatic meanings.[9]

I shall consider these types in relation to *Blade Runner*.

Referential meanings refer to the way in which the spectator constructs the story from a plot and a spatio-temporal world from the diegesis, while *explicit meanings* is when the spectator imputes an intentional meaning to the story and diegesis, such as a specific moral or message. As we have seen, Scott's original cut of the movie was altered, obscuring the final revelation of Deckard's 'replicancy'. Consequently many viewers and critics have had difficulty recovering the film's referential meaning, wrongly assuming that Deckard is human and interpreting the ending as 'a happy marriage of humans and machines'.[10] Exceptions here are the ever-perceptive Robin Wood, and Alan Mackenzie who has documented the institutional background of the film.

Many critics, however, seem to agree on an explicit meaning. The film can be read as a radical social critique, portraying the horrific contradictions of advanced capitalism with its ubiquitous advertising promising the 'good life' to the few who can escape a filthy, over-populated and decayed city. Further, unlike many recent Hollywood films celebrating militarism and violence, *Blade Runner* ends with a renunciation of violence, foregrounding empathy as the prime human trait. In his climactic battle with Deckard, Roy Batty starts as an Aryan warrior but ends as a Christ figure with a nail through one hand and a dove of peace in the other, before saving his opponent from falling to his death. Moreover the film ends with a final act of empathy as Gaff allows Deckard and Rachael to escape.

With *implicit meanings* the critic moves up a further level of abstraction and interprets the film thematically or symbolically. Implicit meaning here may be consistent with referential or explicit meanings or contradict them, for example, through the use of irony. In this context Wood has noted the irony of Roy Batty misquoting Blake:

'Fiery the angels fell: deep thunder rolled

Around their shores, burning with the fires of Orc.'

According to Wood, the single alteration from 'rose' to 'fell' completely inverts Blake's original reference to the rise of the American democratic Revolution and suggests instead its ultimate demise.[11] The explicit meaning of the film, which it reinforces, lies after all in its depiction of oppressive giant monopolies destroying modern civilisation and polluting the planet.

Sources of implicit meaning are to be found not only in irony but also in pastiche and self-reference. The picture's cult status as a 'post-modern' film trades very heavily on this. For post-modernism refers to a whole cluster of concepts which are relevant here: cultural de-differentiation which breaks down the high/popular culture divide, the double coding noted by Umberto Eco which can bring both mass and elite 'readings' of the same cultural object, and finally a self-conscious fascination with style, generic mixing, parody and pastiche. Moreover such intertextualities are a prominent feature of UK television advertising in which Scott was such a seasoned veteran. Pastiche, in particular, is a central feature in the surface or depthless nature of post-modern texts. Images refer only to themselves or other pre-existent images rather than any extrinsic realities. Thus, as Jameson argues, pastiche tends to supplant parody in the stylistic pantheon.[12] Parody assumes consensus over comparison between the object of its wit and a communally agreed normality. If there is no such normality then parody becomes mere pastiche, a neutral paste-up of references whose only function appears to be the provision of the pleasures of recognition.

In *Blade Runner*, examples of this abound. Deckard traces Zhora the replicant snake charmer to a night club, affecting a slightly effeminate voice to disguise his real intent. This is surely a direct reference to the scene where private eye Philip Marlowe (Humphrey Bogart) visits the Geiger book store in the 1946 classic *The Big Sleep*. There is no sense of parody in the playing of the scene, however. The reference is merely available to you provided you have *The Big Sleep* in your textual store. The picture also juxtaposes past styles and texts, referring among other things to Egyptian and Mayan architecture, German Expression-ism and *Metropolis*, forties fashion, *Citizen Kane* and 'film noir', and contemporary punk. In classic Hollywood cinema most settings and props were motivated, that is to say, chosen to serve the needs of the narrative. In post-modern works, however, there is a stylistic excess largely unmotivated by the narrative, which merely allows film-makers to perform a cultural knowledge display, whilst providing the audiences with surfaces on which to pleasurably exercise their own cultural competences. This illustrates a key feature of post-modern texts, the deliberate construction of a 'double reader', one 'naive' and the other 'smart'.[13] Intertextuality then becomes the key method for engaging the 'smart' reader in this play upon 'encyclopaedic competence'.

Symptomatic meanings are ones constructed by the critic which the film represses, or which it expresses 'involuntarily'. Such meanings can usually be traced to economic, political, psychoanalytic or ideological processes. Symptomatic readings of *Blade Runner* have tended to concentrate on gender and racial representations. Here most critics have argued that despite their radical critique of capitalism, the filmic representations are depressingly reactionary and in line with the most of Hollywood output. Gender, for example, is highly stereotyped, pandering to some of the most deplorable male chauvinist fantasies. Ford plays a technocratic white male, possessed of a predictable machismo, who forces sexual relations on Rachael as if it is what she really 'wants', while Rachael in turn submits to this treatment and is rewarded with romantic bliss and the escape to a better life.

The two other female replicants are in different ways both pornographic models of female sexuality. Zhora is a nude snake charmer whom we see showering, then dressing in leather bra, pants and boots under a see-through raincoat. She is shot in the back by Deckard and careers in slow-motion through several plate glass windows. Pris is a 'basic pleasure model' with punk hairstyle, studded collar, leotard, suspender belt and stockings, who tries to kill Deckard by squeezing his head between her thighs. When Deckard first shoots her she has a furious seizure: the second shot produces slow-motion orgasmic pelvic

thrusts. The violent, extended portrayal of these 'retirements' are in
complete contrast to Leon's death, shot once through the head by
Rachael. It is possible to interpret such scenes as economically and
culturally predicated on providing voyeuristic pleasure for the largely
male audience of the film. Sex sells movies and provides product
differentiation from the sanitised network television of the US.

Similarly, racism seems to underlie the ethnic composition of the
figures in the picture, with its 'normal' white hero, and white power
figures, contrasted with the large number of exotic, mainly Asian,
proletarians of the underclass inhabiting the city. This can all too easily
be read as reflecting a white Anglo-Saxon fear of the Western cities of
the future being overrun by foreigners of a different skin colour.

Alternatively, it could be argued that this stark depiction of racial
and gender differences is deliberate. On this logic, *Blade Runner*, rather
than using involuntary stereotypes, is deliberately showing up the
ideological construction of race and gender under capitalism. In
Bordwell's terms of course, this would be an implicit rather than a
symptomatic meaning. But these alternative meanings merely illustrate
a perennial problem of criticism: is it genuinely possible to validate an
unambiguous interpretation of film? It also illustrates a major problem
of social critique in both mass media and high art. How can one
represent oppression without at the same time being implicated in it?[14]
The dilemma here in *Blade Runner* becomes acute. Although it has
some radical potential, its recut version seems to be politically
conservative, providing only an imaginary individual solution to real
social problems. It suggests that human empathy and human values
are *only* expressible in the private sphere of the heterosexual couple and
not in the public domain. Further, escape from human misery is
accessible only to special individuals, not to whole sections of an
oppressed society. From this standpoint, *Blade Runner* can be seen as
largely reflecting in its own time the dominant ideologies of Reagan's
America and Thatcher's Britain.[15]

Notes

1. R. Gustafson 'What's happening to our Pix Biz?' in T. Balio
   (ed.) *The American Film Industry*, Wisconsin: University of
   Wisconsin Press, 1985, p. 579.
2. See J. Monaco *American Film Now*, New York: Oxford
   University Press, 1979, pp. 8-27: M. Litwak *Reel Power*,
   London: Sidgwick and Jackson, 1987, pp. 72-81.
3. G. Murdock and P. Golding, 'Capitalism, communication and
   class relations' in J. Curran, M. Gurevitch and J. Woollacott
   (eds) *Mass Communication and Society*, London: Edward
   Arnold, 1977, p. 40.
4. See *Cinefantastique* vol. 12, no. 5/6, 1982: C. Finch *Special
   Effects: Creating Movie Magic*, New York: Abbeville Press,

1984, pp. 184-98; D. Millar *Cinema Secrets: Special Effects*, London: Apple Press, 1990, pp. 61-6.

5. R. Wood *Hollywood from Vietnam to Reagan*, New York: Columbia University Press, 1986, p. 182.

6. A. Mackenzie 'Blade Runner - death of a thousand cuts' *Voyager* 1, 1982, pp. 61-4.

7. For further details of the making of *Blade Runner* see *Starburst* nos. 50, 51, 53. A. Mackenzie *The Harrison Ford Story*, London: Zomba Books, 1984, pp. 64-83.

8. K. Thompson *Breaking the Glass Armour: Neoformalist Film Analysis,* Princeton: Princeton University Press, 1988, pp. 43-4.

9. See D. Bordwell *Making Meaning: Inference and Rhetoric in the Interpretation of Cinema*, Cambridge, Mass: Harvard University Press, 1989, pp. 8-9; D. Bordwell and K. Thompson *Film Art: An Introduction*, 3rd. ed., New York: McGraw-Hill, 1990, pp. 40-3.

10. M. Ryan and D. Kellner *Camera Politica - The Politics and Ideology of Contemporary Hollywood Film*, Bloomington: Indiana University Press, 1988, p. 251.

11. Wood *op. cit.*, p. 186.

12. F. Jameson *Postmodernism, or, The Cultural Logic of Late Capitalism*, London: Verso, 1991, pp. 16-19.

13. U. Eco *The Limits of Interpretation*, Bloomington: Indiana University Press, 1990, chs. 3 and 5.

14. L. Hutcheon *The Politics of Postmodernism*, London: Routledge, 1989, pp. 2-10.

15. The director's cut was screened for two weeks in Los Angeles in September 1991. Todd McCarthy's review in *Variety* (September 30, 1991, p. 69), argues that the director's version calls for 'a serious upgrading of its critical standing.'

Filmography

Blade Runner (A Warner/Ladd/Michael Deeley/Ridley Scott Production USA 1982.) Starring Harrison Ford, Rutger Hauer, Sean Young, Edward James Olmos, M. Emmet Walsh, Daryl Hannah; Production Design by Lawrence G. Paull: Cinematography by Jordan Cronenweth; Music by Vangelis; Screenplay by Hampton Fancher and David Peoples from the novel by Philip K. Dick *Do Androids Dream of Electric Sheep?*; Directed by Ridley Scott.

14

The narrative sources of Ridley Scott's *Alien*

ROBBIE ROBERTSON

Alien, released by Twentieth Century Fox in 1979, is an exception to the rule in this volume. It is not derived from any single literary text, but rather echoes diverse popular genres in both cinema and fiction. Written by Dan O'Bannon and directed by Ridley Scott, it is an evocative amalgam of two genres, horror and science fiction. Its effects depend on several elements: strong visual interest, particularly the set design; a straight narrative line through which its simple, sometimes implausible story is told; an eye for the unusual and a frightening monster; effective characterisation and a striking pattern of allusion and reference. Last but not least, it has an eye for unusual, surprising detail coupled with an atmosphere of claustrophobic terror. Each of these elements indicates the skills of different professionals – actors, editors, cinematographers, camera operators, production designers, in addition to the screenwriter and the director.

Nearly all feature films begin as written texts, as scripts, and more than half of all commercial films ever made have had their primary sources in a pre-existing print narrative such as a short story, a play, a novel or a documentary account of an actual event. Others, such as *Alien*, have their origin in an original cinema treatment. But these distinctions, it will be argued, are superficial in comparison with the recognition that all narratives have sources within shifting complex patterns of memories, associations and reflections. These patterns may not be immediately recognised, and the writer and other members of the film team would often find it impossible to 'track down' all their sources of influence, should they wish to do so.

Since the origin of any text, including film text, lies in borrowings from earlier experiences, often unconscious but sometimes deliberate, then it is well to recognise the complexity of this process. As films prey on written texts for their inspiration so, now, print preys upon film as in the past it preyed on oral narratives. Films increasingly prey also on other moving and photographic images, films, television, broadcast news, comics and advertising. These, in turn, prey on each other. Such intertextual weavings are fascinating to observe, and intriguing to deconstruct. In essence, however, they are little different from the kinds of borrowings which have been part of the normal currency of literature and living since, one imagines, communication began. We may cite here as an example, *The Road to Xanadu*, written by John Livingstone Lowes in 1927, which is a meticulous unpicking of the sources for *Kubla Khan* and *The Rime of the Ancient Mariner*, two of Coleridge's most famous poems, in an attempt to reveal the forces which underly the process of poetic creation.

Tracing the origins of a film, however, in the same way is much more difficult. Unlike even the most complex poem, a film is the product not of one person's experience and writing, but of the multiple experiences of a highly trained and talented team of professionals and the final text, as final cut, is achieved only by a variety of complex industrial processes. We are confronted with the phenomenon of multiple authorship and thus a whole chain of multiple influences. In looking at *Alien* we not only have Dan O'Bannon's scripting of a story he wrote with Ronald Shusset. We have his work as a visual design consultant along with the designs of the alien ship and the 'alien' by H. R. Giger. But we also have the work of Ron Cobb on the Nostromo sets and the contributions of other visual artists such as Chris Foss and Jean 'Moebius' Giraud. Added to that are the production design of Michael Seymour and the visual flair of Ridley Scott himself, which provide a host of different visual sources and inspirations for the finished product; a veritable case of the multiple authorship of the image operating as a source of multiple intertextualities in which authorship is everywhere and nowhere.

Let us now proceed to the story itself. *Alien* is set in the future. The spaceship 'Nostromo', a conscious borrowing from Joseph Conrad's famous novel of that name, is recrossing the galaxy to Earth from a distant star system, towing an automatic refinery which is busy processing twenty million tons of crude mineral ore. Such is the length of the journey that the seven crew members, two of them women, are in an artificially-induced sleep for its duration. While only halfway home the spaceship's computer, 'Mother', detects signals coming from an unknown planet. The crew's contracts with the Company, a corporate entity as mysterious and formidable as the monster they have yet to encounter, stipulate that any such event must be investigated. The crew are wakened and the 'Nostromo', minus its cargo, makes a landing on a climatically hostile, apparently barren world.

Three crew members, Dallas, Kane and Lambert, all identified by surnames only, leave the slightly damaged ship and follow the signals leading to an alien ship which looms through the duststorms of an eerie dawn. Inside the ship is a dead giant slumped beneath a huge phallic gun and Kane (John Hurt) discovers a gallery filled with large eggs, one of which releases a creature that smashes his helmet and clings to his face. Ash, the scientific officer overrides Ripley who thinks the signals are a warning, and allows the search party to return on board with the unconscious Kane. After a few days the creature dies and Kane, apparently unharmed, is moved out of the hospital bay. After completing repairs, 'Nostromo' lifts off the planet and rejoins its orbiting cargo. The journey back to Earth resumes, but over a final dinner before they return to their artificial sleep, Kane starts to choke and scream in severe pain. His stomach bursts open and 'alien' which has hatched inside him raises its head, bares its bloodied fangs, and wriggles away into the depths of the ship.

There, living amidst the air-shafts, it grows into a creature of frightening cunning and power. Brett and then Dallas, the captain, are killed leaving Ripley (Sigourney Weaver) in command. Ash tries to kill her, but is revealed to be a robot programmed to ensure that the survival of the 'alien' takes priority over the survival of the humans. In the end only Ripley and the ship's cat, Jones, survive. After making her escape in the ship's shuttle, she blows up 'Nostromo', only to discover the 'alien' has escaped along with her . . .

We can now return to the background to the film. Aliens are of course stock ingredients of science fiction. Their history within the genre is a long one and their functions within different texts very diverse. Quite probably monsters from space are already prefigured in the mythical gods and demons of legend and it is not too implausible to argue that aliens are merely the contemporary 'scientific' shapes adopted by those more ancient manifestations of the imagination. The monster in *Alien*, whose 'tongue' is another set of fanged jaws, seems, for example, to belong to the same domain as the jawed demi-gods that decorate the killing grounds of Aztec architecture. But to explore the ethnology of aliens in this speculative way would not really be profitable. Of more interest is the question of what aliens or gods, and the narratives in which they appear, connote? What are their meanings for the imagination? What messages do they convey? The visual attention paid to the alien's bite, for example, echoes the attention paid to the vampire's bite in dozens of previous horror films. As the alien confronts the near-naked Ripley in the shuttle in the film's denouement, do not its predatory teeth convey the sexual threat of Dracula hovering over a sleeping heroine?

Aliens have always been hyperactive creatures and at their best, are more than simple vehicles to convey terror. As monsters whose purpose is to scare their audience, they first appear in popular literature in the nineteenth century. But the invading Martians of *The War of the Worlds* who lay waste the south-east of England can also be read in

H. G. Wells' parabolic text as the analogues of Western colonialists using technological supremacy to subdue less 'advanced' societies. The dread that may have assailed the comfy Victorian reader was given an extra twist by a sense of guilt and a fear of retribution.

Aliens in the American movies of the fifties served as representations of what were perceived to be more immediate threats. In *The Thing from Another World* (1952) the giant vegetable intruder in the Arctic base suggests and reinforces the contemporary fear of invasion from the Soviet Union or from space. In Don Siegel's *Invasion of the Body-Snatchers* (1956) the phobia concerns the loss of self, aroused by fears of brainwashing and an alien socialism, both seeming to constitute a denial of that individuality cherished by American audiences. Both of these films end with encouragement to paranoia. The former tells us to 'Watch the skies!'; in the latter, the hero, unable to convince anyone of the takeover by aliens, runs between streams of freeway traffic shouting 'You're next! You're next!' Messages of a similar kind can be found in many lesser films from the fifties and sixties. Such all-American attitudes were remorselessly satirised in *Night of the Living Dead* (1969) and its sequels, where a space-borne organism roused the dead from their graves and put them to roam through the streets and shopping-malls of America.

The treatments of more recent alien contacts in *2001* (1968), *Close Encounters of the Third Kind* (1977) and *ET* (1982) encourage us to believe in a less threatening cosmos and a far more comfortable niche for humankind within it. Their aliens appear as God-like, their powers closer to magic than to science. In such movies, the progressive treatment of aliens common to literary science-fiction over the past twenty years, is taken on board, re-packaged and humanised for what is often a child audience. The aliens and their technology are mysterious, supernatural, but at the same time unthreatening. The technology is credible because the iconic nature of cinema and the brilliance of special effects allow us to authenticate its 'reality' with our own eyes. There is a consistent attempt to keep the foreground of small-town America and the instruments of space technology credible. We are altogether in a tidier, more controlled and yet more awesome, less intimidating universe.

Such progressive films seem closer to the themes and issues of written science-fiction in the sixties and seventies than is *Alien*. At first sight this belongs to an earlier 'retrogressive' era of pulp science-fiction whose magazine covers would depict bug-eyed monsters menacing scantily-clad women. Both O'Bannon and Giger have cited the influence of H. P. Lovecraft here and particularly the Cthulu tales full of alien monsters and the stench of sexual disgust. Such sources should clearly be borne in mind when considering the sexual politics of the film which works out rather differently. The script was written to be played by either actors or actresses, and it was the director's decision to include women in the space crew without changing it as a result. Hence the relations between the sexes are highly formal with the use of surnames only, of rank that is not gender-related, and a conspicuous lack of the sexual banter one might expect from such relationships at close quarters.

The sources for *Alien* are diverse: comics, print, myth, films and legends only skim the surface. We will focus therefore on the more accessible materials from which the narrative was constructed, and assess the purposes the construction serves. Here there are three important texts to consider: *It! The Terror from Beyond Space* (1958) and *Queen of Blood* (1966). Both in turn share a common progenitor in A. E. van Vogt's *The Voyage of the Space Beagle* (1950). In *It!* the sole survivor of an expedition to Mars is rescued by another space mission. His companions may have been murdered and the new arrivals immediately suspect him. Homeward bound, the real killer, an alien generously endowed with fangs, is a stowaway and the crew are gradually eliminated. The film concludes with 'It' (id?) triumphant and the remaining crew holed up in the forward section of the ship, awaiting their gruesome end. Like *Alien*'s monster, 'It' also shares a liking for storing victims in the air shafts of the ship. In *Queen of Blood*, yet another expedition to Mars picks up the Queen of Mars to bring her to Earth. She has vampiric tendencies, housed this time in a more enticing body, and proceeds to kill the crew. Before she achieves her goal, she cuts herself rather bathetically and bleeds to death, leaving behind – echoes of *Alien* and of Edgar Rice Burroughs' Martian sagas – a clutch of eggs.

The Voyage of the Space Beagle is even more directly an ancestor of Scott's film. An episodic novel collated from short stories and novellas from the late thirties onwards, it is set aboard a spaceship manned by hundreds of crew and scientists which travels faster than light and whose mission is to explore our own and neighbouring galaxies. Two of the aliens the Beagle encounters are plausible models for *Alien*. The first, Coeurl, dating from a short-story of 1947, lives on a deserted barren world ruined by a thousand year winter which follows nuclear war and is described as cat-like with inky black tentacles growing from the shoulders. Its first victim is killed by smashing the face plate of his helmet. As with Ash in *Alien* and Dr Carrington in *The Thing from Another World* the scientists are anxious to keep it alive for study, despite the obvious dangers. Taken on board the Beagle, it proceeds to kill the crew with single-minded ferocity. Like the monster in *Alien* it escapes in a shuttle and it too dies in space. As in *The Thing*, it is the military who rescue the feckless scientists from the consequences of their curiosity and credulity.

The second alien, Ixtl, is found drifting in space and it, too, is allowed entry into the spaceship. It can pass through interior walls as if they were made of mist and shares alien's liking for air-shafts. More important, it plans to use the stomachs of human beings as hatching places for its eggs. When the eggs, having been safely removed from the men's stomachs, hatch in a laboratory the verbal description of the hatching alien is clearly a model for its visual counterpart in Scott's film with its 'ugly, round, scarlet head', 'tiny, beady eyes and a tiny slit of a mouth'. In the story, one of the scientists speculates on the prospect of the alien escaping from the laboratory. Many years later, *Alien*'s horrifying sequence of the alien hatching from Kane's stomach provides a gruesome answer as to what would happen if it did.

The van Vogt story is itself no more than a re-casting of earlier tales of monster visitations, demonic births and the supernatural powers that haunt isolated castles and ships. The unresolved story of the Mary Celeste and the *Rime of the Ancient Mariner* come to mind. We can note that one of Conrad's tales, *The Shadow Line*, concerns a ship with a mysterious visitation aboard and that Scott's first film *The Duellists* was a re-telling of another Conrad story. The message Ripley sends out in the opening minutes of the film: 'This is commercial vehicle Nostromo out of the Solomons . . .' also invokes Conrad in the ship's name, in the rather bizarre locale for its home 'port' and in the sailing-ship language through which its voyage is described. To these intertextual echoes there is no end, but one other may be mentioned. The idea of a spaceship like the Nostromo can be found as early as 1900 in R. W. Cole's *The Struggle for Empire* which describes interstellar travellers who 'towed great masses of valuable rock or precious metals behind their ships.' But Frank Herbert's *The Dragon in the Sea* (1956) with its American submarine towing a huge cargo of stolen Russian oil under the polar ice, can be seen as a parallel model.

All narratives are composed out of elements which present various states of order and disorder. In *Alien* (and in horror films generally) the mechanism of disruption, the monster, produces increasing disorder until by its death a form of order is finally restored. It is important to remember that this process of order/disorder/order is constructed out of different elements: language, camera style, set designs, lighting, characters, music, action and so on. But such listings and categorisations are not in themselves sufficient to define a genre. It is the relationships between the elements and the degrees of emphasis given to each which are crucial. And each must be set against the sorts of expectations possessed by its audience. *Alien* appeals, for example, to a double audience: science fiction buffs and those who like to be scared by scenes they find horrifying. That double audience and the gratifications the film offered to each half, was clearly a major element in its commercial success.

What a genre provides is coherence. Disorder can be 'represented' by discordant, incoherent elements, but to do this successfully within popular art requires a certain familiarity with the conventions out of which the narrative is fashioned. If there is no familiarity then there is a danger that the narrative will lack meaning. The use of a genre ensures familiarity. *Alien* belongs to two distinct, but related genres – horror and science fiction. The very familiarity of these genres gives us the opportunity to be surprised – or terrified – within an entertainment which does us no harm. More importantly, such familiarities help to reinforce the cultural truths to which we subscribe and of which we may be unaware as the meanings of the text unfold. Our readings of genres – and genres themselves – are sustained by and developed within varieties of media narratives. Science fiction, for example, come not merely from films but from our exposure to a multiplicity of discourses found in print, television, comics, styling of toys, children's games and music. Our experiences of genre are also controlled by the conventions of cinema itself.

The cross-over of genres in *Alien* is particularly striking. Although horror and science-fiction have been yoked together, especially at that end of the market which demands a visceral rather than a conceptual response, what the film offers is a sharply defined set of genre specifics whose siting within the same narrative enhances their effect and whose overlapping presentation and history make categorisation difficult. Nevertheless we have to ask which genre, of the two, is dominant. The science-fiction dimension is offered to us as authenticating reality for the depredations of the monster and this has, of course, an influence on our response to the monster itself.

Consider the film's three main sets: the Nostromo, the alien vessel and the planetary surface. The Nostromo set is littered with junk: empty cups, discarded clothing fluttering in the air streams, pin-ups on the wall – effects reminiscent of the inspired clutter in *Dark Star* (1974) which O'Bannon also co-scripted with six others, and in which he starred. As in *Star Wars* such details tend to humanise the sterile configurations of the interior. The ship (screens, sleeping cells, the rather 'old-fashioned' computer room, long corridors, the sense of huge spaces, mysterious wirings, coilings and instrumentation in profusion) is sufficiently well-realised to present the kind of technological reality, fantastic yet formidably 'there' for which *2001* and the comic strips of *Heavy Metal/Metal Hurlant* have prepared us.

In an oppositional sense, helping to join the 'reality' of Nostromo to the phantasmagoric horror of the monster, the alien ship and its dead crew belong equally formidably to an 'elsewhere' for which we are relatively unprepared. We have not seen anything like them before. The imagination of H. R. Giger, developing the work of Foss and Cobb, and using the skills of other craftsmen, has created something truly alien – a ship whose fabric is organic, sinister, and whose entry ports yawn open like vaginal passages ready for an equally monstrous birth. The alien world also possesses a disturbing presence. Its storms, eroded rock, looming skies dominated by a shadowy, ringed companion planet, are credible because though strange and remote from our experience they convey an impression of accuracy gleaned, possibly, from other media images. The experience of the film, then, is established by the concreteness of its science fiction elements which help to give the monster, the true star of the film, a distinctive reality.

The monster is more than just a device to make the audience twitch. Its life cycle has a complexity which combines anatomical verisimilitude with sexual imagery and myths. From the egg it becomes the face hugger with echoes of Sheridan Le Fanu's 'Beast with Five Fingers'. With its ovipositor thrust down Kane's throat, the face hugger arouses the old fear of smothering – familiar in gothic fiction – and at the same time suggests oral sex and with it the mythic penalty for such 'unnatural' intercourse – the birth of a monster. In the adult phase its whole body remains hidden, a convention of the horror genre, until the end of the film. But our attention is directed to the fine detail of the articulating jaws, and their dripping saliva. In a scene edited out of the film because it slowed down the pace of the closing scenes, some of the crew are found cocooned in a monstrous nest, hatching more eggs, one of them undergoing a transformation which will lead to the egg phase found in the alien spaceship.

Through such corroborative effects we are persuaded that the alien, unlike the monsters of horror movies which are usually no more than devices, belongs to the natural world, with the pervasive sexual symbolism of the film's styling and the alien's own phallic form providing further disturbing overtones. The life cycle, its connotations, and the creature's savagery all become emblematic of the strangeness and ferocity to be found, barely-hidden, in nature. That power and ferocity, the otherness that our culture inscribes onto 'nature', itself an invention subject to regular transformations, has the potential to disrupt not only narratives but also, most terrifying of all, our own lives. As the alien disrupts the order of Nostromo, the crew members (mechanics, engineers at best, certainly not, with the exception of Ash, scientists) are helpless before it, and their terror arouses our fearful recognition of our own vulnerability to the effects of nature's darkness.

Yet this broader thematic is contained within a film which belongs, we are told, to the horror genre. In some respects that view is correct. The claustrophobic spaces within the Nostromo, their murkiness, the irruptions of the creature, are certainly designed to terrify in exactly the same way that the 'Thing from Another World', in an earlier picture and similarly sealed environment, terrifies us. But the alien is a more complex creation than the Thing. Its intelligence is marked: it retreats to the shuttle and blends its body, a disconcerting piece of camouflage, into the technology of the vehicle. Although the Thing arrives in some form of complex space vehicle, its failure to reveal much about itself other than its blood-lust, calls into question the imaginative energy which underlay its creation. The alien's drives are also elemental: to procreate and to perpetuate the species. But this emerges from the logic of narrative. Unsurprisingly, given its birth, it is a savage without culture, set within a culture-rich environment which it attempts to destroy.

Alien is in fact richer than those horror movies which it most resembles. The dominant mood of the film is strangeness. The humans cannot effectively connect with each other and with their culture to get rid of the monster. Surrounded by high technology their efforts with cattle-prods and flame-throwers seem woefully inadequate. They are controlled by a computer – 'Mother' – and are easily manipulated. The use of surnames only, the absence of familiarity between the men and the women, suggest an alien culture. The Company is an omnipresent, malevolent power, its interests represented by Ash, the scientific officer, who is a robot and who admires the alien. The Nostromo itself is a mysterious ship, its function and its cargo only hinted at and no more. The film, in fact, is a series of alien experiences in which it is, ironically, only the monster's violence which provides us with feelings of familiarity. In that sense the film subverts the contents of its apparent genre, that of horror. The questions it raises about its own narrative and the world in which it is set, place it firmly within the more demanding discourses of science fiction. To describe it as a Lovecraftian horror movie is to deny the influence of its primary sources and its visual and thematic subtleties. Never trust the teller, trust the tale.

Filmography

Alien (A TCF/Brandywine Production (Walter Hill, Gordon Caroll, David Giler) GB 1979.) Starring Tom Skerritt, Sigourney Weaver, John Hurt, Veronica Cartwright, Harry Dean Stanton, Yaphet Koto; Cinematography by Derek Vanlint and Denys Ayling; Music by Jerry Goldsmith; Screenplay by Dan O'Bannon; Directed by Ridley Scott.

Index